# Understanding and Explanation

# Understanding and Explanation

A Transcendental-Pragmatic Perspective

Karl-Otto Apel
translated by Georgia Warnke

The MIT Press Cambridge, Massachusetts, and London, England

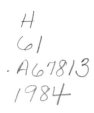
This translation © 1984 by the Massachusetts Institute of Technology Originally published as *Die Erklären-Verstehen-Kontroverse in Transzendental-Pragmatischer Sicht*, © 1979 by Suhrkamp Verlag, Frankfurt am Main.

This book was set in Baskerville by The MIT Press Computergraphics Department and printed and bound by Halliday Lithograph in the United States of America.

**Library of Congress Cataloging in Publication Data**

Apel, Karl-Otto.
  Understanding and explanation.

(Studies in contemporary German social thought)
  Translation of: Die Erklären-Verstehen-Kontroverse in transzendental-pragmatischer Sicht.
  Bibliography: p.
  Includes index.
  1. Social sciences—Philosophy. I. Title. II. Series.
H61.A67813    1984    300'.1    84-12518
ISBN 0-262-01079-8

# Contents

# Translator's Introduction

*Understanding and Explanation* deals with a central controversy in the philosophy of the social sciences. Advocates of a "unified science" such as Comte, Mill, and, more recently, Hempel and Nagel stress the methodological unity of the natural and social sciences, claiming that progress in the social sciences requires adoption of the methods and standards of the natural sciences. We must try to construct causal explanations of human behavior, explanations based on general laws and theories that can be verified by empirical observation and are not influenced by the personal values of the scientist. In contrast, representatives of the *"verstehende* social sciences"—for example, Dilthey and Gadamer, Winch and Taylor—emphasize the affinities between the social sciences and the humanities. They argue that, because of the nature of the objects they study, the social sciences cannot conform to the logic of the natural sciences. Beliefs and practices, norms and values, roles and institutions are inherently meaningful; that is, they stand in some relation to both subjective intentions and cultural traditions. Hence, the task of the social sciences is not simply to specify invariant laws of human behavior but to make this behavior intelligible, to illuminate its rationality in terms of cultural assumptions and subjective intentions. On this view, therefore, the social sciences necessarily involve an interpretive dimension; they cannot rely on observation and explanation alone but must explore the complex of "meanings" that form the context of the actions and practices of a given social group.

The opposition between these two approaches to the logic of the social sciences raises important questions concerning the meaning of social scientific objectivity. Can the social sciences be structured on the model of the natural sciences, or are natural scientific criteria of objectivity completely inapplicable here? Are all social scientific explanations forms of interpretation, and if so, how can they be verified? Are the results of the social sciences true only for particular times and places, or can they achieve a wider validity? Representatives of interpretive social science argue that by stressing causal explanation, general laws, and empirical observation, advocates of a "unified science" endorse a natural scientific concept of objectivity that is irrelevant to the social sciences. Conversely, representatives of "unified science" claim that without the natural scientific concept of objectivity the social sciences become subjective and unverifiable. Indeed, it becomes unclear how any one interpretation can be judged superior to any other.

In this introduction I want to indicate the importance of Apel's work for this controversy by first reconstructing the line of development in Anglo-American thought that has led from the position of "unified science" to the "neo-Wittgensteinian" account of interpretive social science. I shall then turn to Hans-Georg Gadamer's radicalization of this line of analysis and point out certain relativistic implications that can be read out of his position. Finally, I shall indicate how Apel's work challenges these relativistic conclusions.

As Apel explains, the conditions of the possibility of an objective account of history and society have been a concern of philosophy since the nineteenth century. In criticizing Hegel's speculative approach both Ranke and Droysen argued that historical understanding had to begin with recognition of its own historicity; it had to acknowledge that the "whole" of history was not given to it, that it could not make the understanding of particular historical events dependent on an understanding of history's supposed "immanent" goal.[1] If objectivity were to be possible, historical investigation would have to abstract from later historical developments and attain an empathetic identification with its objects. Wilhelm Dilthey made such identification the condition of adequate social scientific understanding as well: only by reexperiencing the context of social actions or practices could one escape the limitations of one's own social and historical position and attain an objective view of one's subject matter.[2]

This was the type of account of the possibility of objectivity in the social sciences that Carl Hempel rejected in applying his deductive-nomological model to social scientific explanation. For Hempel and others, the problem with interpretive social science was that it made the results of research contingent upon the empathetic talents of individual researchers; on this account there could be no verifiable social scientific findings, merely a plethora of competing, unjustifiable interpretations. In his classic essay "The Function of General Laws in History," Hempel argued that the possibility of objectivity depended not on empathy but rather on application of a natural scientific methodology.[3] An event or act was said to be adequately explained if and only if a description of it followed deductively from a set of universal lawlike hypotheses, together with a set of statements specifying initial conditions. Moreover, these premises would have to be capable of empirical confirmation or refutation; they could not refer to such metaphysical entities as Hegel's activity of world-spirit, but would have to cite general laws and regularities that could be tested observationally. To take an example from Hempel, the explanation of why certain farmers suffering from the effects of the Dust Bowl emigrated to California would have to use some general law, such as: "Populations tend to migrate to regions offering better living conditions" together with an expression of the relevant condition—that California offered better conditions. The explanandum would be explained insofar as the sentence stating it followed logically from statements of the law and the relevant conditions, both of which could be confirmed empirically. Further, Hempel maintained that explanations of this type had the same logical structure as prediction. If a description of the event to be explained could be deduced from the stated premises, it followed that on the basis of the same deduction, the occurrence of the event could have been predicted before it happened. That is, it would have been possible to predict the emigration of populations living under certain severe conditions, given the law that stated what populations tend to do, as well as an analysis of the initial conditions. Conversely, occurrence of the event would serve to confirm the law on the basis of which the prediction was made.

Hempel modified this initial, stringent characterization of explanation to make it conform better to historical and social scientific practice and to account for the relative scarcity of general laws in these areas. He argued that many "explanations" were only "explanation sketches," outlines of explanations that pointed to relevant generalizations and indicated the direction in which further investigation would have to proceed but did not amount to strict deductive proof. Such explanation sketches could not generate reliable predictions; nonetheless, they would assist in developing a progressively more complete formulation of relevant laws and antecedent conditions. Hempel also argued that many of the relevant laws in history and the social sciences would be statistical rather than universal in form; instead of explaining the occurrence of a particular event, they would explain the frequency with which it would appear in a given class.

In the 1950s, William Dray called Hempel's account into question.[4] Dray argued that explanation sketches and statistical generalities were no solution to the problem of general laws in history and social science and that Hempel had mistaken the type of generalization relevant to these disciplines. Here, he pointed to an alternative interest of the human sciences—not that of explaining or predicting the occurrence of an event but that of understanding the event's meaning. Dray doubted whether the sole measure of the incompleteness of an explanation sketch was its predictive unreliability. On his view, what an explanation sketch lacked was the capacity to render intelligible a sequence of events. It was the task of the social sciences not only to explain actions as events with causes but to show their rationality as acts with reasons, that is, uncover their meaning or significance for the agents performing them. Following Dray, theorists in the neo-Wittgensteinian tradition went a step further.[5] Social scientific concern with an agent's reasons for performing a certain action was not simply a distinct, independent interest of the human sciences; it functioned, rather, as a necessary presupposition of any attempt to uncover an action's causes. Only if social scientists could understand the internal connection between an act and its motivation could they identify it correctly and thereby try to explain it in terms of laws.

This position can be clarified by referring again to Hempel's example of the migration of Dust Bowl farmers. The explanation provided—that populations tend to migrate to regions offering better living conditions—rests on a number of premises, among them that Dust Bowl farmers wanted to move to a region offering better living conditions and that California was thought to offer these conditions. Such beliefs and desires are culturally specific, however; in order for a group of people to decide on migration as a way of improving their living conditions, they must have a certain conception of the world—for instance, one that allows for change and improvement—and a certain conception of themselves—for instance, one in which, to some extent, they see themselves as the master of their fate. Without some such belief structure, the migration to California could not be explained in terms of the general law to which Hempel points. The argument here is that if one is to subsume an action under law, it must be a law that properly characterizes the action in its relation to the situation in which it occurs. Hence, one must have some familiarity with the norms, world view, and self-understanding of the group in question.

This argument is fundamental. It is not simply that social science must acknowledge that the activities it studies are already interpreted by those that engage in them. If that were the only point, it would not be clear why one could not simply replace an agent's understanding of his or her action with a more sophisticated scientific understanding.[6] The point, as formulated by such theorists as Peter Winch and Charles Taylor, is, rather, that the institutions, practices, actions, etc., under study are constituted in part by the participants' understanding of them. They are possible only within specific constellations of beliefs and practices and are internally related to the norms, values, and assumptions to which a particular culture subscribes. As Taylor points out in his essay, "Interpretation and the Sciences of Man," the practice of negotiation is connected to a series of concepts and activities peculiar to advanced industrial societies, such activities as making an offer, bargaining, and breaking off negotiations.[7] These activities, in turn, are supported by a larger set of assumptions, for instance, notions of individual autonomy, contractual obligation, economic freedom, and voluntary association. These premises are as constitutive of the practice of negotiation as are the verbal and physical motions of the participants; indeed, they give the latter their sense. But this means that in order even to identify acts of negotiation, one must be able to understand the meaning of words and motions in terms of the conceptual or semantic system to which they belong. To that extent, understanding the meaning of beliefs and practices, and hence, attention to the conceptual framework of the society under study, is a presupposition of attempting to formulate nomological connections with regard to these beliefs and practices.

Along these lines, then, the neo-Wittgensteinians argued against Hempel that the possibility of identifying regularities and laws of behavior within a society already presupposed a familiarity with its norms and beliefs. As a result, objectivity in the social sciences could not be secured solely through application of laws, for such applications were themselves founded on a prior understanding of the meaning of the actions at issue. The question that had to arise was how an understanding of this kind could be verified, how it could be shown to represent an objective account and not simply the idiosyncratic interpretation of an individual researcher. The virtue of the deductive-nomological account had rested precisely on this point: To be valid, any logically conclusive, social-scientific explanation had to be corroborated observationally. The neo-Wittgensteinian account undermined this criterion of objectivity by pointing out that what one "observes" is itself a matter of interpretation, that is, a matter of correctly relating external behaviors to the relevant system of norms and assumptions. The question, therefore, was how to discriminate between competing interpretations, how to decide on the correct relation.

The neo-Wittgensteinians did not resolve this problem; for the most part they were concerned simply to indicate the inapplicability of the natural scientific criterion of objectivity. Thus, in *The Idea of a Social Science and Its Relation to Philosophy*, Winch argued against Max Weber, that the validity of social scientific interpretation could not be "checked" by means of statistical analysis. Since establishing correlations between kinds of behavior did nothing to clarify the point of the behavior, if a given interpretation were wrong, what was required was "a better interpretation, not something different in kind."[8] Moreover, "better interpretations" required greater familiarity with, or better "socialization" into, the life of the community under investigation, rather than the use of methods borrowed from the natural sciences. In a later essay, Winch noted that all societies partook of certain universal "limiting notions" insofar as all recognized the importance to human life of birth, death, and procreation.[9] He argued that, for this reason, a culture's particular attitude toward these phenomena could give the social scientist a means of access to its beliefs and practices. Of course, this argument left open the question of the adequacy of such access; indeed, it left open the question of how, given the variety of cultural responses to the phenomena of birth, death, and sexual relations, one set of attitudes could provide the basis for a correct understanding of any other set.

For his part, Charles Taylor argued that interpretation always demanded a certain measure of insight and that such insight could not be formalized; understanding another society or historical period might entail developing one's intuitions, and even changing one's life. On his view, an interpretation capable of both interpreting the phenomenon in question and showing the inadequacy of other interpretations was superior to them. Taylor was forced, however, to admit that this criterion of interpretive adequacy would convince only those who had already adopted the "superior" position, hence, that the scope of the validity of an interpretation might be quite limited.

Gadamer's reflections in *Truth and Method* mark a significant turn in the discussion of this problem, inasmuch as he suggests that it is precisely a concern with objectivity that blocks an adequate account of the structure of understanding. On his view, this concern betrays an underlying affinity of interpretive approaches, such as Dilthey's, to the position of unified science.[10] They, too, assume that the validity of social-scientific findings depends upon intersubjective confirmation and repeatability. For "positivists" such as Hempel, this is secured by duplicating observations and experimental results. For *Verstehen* theorists such as Dilthey, it depends on duplicating experiences, that is, reexperiencing events as the participants themselves originally experienced them. Hence, in both cases the adequacy of social-scientific explanation depends on eradicating the influence of the investigator's own perspective; only those explanations or interpretations are "objective" that can be accepted by different investigators irrespective of cultural differences or temporal distance. It can be argued that the neo-Wittgensteinians were less "positivistic," in that they saw the question of objectivity in terms of the possibility of extending, not eradicating, the social scientist's perspective. Understanding another society or historical epoch did not require that one suspend the norms and values of one's own culture, only that one surmount a naive cultural parochialism. Nonetheless, this position still did not directly question the possibility of achieving a uniquely correct interpretation, the validity of which would extend beyond the investigator's cultural and historical purview. From a Gadamerian point of view, it thus continues to conflate objectivity, impartiality, and the idea that valid social scientific results should be the same for all investigators at all times. In contrast, Gadamer suggests that we must not only reject observation and prediction as the proper mode of verifying social scientific analyses, we must also give up our concern with intersubjective verification itself.

Gadamer's position emerges most clearly from his account of the influence of prejudice and tradition on different forms of human knowledge. Taking the phenomenological investigations of Husserl and Heidegger as his point of departure, Gadamer argues that all forms of human understanding are understandings of something *as* something. In other words, the content of an experience involves a projection of meaning that goes beyond the actual constituents of the experience, which are always one-sided and perspectival. For example, the perception of an object as a desk does not evolve from an unconditioned, total apprehension of all sides of it at once; rather, it is an interpretation based on a limited, one-sided perspective. Analogously, textual understanding develops on the basis of a kind of part-whole understanding. Here again, one understands a given part in terms of a projection of the meaning of the whole, and revises that projection of the whole on the basis of a reading and interpretation of its parts. This projection of meaning is grounded in a network, or "horizon," of expectations and assumptions. Thus, if I understand a given text as a detective novel, this presupposes that I know what a detective novel is, and, more generally, that I am familiar with other literary forms from which I can distinguish it. Similarly, to see something as a desk I must know what a desk is, as well as be familiar with the acts of writing, studying, and reading that distinguish desks from other writing surfaces. On this view, any apprehension of the immediate data of experience is theory-laden; the apprehension reflects the experience and values of the culture and society to which one belongs.

It is such projections of meaning that Gadamer refers to as "prejudgments" or "prejudices"; they are the basis for his insistence on the importance of historical tradition. If projection of the meaning of a cultural object is rooted in the culture to which one belongs, then it is also rooted in the history of that culture, and hence in tradition. The projection of meaning is neither a purely individual assumption on the part of the interpreter nor an arbitrary decision. What is projected as meaning is, rather, a historical prejudice, an anticipation based on previous interpretations and approaches to the object in question. It is only to the extent that one anticipates the meaning of something that it appears as anything at all. But this anticipation is not itself ungrounded; rather, it draws on a cultural tradition. In Gadamer's view, the operative force of this tradition is not neutralized by the introduction of "method" into history and the social sciences. Instead, the way in which one defines or describes the explanandum, the focus one gives to social scientific questionnaires, the facets of history one emphasizes, all reflect a conceptual orientation informed by a specific cultural and intellectual history.

This is a central aspect of what Gadamer means by his notion of effective history: the force of tradition operates upon knowledge in such a way that all projection of meaning is already prejudiced. Another aspect is equally important: These prejudices constantly undergo revision in and through the very act of interpretation. Gadamer argues that the goal of interpretative social science cannot be to duplicate or confirm previous research; rather, its task is to illuminate new dimensions of a phenomenon opened up by the phenomenon's involvement in a later stage of the historical tradition. Because we always understand on the basis of our own historical situation, and because history is always changing, any event, artifact, or practice comes to be associated with different events, artifacts, and practices and will be continually reinterpreted in light of subsequent developments. Thus, on the one hand, all interpretation is a projection of cultural prejudices; on the other hand, because historical phenomena are always interpreted from a different historical perspective, the prejudices that are projected are always changing. Indeed, they are necessarily revised in the very course of being projected. Thus, on Gadamer's view, the process of interpretation is a *dialogical* one in which one apprehends meaning in terms of one's own prejudices and at the same time is forced to reconsider these prejudices in light of the questions provoked by confrontation with the object of interpretation.

For Gadamer, therefore, the human sciences are forms of historical self-consciousness. They do not express objective truths about human behavior or actions, truths available to any interpreter from any cultural or historical perspective. Rather, they exemplify phases in a culture's understanding of itself. That is, they reflect stages in a culture's confrontation with its own history and tradition and hence stages in the development of that tradition. Thus, the validity of the scientist's results cannot depend upon their consistency with the findings of other scientists. Different cultural, historical, personal situations, permit insight into different dimensions of the phenomenon at issue.

This argument entails that objectivity in the social sciences cannot be a question of the repeatability of results or of intersubjective verification. If the concept of objectivity retains any significance within Gadamer's analysis, it means that one is aware of one's participation in the unfolding of a tradition. Indeed, the concept amounts to a plea for modesty in one's conclusions, for no interpretation can claim to be uniquely correct or to possess a privileged position of insight. Gadamer does claim that not all interpretations will be equally valid; nonetheless, the question of their validity cannot be settled by appealing to an ahistorical standard of objectivity. The objectivity of an interpretation is, rather, a question of its "fruitfulness" in revealing new dimensions of a phenomenon, together with its historical self-consciousness with regard to the scope and significance of the aspects it has disclosed. Objectivity in interpretation thus involves recognizing the limits of one's understanding and acknowledging the force of the tradition to which one belongs.

This is a position that Apel never tires of criticizing, one that serves as a catalyst for his own "transcendental-pragmatic" perspective. On his view, despite Gadamer's criticism of "scientism" and "objectivism" in the social sciences, Gadamer remains guilty of a "scientistic fallacy": like those he attacks, he supposes that the natural sciences possess a monopoly on the meaning of "science" and "objectivity," and that social scientific or historical understanding must, therefore, dispense with both the claim to science and the search for objectivity. Apel seeks to reverse the thrust of this argument: The notions of science and objectivity need not be abandoned to the natural sciences; what is required, instead, is an expanded conception of scientific rationality in general. Finally, I want briefly to trace one main strand of Apel's analysis. Its point of departure is Georg Henrik von Wright's book, *Explanation and Understanding*, in particular von Wright's discussion of the limits of the Hempelian conception of causal explanation.

For von Wright, the concept of causal necessity involves our capacity to manipulate natural systems that are sufficiently closed to external disturbances. He argues that we are able to form the notion of the causal necessity of certain connections between events only because we can actively produce or hinder effects by intervening in natural sequences. In Apel's view, this analysis provides a clue to the "transcendental-pragmatic" conditions of the possibility of causal explanation. He maintains that the capacity to manipulate and direct natural chains of events forms the transcendental ground of causal explanation inasmuch as it provides the foundation for our understanding of the connection between events. In contradistinction to Kant, Apel describes the ground as transcendental-*pragmatic*; that is, the concept of causality is no longer regarded as a category of the "pure understanding" but rather as a product of our ability to interfere with natural chains of events. It is tied intrinsically to the possibility of experimental action. Apel argues further that such action cannot itself be subjected to a deductive-nomological account without undermining the meaning of the concept of causality itself:

If we want to understand an experimental, interventionist action as such we cannot objectify it as an observable nexus of events in the external world. If we could, we would naturally again confront the Humean problem and be unable to infer any causal necessity from the conjunction of phenomena.[11]

By interpreting von Wright's analysis as a transcendental argument about the conditions of the possibility of the concept of causal explanation, Apel is able to add an important twist to the neo-Wittgensteinian position. As we saw, such theorists as Winch and Taylor have argued that the possibility of explaining actions in terms of general laws depends upon prior understanding of the meaning of the actions in question. Apel now argues that the conditions of possibility of causal explanation in general include the concept of the freedom of action. It follows that action cannot be universally reduced to an observable event with a causal determination without destroying the meaning of causal necessity itself. Hence, an interpretive study of action in terms of intelligible reasons must be a legitimate concern of science.

In the form of what he calls his "complementarity thesis," Apel asserts that there are two distinct and valid "interests of knowledge" within the social sciences: an interest in explaining events in causal terms, and an interest in understanding the meaning of actions in terms of cultural norms and subjective intentions. Transcendental-pragmatic reflection on the conditions of the possibility of causal explanation does *not* preclude the possibility of explaining actions as events with causes; it *does* preclude the claim of proponents of a "unified science" that such explanation is the *sole* "scientific" approach to human action. Unless social inquiry also includes understanding, the transcendental basis of the concept of causal explanation is itself undermined. If the condition of the possibility of the concept of causality is the possibility of "free" purposeful action, the purposes or reasons behind such action must be a legitimate concern of science. Hence, the joint neo-Wittgensteinian and hermeneutic emphasis on intersubjective norms of action is validated as a necessary theme of an expanded notion of science. In other essays Apel makes the same point by referring to the conventions and norms of scientific practice itself. As he writes in "Scientistics, Hermeneutics and the Critique of Ideology,"

A natural scientist, as solus ipse, cannot seek to explain something for himself alone. And in order merely to know "what" he should explain he must have come to some agreement with others about it. . . . Yet this agreement at the level of intersubjectivity, precisely because it is the precondition for the possibility of objective science, can never be replaced by a mode of procedure of objective science. Here we confront the absolute limits of any programme for objective-explanatory science. Linguistic agreement concerning what one means and what one wants is complementary to objective science. . . . [12]

This analysis constitutes the core of Apel's defense of the validity of the interpretive position in the social sciences. Can he now avoid the relativistic consequences to which this position seems to have led? Although Apel follows Dray and the neo-Wittgensteinians in emphasizing an autonomous interest of knowledge in exhibiting the intelligibility of human action, in his view, this interest would be sufficient in and of itself only if social action were always rational or intelligible. The problem with a purely interpretive social science, he argues, is that it cannot deal with unintended consequences and causal connections that go beyond an agent's or society's understanding of actions. In particular, it cannot deal with self-misunderstandings and systematic distortions that affect the entire framework of action and interpretation. Apel points to psychological illness as an instance of this kind of debilitating self-misinterpretation. In this case, individuals cannot give adequate accounts of themselves or their actions; in fact, the very terms they employ in attempting to do this are part of the problem. Thus a therapist must look behind the accounts that patients give of themselves to uncover the unacknowledged elements that condition both the pathological behavior and the language in which it is interpreted. Decoding the "actual" meaning of the action thus requires something more than mere interpretation. Apel maintains that it requires a combination of understanding and explanation: since the behavior cannot be understood in the terms that the agents employ, understanding must be coupled with an explanation of the unconscious factors that affect the action and its interpretation. Another instance of self-misinterpretation—this time at a societal level—is the ideology of fair exchange under liberal capitalism. Here, the "critique of ideology" claims that it is necessary to go beyond society's understanding of itself in terms of the principles of justice and equality, to reveal the difference between these principles and the actual practice of economic exploitation. Again, interpretive insight is not enough, for the problem affects the framework of interpretation itself.

At first glance, these considerations seem not to detract from the validity of Gadamer's account of hermeneutic understanding, for he too holds that understanding always goes beyond an agent's or society's self-interpretation, that, in understanding, one always sees actions, practices, norms, etc., within a wider historical context, and hence, reveals their unintended consequences and connections. Yet, in Apel's view, Gadamer's analysis is, in fact, subject to the same limitation: It cannot deal with the causal connections or unintended consequences of the tradition of interpretation itself; nor can it deal with systematic distortions within this tradition's self-understanding. Hermeneutic interpretation alone is incapable of breaking free of the tradition to which it belongs in order to uncover external influences on its force and direction. Hence, understanding must be combined with a form of theoretical explanation, or "critique of ideology," capable of appealing to a reference system outside the tradition's account of itself.

Therefore, both the "critique of ideology" and psychoanalysis differ from straight hermeneutic studies, insofar as they deny the adequacy of an agent's, culture's, or tradition's self-understanding. In particular, because this self-understanding may be subject to ideological or pathological disturbances, it becomes necessary to supplement it with an explanation of the causal factors, connections, and consequences that remain opaque to it. As Apel points out, however, both forms of knowledge also differ from deductive-nomological sciences; for the point of uncovering the causal elements of the behavior in question is not to assist possible prediction and experimental control. Rather, such a "science" attempts to aid in the self-reflective processes of the agent, society, or tradition and thus promote its own self-understanding. As Apel's colleague, Jürgen Habermas, has explained: The aim of such sciences is to "dissolve" the "causality of fate," that is, to liberate

the "subject-objects" of causal explanation from the operative force
of causes of which they are unaware.[13] In Apel's words, "The point
here is to deepen the self-understanding of human actions from the
inside, so to speak, by understanding their irrational and alien determinations, determinations that at first can only be explained."[14]

In summary, then, Apel differentiates three legitimate approaches
to the social sciences, connected with three "knowledge-constitutive"
interests: deductive-nomological sciences correspond to a "technological" interest in predicting and controlling behavior; historical-hermeneutic sciences correspond to the interest in expanding
communicative understanding; and critical-reconstructive sciences
pursue an interest in emancipation from pathological or ideological
impediments to understanding.[15] In Apel's work this theory of interests
is part of his transcendental-pragmatic transformation of Kantian philosophy. Rather than attempting to sketch his overall project, however,
I would like to close this introduction by indicating the importance of
Apel's expanded "philosophy of science" for the question of objectivity
in the social sciences.

As against Gadamer's hermeneutics, Apel's analysis means that it
is no longer necessary to replace the natural scientific concept of
objectivity with a notion of participation in cultural tradition. Instead,
the methodological combination of explanation and understanding
entails the possibility of monitoring the rationality of the cultural tradition itself. The norms, values, and self-interpretations of the tradition
need not be accepted at face value; they can be explained in terms
of the social and historical conditions affecting them. What Apel per-
ceives as a dangerous "hermeneutic idealism" is thus supplemented
by introducing a theoretical explanation that refers to factors outside
the tradition's own account of itself. From a hermeneutic perspective,
this attempt to correct "understanding" with "explanation" would be
seen as a reflection of the same "objectivistic illusion" characteristic
of deductive-nomological science; it supposes that the use of explanatory "method" removes the pitfalls of historicism and subjectivism,
when it is itself part of the tradition of interpretation. For Apel, however,
this objection would be telling only if it were possible to assume an
absence of ideological confusion in a culture's view of itself. As long
as this assumption continues to founder on obvious discrepancies between social values and actual practices, political ideals and concrete
policies, the need for critique and distanced "objectivity" remains.

# Author's Preface

The specific occasion for the following study was a colloquium on Georg Henrik von Wright's *Explanation and Understanding* held in Helsinki in January 1974. My own contribution came too late to be printed in the book that J. Manninen and R. Tuomela published in connection with this colloquium (*Essays on Explanation and Understanding*, Dordrecht, Holland, 1975). A shortened version of my essay did appear in G. Ryle's *Contemporary Aspects of Philosophy*, under the title "Causal Understanding, Motivational Explanation, and Hermeneutical Understanding: Remarks on the Recent Stage of the Explanation-Understanding Controversy." In addition, Manninen, Tuomela, and I agreed to collaborate on a volume in the Suhrkamp Discussion Series containing German translations of some of the essays in the English book, together with other German contributions. This collection has now appeared under the title *Neue Versuche über Erklären und Verstehen*. Although I had intended to include the German version of my article in this volume, it had to be excluded again since in the meantime it had become a book. Nevertheless, although my contribution is appearing as an independent publication, I want to emphasize its close relation to the original intention of the Discussion Series. Indeed, it can be viewed as the second volume of *Neue Versuche über Erklären und Verstehen*. I would like to thank G. H. von Wright, the participants in the Helsinki conference, and the authors of the essays in the Suhrkamp volume for providing the impetus to reconstruct an old dispute within the German philosophical tradition, a dispute which I, for one, have never considered either resolved or irrelevant. (See the appendix to this volume.)

In recent years a series of important publications has appeared in Germany on the same theme. Because I have not been able to take sufficient account of these publications in the text, I would like to draw attention to them here. In 1977 Suhrkamp published G. Meggle and A. Beckermann's two-volume collection *Analytische Handlungstheorie* (Vol. I, *Handlungsbeschreibungen*; Vol. II, *Handlungserklärungen*). In 1976 C. H. Beck, in Munich, published O. Schwemmer's *Theorie der rationalen Erklärung: Zu den methodischen Grundlagen der Kulturwissenschaften*, a work which comes from the Erlanger School of constructivism and is, next to Dray's and von Wright's investigations, the third most ambitious monograph on this theme. My own investigations have the extraordinarily important relation between hermeneutic and ethical rationality as one of their foci; however, I could only suggest the significance of the criterion of "meaning-rationality" that Schwemmer postulates in addition to that of purposive-rationality. Two studies seem closely tied to my transcendental-pragmatic interpretation of von Wright's theory of interventionist causality: H. J. Schneider's "Die Asymetrie der kausal Relation," in *Vernünftiges Denken, Studien zur praktischen Philosophie und Wissenschaftstheorie*, eds. J. Mittelstrass and M. Riedel (Berlin and New York, 1978); and A. Wellmer's "Georg Henrik von Wright über 'Erklären und Verstehen'," *Philosophische Rundschau* (1979). Finally, I was familiar with pertinent works by G. Meggle ("Eine Handlung verstehen," in *Neue Versuche über Erklären und Verstehen*, and "Eine kommunikative Handlung verstehen," in G. Grevendorf, ed. *Sprechakttheorie und Beudeutung* [Frankfurt, 1979]). Here I can only point out that, for the first time in Germany, these studies use the full technical and formal-logical sophistication of analytic philosophy to the advantage of the other, hermeneutic side.

At this point I wish to express my thanks to those who helped me prepare this text for publication: Cornelia Tutuhatunewa, for producing the manuscript; Matthias Kettner, for help in correcting it; and Joachim Leilich, for his assistance in reading the galley proofs and compiling the index.

# Understanding and Explanation

# Introduction

Johann Gustav Droysen's *Grundrisse der Historik* appeared in manuscript form in 1858. (It first appeared as a book in 1868.) Here, Droysen writes: "According to the object and nature of human thought there are three possible scientific methods: the speculative (formulated in philosophy and theology), the mathematical or physical, and the historical. Their respective essences are to know, to explain, and to understand."[1] As far as I know, this is the first time the distinction between explanation and understanding is used to ground the historical sciences methodologically and to distinguish them from the natural sciences (or, more precisely, from mathematical physics). Both were further to be demarcated from the "speculative knowledge" of philosophy and theology, which, for Droysen and his contemporaries, meant German Idealism and, in particular, Hegel.

Droysen elaborates his concept of understanding (*Verstehen*) in definitions that remain epistemologically relevant:

The possibility of understanding consists in the fact that the expressions which are present as historical material are congenial to us. It is determined by the condition that the sensuous spiritual nature of mankind manifests (*äussert*) every inner process to sensuous perception and in every outer expression (*Äusserung*) mirrors inner processes. In being perceived the outer expression provokes the same inner processes by projecting itself into the inner of the perceiver.[2]

The individual expression is understood as an expression of the inner through an inference back to this inner; the inner is understood through the example of the expression and as a central force which represents itself in this example as in every one of its peripheral effects and expressions.[3]

The analysis of *Verstehen* as an inference back from the outer to the inner reveals the epistemological dependence of Droysen's *Historik* on Schleiermacher and Boeckh's grounding of "hermeneutics."[4] Both of the latter sought to answer the question as to the conditions of the possibility of understanding in part by refering to Leibniz and Herder's theory of monads of psychical force (*pyschischen Kraft-Monaden*). In addition, Schleiermacher furnished the methodological topos of the hermeneutic circle, a topos he uncovered by philosophically appropriating and assimilating the tradition of hermeneutics that Protestant theology, humanist philology and jurisprudence developed as a pragmatic theory of textual interpretation.[5] In Droysen's work the topos appears as follows:

The individual is understood from the whole and the whole from the individual. Because he is an "I," a totality in himself just as he whom he has to understand, the person who understands completes the latter's totality from the individual expression and the individual expression from the latter's totality. Understanding is just as synthetic as analytic, just as much induction as deduction.[6]

Schleiermacher's new philosophical grounding of the tradition of hermeneutics is also oriented towards the paradigm of linguistic understanding stemming from Italian humanism. Droysen writes: "Our historical understanding is completely the same as our understanding of those with whom we speak. It is not merely the individual word of the individual sentence that we comprehend; this individual expression is rather for us an outer expression of its inner."[7]

Finally, we find in Droysen, as in Hegel, an indication of the revolutionary consequences of the hermeneutic-dialectic starting point in philosophy: the hermeneutic circle has implications that are anthropologically and ethically relevant insofar as it supersedes the methodological solipsism of the traditional philosophy of consciousness. "Humanity becomes what according to its analysis it is—totality in itself—only in understanding others, in being understood by others, in ethical communities (family, folk, state, religion, etc.)."[8]

Above all, Droysen exhibits a philosophical consciousness of the necessity and importance of the methodological dichotomy between explanatory sciences and those involving understanding:

Historical research does not intend to explain, i.e., to derive the later from the earlier, or to derive phenomena from laws in terms of which they can be seen to be necessary, to be mere effects or developments. If the logical necessity of the later lay in the earlier, there would be an analogue to eternal matter and material processes, not the ethical world. If historical life were the reproduction of what always remains the same, it would be without freedom or responsibility, without ethical content, hence only organic nature.[9]

This paragraph documents the philosophical point at issue in the controversy over explanation and understanding (or *Verstehen*) upon which the present work focuses. (Hereafter, we also refer to it as the E-V controversy.) Of course, the historically significant form of the debate began not with Droysen but later, with Wilhelm Dilthey. In 1883, in his *Einleitung in die Geistesiwissenschaften*, Dilthey made the dichotomy between understanding and explanation the terminological foundation for distinguishing between the natural sciences annd Geisteswissenschaften as a whole. Furthermore, he explicitly connected the dichotomy to the demand for an epistemological grounding of the Geisteswissenschaften in the sense of a "critique of historical reason" analogous to Kant's "critique of pure reason." In this way Dilthey attempted to answer John Stuart Mill's *Logic*, in which the "moral sciences" (Dilthey's Geisteswissenschaften) were adapted to the positivist program of causally explanatory sciences or the model of the natural sciences.[10]

From a contemporary perspective Dilthey's earlier exposition and grounding of the method of *Verstehen* seems a partial step backward, or a deviation, in comparison to Droysen. Dilthey proclaimed an "interpretive" psychology to be the philosophical foundation for the Geisteswissenschaften and, accordingly, emphasized primarily the aspects of psychological understanding in Schleiermacher's foundation of hermeneutics. This position has become absolutely decisive for the E-V dichotomy; it is represented in the following explications:

We explain through intellectual processes, but we understand through the cooperation of all dispositional and spiritual forces (*Gemütskrafte*) in understanding and their submergence in the object.[11]

The Geisteswissenschaften are distinguished from the natural sciences insofar as the latter have as their objects facts which enter into consciousness as if from outside, and are given as phenomena and individuals. In contrast, the objects of the Geisteswissenschaften originally enter consciousness from inside, as reality and as a living relation. Hence, for the natural sciences a connection in nature arises only through supplementary inferences, by means of an association of hypotheses. However, for the Geisteswissenschaften it follows that, in them, the connectedness of psychical life is thoroughly basic as an originally given one. We explain nature, but we understand psychical life.[12]

In contrast to an atomistic, natural-scientific psychology, interpretive psychology starts from "experienced relations which are given with original and immediate force."[13] Dilthey further states that "the transition of one condition into another, the effect which leads from one to the other, falls within inner experience." Thus, on the foundation of the structural relation that we "experience, which comprehends all passions, pains and fortunes of human life," we should "understand human life, history, and all the depths and precipices of mankind."[14] "The experienced connectedness of psychic life" is, and remains, "the firm, experienced and immediately certain foundation of psychology." This contrasts with the natural sciences, where "a causal connection is added supplementarily to the given through the construction of hypotheses."[15]

To be sure, the new philosophy and epistemology on which Dilthey wanted to ground his "critique of historical reason" is not unequivocally represented by psychology. It is more appropriately associated with the notion of transforming Kant's transcendental philosophy of consciousness into a quasi-transcendental philosophy of life. In it, the Kantian functions of the understanding in constituting objects are to be replaced or expanded by life relations (*Lebensbezüge*) as the conditions for the possibility of world significance, whether in the sense of the structural connections of psychical life or the sense of the naked opposition that the real world qua nature presents to the will. The former sense can be experienced or reproductively understood in its expressions; the latter reflects a sideshow of the former, and its connections can be established only externally, by means of explanatory hypotheses. Dilthey retained this new fundamental approach in *Der Aufbau der geschichtllichen Welt in den Geisteswissenschaften*. Here, under the influence of the neo-Kantian and Husserlian critique of psychologism, he abandoned the view that psychology forms the basic science and gave his *Verstehen* epistemology an objective turn, one oriented in part toward Hegel and, to this extent, in part returning to Droysen. The following positions are characteristic of this "late phase," to which, at first, the E-V controversy paid too little attention.

Dilthey now calls it an error "to employ psychology for our knowledge of the inner side of psychical life" that the Geisteswissenschaften are to understand. "The understanding of this spirit [as it is expressed in Roman law] is not psychological understanding; it is the return to a spiritual form with its own structures. . . ."[16] At issue here is the understanding of "objective spirit" or its "objectification" in the form of meaning. For the late Dilthey, "objective spirit" is a sphere of commonality that mediates between individual "spiritual" subjects and thus serves as the condition for the possibility of understanding:

Each individual life-expression represents something common in the realm of objective spirit. Every word, every sentence, every gesture or form of politeness, every work of art and every political act is intelligible only because a commonality binds those who express themselves in them with those who understand them. The individual experiences, thinks and acts constantly only in such a sphere of commonality and only in it does he understand.[17]

Of course, understanding remains epistemologically bound to the internal connection of experience and expression (*Erleben* and *Ausdruck*):

The Geisteswissenschaften have the objectification of life as that which is comprehensively given to them. To the extent, however, that the objectification of life is something intelligible to us, it contains throughout the relation of the outer to the inner. Accordingly, this objectification is everywhere related in understanding to the experience in which its own content is disclosed to a life-unit and which allows the interpretation of all others.[18]

The interrelation between life, expression and understanding [comprehends] not only the gestures, facial expressions and words with which human beings communicate with one another, nor only the lasting spiritual (*geistige*) creations . . . or the continuing objectification of spirit in social forms; . . . even the psychological unity of life is known to itself through the same double relation of experience and understanding; it becomes aware of itself in the present, rediscovers itself as something past in memory . . . and, on the other hand, we understand ourselves and others only insofar as we bring our experienced life into every kind of expression of our own or alien life. Thus, in all cases, the interrelation of experience, expression and understanding is the characteristic procedure through which humanity is present as the object of the Geisteswissenschaften.[19]

In comprehending the world speculatively as the alienation of spirit, Hegel had already claimed a dialectical identity of the subject of knowledge with the object of knowledge. Dilthey makes a similar assumption with respect to grounding the intersubjective validity of the empirical Geisteswissenschaften. Moreover, in his revived philosophy of spirit he connects this premise as to the identity of subject and object with a revival of the basic principle of Giambattista Vico's *Scienza Nuova*,[20] according to which we are able to understand history because, in a certain way, we ourselves have made it:

In the understanding of a historical product, as in the understanding of the expression of something inner, no logical identity is embodied but rather the unique relation of a sameness among different individuals. . . . These individuals understand each other not through their uniformity. . . . They understand each other rather through possibilities which the individual possesses within certain limits, possibilities which allow one to start with the expressions and effects of a completely differently formed individual and to reexperience the latter's inner states and processess as the inner belonging to him. For the individual has possibilities in himself which extend beyond what he can realize as his own life.[21]

The first condition for the possibility of the Geisteswissenschaften lies in the fact that I myself am a historical being, that he who investigates history is the same as he who makes history.[22]

Thus, according to the scope of the phenomena which fall within it, the concept of the Geisteswissenschaften is determined by the objectification of life in the external world. Only [that which] spirit has created does it understand. Nature, the object of the natural sciences, comprises the reality produced independently of the effect of spirit.[23]

This attempt to ground the methodological, epistemological claim to the autonomy of the Geisteswissenschaften was adopted in modified form by Weber and the neo-Kantians. It was criticized by positivists and neopositivists, and thus began the controversy over explanation and understanding that continues to this day. The logic of explanation promoted by "unified science" has not had the last word even within analytic philosophy. Rather, the pragmatically oriented post-Wittgensteinian analysis of language games—of the interweaving of language use, actions, and paradigmatic experiences—has in some ways renewed the basic positions of the hermeneutic philosophy of the Geisteswissenschaften. This is especially true of William Dray's *Laws and Explanation in History* and Peter Winch's *The Idea of a Social Science and Its Relation to Philosophy*, both of which were already known in Germany in the 1960s.[24] It is also true of Georg Henrik von Wright's more recent work, *Explanation and Understanding*, the book that inspired the present analysis.

The methodological approach and strategies of argumentation involved in the post-Wittgensteinian analysis, of course, differ in important respects from those of the pre-analytic philosophy of the Geisteswissenschaften. The neo-Wittgensteinian's new fundamental approach actually was not motivated by scientific theory. Although the three works cited above explicitly draw consequences for the theory of science (e.g., with regard to the rules of language games and forms of social life and with regard to the teleological structure of intentional actions, they concentrate on detailed logical problems. In this regard they differ both from Dilthey's global focus on "historical-social reality" and from Max Weber's methodological reflections. Even in its cautious broadening of pragmatic horizons, the logical analysis of language seeks to comply with the standards set by logical semantics. But it is precisely for this reason—because of the level of sophistication it involves—that I think it is imperative to use the perspective of the dialectical-hermeneutic and transcendental-pragmatic tradition to look at the newest phase of analytic action-theory as represented in von Wright's book and in the ensuing discussion.

Our discussion must comply with two demands. On the one hand, it must establish a relation to the wide horizon of problems in philosophy and the theory of science within which the twentieth century has raised its questions. It must also establish a relation to the radical claims that neopositivism opposes to the hermeneutic philosophy of the Geisteswissenschaften. On the other hand, it must pursue the details of post-Wittgensteinian language analysis, and therefore necessarily screen out many important problems in a global theory of the Geisteswissenschaften or social sciences.[25] In what follows, I attempt to fulfill these two tasks by concentrating on the central problem of a critical reconstruction of the E-V controversy, especially the solution of the disputed questions at its foundation.

In the first part of the book I attempt to reconstruct the "dialectic" of three phases, or rounds, of discussion in the controversy, which is a presupposition for understanding the present problem situation. In doing so, however, I do not undertake the hopeless and, I think, fruitless attempt to present a value-neutral report. From the beginning, I shall bring the transcendental-pragmatic approach into play as the heuristic and normative standard of reconstruction. Naturally, this does not mean that disagreeable facts are to be ignored or that norms are to be derived from facts. In order to assess the problem of evaluation in a hermeneutic reconstruction of intellectual history (*Geistesgeschichte*), it is advisable to consider that Max Weber's concept of the Western process of "rationalization" represents an interpretive perspective that is both fruitful and not value-neutral. The following consideration is even more radical: Weber ultimately postulated the value-neutrality of social science because he assumed that only such a science could guarantee the intersubjective validity of its results, and thus historical progress. Hence, the value freedom of science can be demanded only in the name of an ultimate evaluation, and the question arises, whether it is justly demanded in this name. With regard to natural scientific and quasi-natural scientific descriptions and explanations, the question is certainly to be answered in the affirmative; with regard to the critical reconstruction of intellectual history in terms of possible progress, it is not. Reconstructing the E-V controversy involves doing the latter.

The second part of the present work is devoted to a critical interpretation of von Wright's book and some of the critical reactions to it. I focus on the question of whether the neo-Wittgensteinian or language-analytic distinction between the onto-semantic frameworks of causal explanation, on the one hand, and of teleological explanation, on the other, can help decide old disputes in the E-V controversy. As we shall see, because this question cannot be given a clear affirmative answer, it is necessary to collect the results of the second part of the book in a third part. There, I shall present the beginning of both a transcendental-pragmatic solution to the E-V controversy and a theory of science that is differentiated according to cognitive interests.[26]

# I

## Toward a Critical Reconstruction of the Problem Situation

# 1
## The Three Phases of the Explanation-Understanding Controversy

### 1.1 Grounding the Interpretive Geisteswissenschaften or Cultural Sciences

At the beginning of the nineteenth century, in close connection with the new foundation of the philological and historical disciplines as sciences, Schleiermacher provided a new foundation for "hermeneutics," and Droysen founded the principles of history (*Historik*) in light of that foundation. Then, with reference to the dichotomy between explanation and understanding, Dilthey grounded the Geisteswissenschaften, first, on a psychological foundation and subsequently on a quasi-transcendental life philosophy. Both strategies signaled his opposition to Mill's integration of the "moral sciences" into the unified science of nomological explanation. In the following period the dichotomy between explanation and understanding was, for the most part, associated with Dilthey's views and further elaborated in various, initially German studies. At the beginning of the twentieth century, contributors included:

(1) the Dilthey school itself, oriented toward "life philosophy, and later toward neo-Hegelianism;[1]

(2) the antipsychological and anti-"life-philosophy" school of neo-Kantianism in Heidelberg, associated with Wilhelm Windelband and Henrich Rickert,[2] and finally related to the latter school;

(3) Max Weber's concept of a *verstehende* sociology proceeding from the ideal-typical paradigm of purposive-rational understanding.[3]

The entire period of the attempt to ground the interpretive (*verstehende*) Geisteswissenschaften, or cultural sciences, must be understood against the contrasting background of the earlier positivism or scientism. I would like to characterize it as the first phase of the controversy between explanation and understanding.

In beginning our discussion, I think it is important to note at least some of the points in which the epistemological conceptions of Dilthey, the neo-Kantians, and Weber diverge. Dilthey first intended to transform the transcendental philosophy of consciousness by referring to the structural interconnection of life (or the life relations that ground experience and significance), expression and understanding,[4] but he was unable sufficiently to free this intention from the general psychologism of his time. Later he was even less able to avoid the danger of a quasi-positivistic historicism or relativism in his program of an empirical objectification of spirit and in his universal understanding of historical life. Windelband and Rickert therefore understood their attempts to found the "cultural sciences" as a corrective both to Dilthey's psychologism and the historicism or relativism of his "life philosophy."

Critique of Dilthey's Psychologism

The neo-Kantians sought to avoid Dilthey's psychologism by detaching *Verstehen* from its relation to experience, on the subjective side, and, on the objective side, from the real psychic processes it is supposed to reproduce. In contradistinction to natural scientific (physical or psychological) explanation, understanding was to be correlated with the binding, value-related or "irreal" meaning of individual human cultural activities. Thus, Rickert asserts, "To put the problem clearly [is always to ask] (i) whether by *Verstehen* one means the reexperience of individual psychic being or the comprehension of a supra-individual unreal meaning which grants to psychic being its historical interest, and (ii) how these forms of understanding are interrelated."[5]

Signs which are given "externally" must be perceived as more than simply the expression of a real "inner." Otherwise they remain unintelligible.[6]

We can always call the grasp of an irreal meaning an "understanding" and thereby distinguish it from the explanation of the merely actual psychical and physical material. . . . The real is understood [only] to the extent that and insofar as it is the bearer of an irreal meaning.[7]

The historian may consider not only his material as something unitary. He may also conceive his reexperiential understanding of a meaningful inner life of the past so much the unified act of his scientific knowledge that he characterizes it as "empathy with an alien soul." Nevertheless, the understanding of irreal meaning which is thereby accomplished and the reexperiencing of the real psychic processes which expire temporally are not identical.[8]

Only the irreal meaning can build the bridge between the processes of one's own inner life and those of a foreign psyche because, as irreal meaning, it is neither one's own nor foreign."[9]

In this way it seems that the neo-Kantians were able to presuppose that the problem of understanding, or *Verstehen*, involved a clear relation between subject and object. In other words, they were able to avoid a dimension of the problem which both hermeneutic and dialectic approaches take for granted: namely, the identification between the knowing subject and the subject's subject-object. In contrast to Dilthey, Rickert's account of the "sense data" given in hermeneutic experience could conform entirely to Kant's epistemology since Rickert saw no difference between these "sense data" and those of the natural sciences. In his view, the distinction between the constitution of the objects of the natural sciences and that of "individuals" as objects of cultural scientific understanding could be resolved exclusively in the formation of concepts. One need only distinguish individualizing, value-related concepts from the generalizing concepts of the natural sciences.

Phenomenologically speaking, the steep price exacted for this solution consisted in abandoning the question that Dilthey posed—whether a hermeneutic understanding concerned with expression (e.g., with linguistic signs) does not represent a form of experience that differs from the natural scientist's observation of "sense data" that are "expression-neutral" (semiotically put, of causally relevant indices). If one reflects on the fundamental shift in the constitution of phenomena that occurs in the transition from communication with persons or texts to the mere observation of verbal data or audiovisual material, then it no longer seems possible to reduce the difference between understanding and explanation simply to the question of concept formation. Rather, the question arises whether the synthesis of experience involved in apprehending meaning (e.g., qua empathy with the data of expression) does not differ from that involved in experiencing the physical world.

Dilthey raises this set of problems in demanding the transformation of the Kantian concept of experience in terms of the "life relations" he considered constitutive of the objects of the Geisteswissenschaften. It is not only these problems that the neo-Kantians avoid, however; they also evade—or rather, because of their "logism," overlook—the issue of Dilthey's transformation (in the sense of a "revivification") of the notion of the transcendental subject of knowlege. With this oversight they move in the direction of logical positivism's pure logic of science. Indeed, they stop short of it only because of their epistemologically and methodologically relevant theory of the object-constitutive "value-relevance" of knowledge.

## Historicism of Dilthey's "Life Philosophy"

Two aspects of Dilthey's historicism or relativism must be distinguished in order to clarify the neo-Kantian attempt at providing a corrective to it. As I have noted, Dilthey's historicism-relativism is connected to his empirical notion of the objectification of spirit (which includes both Hegel's objective spirit and his absolute spirit—art, religion, and philosophy) and to the account of the universal self-understanding of historical life. On the one hand, both Dilthey and the neo-Kantians followed the Kantian perspective in drawing a parallel between the natural and cultural sciences or Geisteswissenschaften with respect to the problem of the objective validity of knowledge. Both were concerned to secure the objective validity of understanding and thus its capacity for progress against the limitation of a particular historical standpoint. On the other hand, a deeper and, for Dilthey and Troeltsch, disturbing problem is involved here, which is characteristic of the special status of the cultural sciences or Geisteswissenschaften. This problem concerns the question whether the possibility of the epistemological validity or truth of understanding is not bound ultimately to the condition under which understanding, as valid *interpretatio*, can evaluate the normative validity of the *interpretandum*.[10]

The neo-Kantians were interested in guaranteeing the objective validity of *Verstehen* primarily in the first sense noted above—as it were, scientistically. They prepared the ground for Weber's demand for value-free understanding by distinguishing between an empirical, nonevaluative understanding of the "individual," resting on its historical relation to general cultural values, and a philosophical grounding of the validity of values immanent to history. To be sure, unlike Weber, Rickert did not think that the cultural sciences can be established satisfactorily in complete independence of a philosophical solution to the problem of the validity of cultural values. On the contrary, he believed that, in the last analysis, the objective validity of the results of the empirical cultural sciences remained dependent on the capacity of philosophy to ground the unity and objectivity of an order of values and therefore to secure the value rationality of understanding (*Wertrationalität des Verstehens*).

Max Weber was the first to relinquish this presumption. In his concept of value-free understanding, and particularly in the notion of purposive-rational understanding which he emphasized as an ideal type, an alternative premise is characteristic. The tendency toward "disenchantment" means that an objectively valid order of values can no longer be rationally founded. Hence, the Western process of rationalization and, within it, the progress of objectively valid sciences involve renouncing the assumption of one objectively valid order of values and substituting for it a "polytheism" of values which leaves to the individual an ultimate, prerational choice.

According to Weber, empirical science cannot derive objectively binding norms or values from facts even where it serves to interpret them. The illusion of a legitimate, evaluative Geisteswissenschaften, or cultural science, can last only as long as historical understanding does not objectify the ultimate, unreflective, and traditionally determined judgments that the scientist makes as a person. Thus Weber's reflections result in a historicism highly similar to that of Dilthey. Whereas Dilthey's pantheistically tinged historicism-relativism involves the universal understanding of all life expressions, however, Weber defends a rigorous dualism that is ethically motivated by the "dualistic idealism of freedom" in Dilthey's sense of "types of world-view." This dualism consists in an existential decisionism with regard to private world-orientations and in a scientism or instrumentalism with regard to the sphere of rational, intersubjectively valid information and practically relevant grounding procedures. Weber thus became a founder of the contemporary Western system of ideology which, in contrast to the Eastern system of integration, counterposes a public scientism and pragmatism with a private existentialism. (I will return to this consequence of historicism in the cultural sciences.) It is important to note, however, that Weber's doctrine of value-freedom, and particularly of value-freedom in the scientific understanding of norms and values, represents a confirmation of scientism on different methodological levels.

For the present inquiry, another feature of Weber's theory is more important: the analysis of interpretive explanation (*verstehenden Eklären*) or explanatory understanding (*erklärenden Verstehen*) in which, again, Weber at least approximates the scientism that follows the model of the natural sciences. On the one hand, with the neo-Kantians and implicitly with Dilthey, Weber emphasizes intelligibility (*Verständlichkeit*) as the distinctive characteristic of the objects of the cultural sciences. In this regard he apparently was inspired by the neo-Kantian idea I mentioned earlier, that for the cultural sciences the understanding constitutive of objects involves the formation of individualizing, value-related concepts. Weber thus argues for the methodological relevance of a type of understanding that precedes the reply to the ambiguous "why" question—whether the reply involves understanding, explanation, interpretive explanation, or explanatory understanding. He refers to this type of understanding as "direct observational understanding" (*aktuelles Verstehen*), meaning by it the answer to the question arising at the level of describing actions, institutions, or works in regard to what is actually present. In his view, this is to be determined by an understanding that refers not to nomological theories but to historical complexes of cultural values (state, religion, economy, art, etc.) Weber's account here deserves special emphasis since, in his subsequent neopositivist phase, he talks more about describing observable data and about describing data in the light of nomological theories. The notion of direct, observational understanding disappears from view.[11]

It is characteristic of Weber's earlier work that, although he answers the "why" question by referring to "connections" and "regularities," he recognizes the necessity for a methodologically relevant combination (or, better, of a differentially accentuated mediation) of understanding meanings and explaining events. Here again, he first emphasizes the necessity of the understanding peculiar to the cultural sciences: "What, however, at least in the full sense is appropriate only to human behavior are connections and regularities whose course can be clarified as intelligible. An understanding of human behavior gained through interpretation contains a specific, qualitative certainty (*Evidenz*) in very different magnitudes.”[12] To this extent, the types of rational understanding that he distinguishes—understanding in the sense of objectively correct rationality (*Richtigkeitsrationalität*), objective or subjective purposive-rationality (*Zweckrationalität*), and meaningful intelligibility (*sinnhafter Verstandlichkeit*)—form not merely psychological but logical, ideal-typical presuppositions of all causal explanation in the social sciences:

The most immediately intelligible form of meaningful structure in an action is the subjectively strictly rational action oriented towards means which are held (subjectively) to be unequivocally adequate to the attainment of (subjectively) unambiguously and clearly conceived ends. This is the case for the most part where the means seem appropriate to the goal for the investigator as well (where the criterion for objective purposive-rationality seems to be fulfilled for the investigator). . . . If one explains such behavior, this certainly does not mean that one explains it in terms of psychical states of affairs.

(In the latter case one is practicing a causally explanatory psychology which, for Weber as for the neo-Kantians, counts as a natural science.) Rather, it means “precisely the opposite: that one intends to derive it from the expectations which were subjectively entertained with respect to the behavior of the objects (subjective purposive-rationality) and which, according to suitable experience, could have been entertained.” This understanding in the light of normatively relevant criteria of rationality is the logical presupposition for the causal explanation of that which is no longer intelligible, for instance, of the irrational:

Conversely, each explanation of irrational phenomena, e.g., a panic on the stock market, requires, above all, a determination as to how, in the rational ideal-typical limit-case of purely purposive and correct rationality the matter would have been handled. Only if this is established, as the most basic considerations indicate, can the causal imputation regarding objectively as well as subjectively irrational components within the course of events be accomplished.[13]

Weber summarizes this conception of the normative and methodological necessity of presupposing rational understanding in causal explanation as follows:

Objectively correct rationality serves as an ideal type with respect to rational action, purposive rationality with respect to what is meaningfully intelligible on a psychological level, and the meaningfully intelligible with respect to unintelligibly motivated action. It is in comparison with these ideal types that the causally relevant irrationalities which are necessary to causal imputation are established.[14]

Despite his emphasis on the intelligibility of the objects of the cultural sciences, it is not Weber's opinion that causal imputation is to be undertaken only in the limit case of a failure to understand, in other words, with respect to "subjectively as well as objectively irrational components"; for, he also writes, "an interpretation which possesses certainty (*Evidenz*) to an especially high degree [specific qualitative certainty for understanding] proves nothing in itself with regard to its empirical validity. . . . Rather, understanding of content must always be checked through the usual methods of causal imputation before any interpretation, no matter how evident, becomes a valid 'interpretive explanation'."[15] Therefore Weber denies "that *Verstehen* and causal explanation have no [positive] relation to one another,"

even though it is true that they begin their work from opposite poles of the event, that the statistical frequency of behavior makes it in no way more intelligible, nor does optimal intelligibility say anything about frequency, that with respect to absolute subjective purposive-rationality, intelligibility even speaks against frequency. For, irrespective of all this, certain meaningfully understood psychic relations and certain currents of motivation which are especially oriented by purposive-rationality are, for sociology, best qualified to serve in a causal chain—those, for example, which begin with external circumstances and lead in the end back to external behavior.[16]

Weber thus moves in the direction of a methical mediation of understanding and causal explanation that will be very significant for our analysis of the second and third phases of the E-V controversy. On the one hand, the theory of "interpretive explanation" seems to foreshadow the neopositivist view according to which understanding has a merely prescientific or heuristic function in the service of causal explanation. On the other hand, Weber's remarks point to a crucial aspect of *Verstehen*: Even if, in itself, *Verstehen* is relevant from a methodological standpoint, it may be not only possible to show that "understood" grounds are causally effective motives; this may be necessary for confirming the empirical accuracy of the "interpretive explanation." This suggestion will be important in our critical discussion of the post-

Wittgensteinian revival of the E-V dichotomy, which, in the form of a "New Dualism," distinguishes two language games, one in which actions are understood and one in which phenomena are causally explained.

It is essential to note that, in spite of his demand for "causal imputations," Weber retained Windelband's and Rickert's distinction between individualizing (ideographic) and generalizing (nomothetic) methods. Like Rickert, he was convinced that the relation to general value-ideas was as significant for the selective constitution of objects in the cultural sciences as was the search for laws in the natural sciences. This distinction (itself determined by a prior distinction in cognitive interests) led him to conclude that, whereas more general laws were most important for the exact natural sciences, for the knowledge of historical phenomena they were the emptiest in content and the least valuable. If this thesis is correct, the historical sciences confront the following problem: How can one impute causes to individual actions, conceived as events, without assuming the possibility of employing universal laws to deduce and predict them in their intelligibility? I shall return to this problem.

## 1.2 The Neopositivist Logic of Explanation in "Unified Science"

The point of departure for a second phase of the E-V controversy in the twentieth century was provided by the deductive-nomological (D-N) model of causal explanation formulated by Karl Popper,[17] Carl Hempel,[18] and Paul Oppenheim, which, within neopositivism at least, has been associated with the program of "unified science" or "methodological unity."[19] Hempel's essay "The Function of General Laws in History" is the classic starting point of this more recent discussion. With regard to reconstructing the E-V controversy, the challenge it raises can be summarized in three main points:

1. At the most fundamental (and, therefore, least considered) level, the premise is that the work of "scientific explanation" or "understanding" lies in answering the question why something was to be expected as an event. This delineation of their task holds for all empirical sciences to the extent that they go beyond the description of data.[20] In later works, which are in part a response to William Dray, Hempel clarifies this implicit thesis.[21] He writes, for example: "Science seeks

to answer not only the question as to what has happened, happens or will happen in the world, but also the question as to why it is so. Questions of this second kind are answered through scientific explanation." In the case of explanation in terms of "good reasons" or "systems of rules," "we are not justified in saying that, if what the explanans sentences state is the case, then it was to be expected that S would decide against A."[22]

2. The second thesis of unified science is that in all empirical sciences (and, therefore, in history), explanation consists in the subsumption of the explanandum under "general laws" (i.e., "universal empirical hypotheses"). Explanation in this sense takes the form of a deduction of the explanandum from the explanans, that is, from at least one law and antecedent conditions. Ordinarily, however, historical explanations do not refer to general laws. Hempel sees two reasons for their absence. On the one hand, the presupposed individual-psychological or social-psychological laws belong to everyday experience, and thus are assumed to be self-evident. On the other hand, given the present state of the science, the explicit specification of implicitly applied laws remains too difficult. Hence the historian makes do with "explanation sketches." (At this point the question arises whether it is possible, in principle, to complete the "because" sentences of the historian by identifying general laws; this question forms part of our further discussion.)

3. Most instructive from the standpoint of reconstructing the dialectic of the E-V controversy is the strategy with the help of which Hempel dismisses the methodological claims of the "interpretive" Geisteswissenschaften. Elaborating on an aperçu by Otto Neurath,[23] Hempel detaches the moment of empathy from the structure of hermeneutic knowledge to which it has belonged since Schleiermacher.[24] Although this structure includes the operation of verifying or correcting conjectures, Hempel considers empathy relevant only as a psychological-heuristic procedure prior to science proper. Thus its function consists only in discovering hypotheses that can be employed in a causal-nomological explanation, that is, in an explanation viewing motives as causes and maxims as laws.[25] To my knowledge, this strategy has never been examined adequately. Ultimately it is connected with Hempel's designation of the causal explanation that answers the question why a certain event occurs as the only possible form of scientific explanation and understanding (see thesis 1 above). Having reduced

hermeneutic understanding to empathy and placed it in the service of causal explanation, Hempel can dispute its logical-scientific function by using an argument, the sharpest formulation of which runs as follows:

But the existence of empathy on the part of the scientist is neither a necessary nor a sufficient condition for the explanation of the scientific understanding of a human action. It is not necessary, for the behavior of psychotics or of people belonging to a culture very different from that of the scientist may sometimes be explainable and predictable in terms of general principles even though the scientist who establishes or applies those principles may not be able to understand his subjects empathetically. And empathy is not sufficient to guarantee a sound explanation, for a strong feeling of empathy may exist even in cases where we completely misjudge a given personality.[26]

The following questions can be raised with respect to both of these standard arguments.[27]

1. For a representative of a hermeneutic methodology, empathy contributes to the understanding of intentions, goals, and reasons. Thus we can question whether he would accept the reference to psychotics and members of foreign cultures as an argument for the possibility of circumventing understanding. He would rather consider it proof of the relevance of understanding for interpreting human actions; it is only in the limit case of pathology (and by no means in regard to members of foreign cultures) that understanding must be abandoned in favor of causal explanation or prognostically relevant generalizations along the lines of a natural science.

2. With regard to the second argument, the hermeneutic social scientist could ask why the method of understanding should guarantee the accuracy of its hypotheses.[28] The decisive question here is whether methods of empirical verification in the case of understanding can be the same as those in the case of explanation, namely, repeatable observations and experiments. Alternatively, the "hermeneutic circle" that Schleiermacher and Boeckh established points to a different process for verifying and correcting philological-historical conjectures, one involving a communicative-interpretive experience in further reading and deeper penetration into texts or sources. The significance of the dichotomy between the two procedures emerges in an example Hempel himself cites concerning the emigration to California of "Dust Bowl

farmers."[29] According to the example, this emigration was forced by the constant drought and sandstorms that made life in the Dust Bowl more and more difficult. But can we verify this hypothesis by observationally testing the hypothetical law: "Populations tend to emigrate to areas that offer better living conditions"? Even if as many farmers as possible are observed, must we not rather confirm the hypothesis by reading the relevant sources on the settling of the United States and by communicating with farmers indirectly, that is, through the mediation of historical tradition? The point becomes even clearer in imagining how one could empirically test a hypothesis as to the circumstances of Cleopatra's suicide. Cleopatra let herself be bitten by a snake because she refused to be put on display in Octavius's triumphant march into Rome and because she wanted to become immortal. How can this thesis be verified by observing (living?) women (or queens?)?

More important in view of the later phases of the E-V controversy is Hempel's discussion of the opposition of teleological and causal analysis in the examination of purposive behavior.[30] As we have seen, Hempel understands explanation as a scientific answer to the question why an event occurs. Hence he considers teleological explanation referring to motives as an alternative answer to this question, such that a motive which lies in the future is to function as a cause (*causa finalis qua causa efficiens*). On the basis of this pre-Galilean supposition, Hempel can argue in the following way: Even in the case in which a goal is projected but not achieved, a motive must be presumed to exist and must be empirically identified, although, as always, the identification is indirect. The motive must therefore be considered a cause, that is, an antecedent condition within the framework of the D-N model. Hempel thus comes to the view that the causal complex in a motivational explanation can be characterized by: (a) the desire to attain a certain goal, and (b) the conviction that a certain mode of action is the most likely means to its achievement. Given the premises of Hempel's concept of explanation, this is a strong argument for his view of the volitional-cognitive causal complex, as, indeed, the entire subsequent discussion demonstrates. To be sure, from the hermeneutic perspective (in this case from the perspective of Max Weber's purposive-rational understanding but not reinterpreted to mean an "interpretive explanation"), one can ask whether understanding goals (for example, the future-related programs of human beings, even those not realized) is not an autonomous task of the Geisteswissenschaften alone, one that a comprehensive scientific enterprise also in fact performs in a methodologically successful way. Obviously, the same objection obtains for understanding grounds, maxims, and convictions, as well as for understanding actions of a specific type insofar as they are guided by specific grounds, maxims, or convictions.

This much is already clear with regard to Hempel's conceptual specification of scientific explanations (and understanding), on the one hand, and hermeneutic understanding, on the other. Together with his implicit premise that this categorial determination embodies a thorough disjunction of methodological and merely heuristic relevance, it constitutes a decisive assumption for the reductionist notion of a "unified science" or "methodological unity." Moreover, it threatens (at least partially) to block the E-V controversy through a petitio principii; the danger arises that the arguments for and against the methodological independence of the Geisteswissenschaften or social sciences will be obscured by the dispute over the meaning of the two terms, understanding and explanation.

For this reason it is important to draw attention to differences in the paradigmatic formulations of the question that distinguish the various phases of the controversy. For those interested in grounding the Geisteswissenschaften, the essential question involves the relation between explaining natural events and understanding meaning. Hempel shares his preconception of explanation with this first phase. From the outset, however, he ignores the question whether the understanding of meaning might be methodologically relevant. (Indeed, he seems not to know the tradition of hermeneutics that is pertinent here). He asks only if there can be an explanation of the occurrence of spatio-temporal phenomena that does not correspond to the type he himself has explicated, and he denies this possibility for convincing reasons. The subsequent discussion in analytic (primarily Anglo-Saxon) philosophy has adopted Hempel's formulation of the question. That means it addresses the question of the possibility of alternative types of explanation but seems neither sufficiently familiar with the first phase of the E-V controversy nor sufficiently aware of the idiosyncratic character of Hempel's notion of explanation. In explicating different types of explanation, such as rational and teleological explanation, it de facto more or less renews the original methodological interest in grounding the Geisteswissenschaften.

Hempel dismisses each proposal by referring back to the undeniable fact that no alternative model corresponds to his preconception of explanation. Thus, in response to Dray's explication of "rational explanation" or of a "good reasons" essay (which practically confirms Weber's theory of "rational understanding" and, in particular, of "purposive-rationality"), Hempel argues: even if such a criterion were available,

[a criterion of rationality which, for the given kind of situation, singles out one particular course of action as the thing to do] an account of the form here considered cannot possibly explain why A did $x$. For, according to the requirement of adequacy set forth in . . . this essay, any adequate answer to the question why a given event occurred will have to provide information which, if accepted as true, would afford good grounds for believing that the event did occur.

In conformity with the standard of the causalists,[31] he adds: "The information that A was in a situation of kind C and that in such a situation the thing to do is $x$ affords grounds for believing that it would have been rational for A to do $x$ but no grounds for believing A did in fact do $x$."[32]

If Dray's schema of rational explanation is to be adapted to Hempel's demand for an explanation that answers the question "why the event occurred or was to be expected," then this adaptation takes the following form:

A was in a situation of type C.
A was a rational agent.
Schema R:     In a situation of type C, any rational agent will do $x$.

Therefore A did $x$.[33]

Here the new antecedent condition "A was a rational agent" is added, and the normative principle of action is replaced by a general empirical proposition or a quasi-nomological hypothesis. By means of this formal reductionism, Hempel reproduces the D-N model of unified scientific explanation. Further, he interprets the content of the premise "A was a rational agent" as the identification of a disposition and the content of the premise "A was in a situation of type C" as the designation of a contingent cause. Hence he suggests an analogy between a "rational explanation" and a causal explanation and thereby completes unified science's material reductionism.[34]

At this point, we can postpone the wider horizon of the question whether Dray (and before him, Weber) has not undermined Hempel's claim that the explanation of events has a monopoly on the cultural sciences. I think Hempel's restitution of the D-N model can be criticized on a more narrow basis. First, we can ask whether the "new antecedent condition" can be viewed as the identification of a disposition; for, as a disposition, it would have to be explicated in terms of an if-then regularity that could be operationalized empirically and thus would be open to empirical falsification. Dray has already shown, however, that, unlike hypotheses about laws, rational principles are not falsifiable. Hence we can ask further whether rational principles can be reformulated in Hempel's sense, as general empirical propositions that are, in principle, falsifiable. The difficulty that emerges here is, we must exclude the possibility of always placing the blame for the failure of a prediction on the fact that antecedent conditions and, in particular, the claim to rationality, have not been fulfilled.

If this possibility cannot be excluded, then at least the suspicion must arise that Hempel's reduction of Dray's explanation schema amounts to a formalistic obfuscation of the structure of rational understanding, that is, of the understanding of actions in terms of reasons and principles or, in other words, in terms of norms as subjective maxims. In this case we have to return to the larger horizon of the E-V controversy. The question arises: must not understanding in the Geisteswissenschaften or cultural sciences be viewed as the answer to a different question than that presupposed by Hempel's notion of explanation? Indeed, we can follow Weber in reversing the roles of explanation and "rational understanding" in the social sciences. That is, we can raise the possibility of the existence of quasi-nomological explanations that must be confirmed by empirical hermeneutic methods and which serve as heuristic preliminaries to the results of "rational understanding."

In *The Poverty of Historicism*, Popper shows that historically relevant actions—thus, for example, scientific innovations and similar, creative cultural accomplishments—cannot, in principle, constitute the subject of possible prediction or nomological theories. They are the subject only of an ex post understanding.[35] If I understand it correctly, this claim converges with Dray's denial of the possibility of laws in historical explanations.[36] We can therefore formulate our previous question more precisely: Is it possible to construct quasi-nomological explanations in which understanding plays a mediating role in at least certain social sciences, namely, in those that abstract from the historicity of actions as innovative cultural acts and concentrate on analyzing modes of action that are historically and innovatively determined but that, in the cross section, are relatively fixed? I will return to this question in the second and third parts of the present investigation.

## 1.3 The Neo-Wittgensteinian New Dualism

William Dray's investigations in *Laws and Explanation in History* to which I have referred indicate a new post-Wittgensteinian phase of the analytic philosophy of language. This phase surprised those accustomed to equating analytic philosophy with a neopositivistic or at least a scientistic logic of science, in that it questions the model of unified science and its subsumption theory of "covering law" explanation. Of course, Dray's investigations are indebted to R. G. Collingwood and hence to the preanalytic tradition. Even more characteristic of the neo-Wittgensteinian approach in the third phase of the E-V controversy is a series of works that began to appear in the late 1950s and that have been grouped together as the New Dualism.[37] Based on a language-analytic approach, all criticize the monopoly of subsumption-theoretic causal explanation and, implicitly, the probabilistic form of such explanation as well.

The "New Dualists" start from the late Wittgenstein's basic thesis, or better, suggestion that things can be meaningfully discussed only within the framework of consistent language games in which are interwoven the use of language, activities, and paradigms of world interpretation. Gradually this thesis led to a suggestive distinction between two fundamentally different language games, or rubrics, of concept formation. One language game discusses strictly observable (natural) events, their causes and regularities or laws that hold without exception. This language game can be identified approximately with the conceptual framework of the neopositivistic and scientistic model of subsumption-theoretic explanation (at least to the extent that one ignores the fact that the concepts of cause and causal law in the neo-Humean metatheory of the D-N model have been replaced with conceptions less substantial in pragmatic terms). The other language game accounts for human actions as well as the meaning intentions, reasons, aims, or goals that are bound up with them and the rules, norms, or maxims to which they refer. In no sense do the latter hold without exception, but, rather, are constituted precisely by the possibility of deviation or nonobservance.

If one interprets this dichotomy of language games in epistemological and methodological terms instead of ontological—or, more precisely, ontosemantic terms—then one can see it as a language-analytic reconstruction of the dichotomy between explanation and understanding developed in the nineteenth century. Of course, for the neo-Wittgensteinians, as for post-Heideggerian phenomenology, the E-V controversy raises a problem. At the prescientific level, the two language games correspond to two different modes of a preunderstanding of the world. Subsequently, at the level where scientific concepts are formed, the two language games divide into two forms of explanation or, as I want to suggest, into explanation, on the one hand, and methodical (hermeneutic) understanding, on the other.

The following works serve to represent stages in the neo-Wittgensteinian renewal of claims involved in the language game of action, claims connected to practical philosophy and the theory of the social sciences.[38]

In 1957, G. E. M. Anscombe's *Intentions* appeared. Here, she explicates the fundamental distinction between the description of natural events, in particular, those on which actions are based, and the many varied descriptions of the corresponding actions, descriptions that in each case depend on understanding the intentions. By referring back to Aristotle, Anscombe illuminated the possibility of explaining intentional actions in terms of the "practical syllogism." The year 1958 saw the appearance of R. S. Peter's *The Concept of Motivation* (a new, intentionalist, anticausalist explication of the basic concept of philosophical metapsychology and psychoanalysis) and Peter Winch's *The Idea of a Social Science and Its Relation to Philosophy*. Winch's book presents for the first time a quasi-hermeneutic interpretation of Wittgenstein and uses it to ground a sociology, the theme of which is not the concept of intentional action but that of "incommensurable" basic rule conventions and the forms of social life corresponding to them. A. I. Meldon's *Free Action*, which appeared in 1961, examines the consequences of the neo-Wittgensteinian dualism in language games for the problem of free action. In 1964, Charles Taylor published *The*

*Explanation of Behavior*, in which he connects the neo-Wittgensteinian point of view with the phenomenology of Merleau-Ponty and introduces the concept of "teleological explanation" as the foundation of the science of behavior or action. Finally, in 1971, G. H. von Wright's *Explanation and Understanding* appeared after a series of studies concerning the relation of actions and norms. Von Wright's book employs the neo-Wittgensteinian dichotomy between language games, on the one hand, as a basis for reconstructing the E-V controversy in the theory of science (in the extremely wide sense of contrasting the Galilean and Aristotelian traditions) and, on the other, as the starting point for a new theory of causality and teleological explanation in the social sciences.

In what follows I want to focus on the question of the significance of the neo-Wittgensteinian framework, and particularly of von Wright's work, with regard to resolving disputed points in the E-V controversy. Before examining this third phase of the debate or its most recent stage more closely, however, I want to review the background and presuppositions of the first two phases, this time from a greater philosophical and historical distance. This preliminary review will prepare the heuristic horizon for our discussion of the present state of the controversy.

**2**

# On the First Phase
# of the Controversy:
# The "Interpretive"
# Geisteswissenshaften

## 2.1 Renouncing the Teleological and Sympathetic Understanding of Nature and Its Consequences for the Cultural Sciences

The foundation of the exact natural sciences at the beginning of the seventeenth century presupposed renouncing the teleological and empathetic understanding of nature and enforced this interdiction against the Renaissance's neo-Aristotelian and neo-Platonic-pantheistic philosophy of nature. It was this rejection of an understanding "from inside" that first opened up nature as a nexus of relations that could be analyzed mathematically.[1] To be sure, the founders of modern natural science first replaced the internal understanding of nature with the speculative and heuristic notion of understanding or reconstructing natural laws as God's normative thoughts with regard to creation. For this notion, the idea of understanding the logical or metaphysical necessity of the relation between cause and effect remained appropriate. When David Hume established the logical contingency of this relation in the eighteenth century, however, he not only implicitly raised the problem of the conditions of the possibility of objectively valid natural laws, but accelerated the renunciation of the internal understanding of nature that served as the basis of the exact natural sciences. Hume denied that the regular connection between events or states that we characterize as cause and effect can be understood "from inside," as logically or metaphysically necessary. The consequence of this situation was the first subsumption-theoretic definitions of causal explanation by Kant, Comte, and Mill.[2]

Irrespective of the difference between transcendental-idealist and empirical-inductivist premises, these definitions agree that laws establishing necessity must be imposed on sense data "from outside," even though such hypothetical laws are to be verified empirically by observing the data. Put negatively, the sense data that constitute the original material or test material for the natural sciences do not involve phenomena that express "meaning" or anything "inner." They express neither the inner necessity of the causal connection nor any intentions with regard to goals or meanings. Correspondingly, the knowing subject on whom at least Kant explicitly reflected is no longer presumed to possess the capacities for sensuousness or interpretive empathy that it retained for the Renaissance philosophers Patrizzi, Telesio, Campanella, and Bruno, as well as for Herder.[3] In other words, in natural scientific knowledge, the relation of subject to object is assumed to be one of absolute difference, and it contains no possibility for mediation in the sense of the self-understanding of the one in the other. A reconciliation between subject and object occurs not on any premise such as that of the philosophy of identity, but only as a consequence of the observational testing of hypothetical laws and regularities in experiment.[4]

This was the problem situation in which the nineteenth century found itself in beginning its epistemological and methodological reflections on the foundations of philology and history, the central disciplines of what were later called the Geisteswissenschaften.[5] As noted, the development from Galileo to Hume and Kant involved an increasingly radical renunciation of the internal understanding of nature, the compensation for which lay in explanation on the basis of nomological hypotheses. Hence the question necessarily had to arise, whether the condition of the scientificity of the sciences of the "historical-social world" (Dilthey) did not lie in a similar development. Or did the problems of these latter sciences differ so greatly that they required restoring the validity of the claims for understanding eliminated at the beginning of the modern "instauratio magna scientiarum"— claims such as Aristotle's teleological understanding and the philosophy of identity's mediation of subject and object, perhaps reduced in its cognitive claim?[6]

## 2.2 The Positivist Radicalization of the Theoretical Separation of Subject and Object: Orientation of the Humanist Geistesweissenschaften toward Problems of Practical Reason

The positivist response to the question posed above followed from its naturalistic or causalist theory of the will, as well as from its related view of action as an effect of the will that could be determined inductively. These theories seem to have appeared as early as the late period of nominalist scholasticism in place of an intentionalist view of mental (*geistige*) acts, which then played no role until rediscovered by Franz Brentano. Hobbes was the first to develop a consistent theory of will formation, grounding the theory causally in impulses of the passions and viewing action as its causal effect. He thus refers to the will as an "appetite resulting from a precedent deliberation."[7] Hume, however, denies the capacity to perceive a logical connection between cause and effect, not only in the case of observing external sensuous objects but also with regard to reflection "on the operations of our own mind and on the command which is exercised by the will both over the organs of the body and over the faculties of the soul." Hume can no more admit an internal understanding of causal connection in the case of the "union of soul with body" than he can in the case of the "mutual operation of bodies." "We learn the influence of our will from experience alone. And experience only teaches us how one event constantly follows another, without instructing us in the secret connection which binds them together and renders them inseparable."[8]

In this way, Hume conceived of the actions of the will as objects of experience and of causal analysis, identical in this respect to the objects of external observation. Moreover, because in both cases he denied any possibility of understanding inner connections within the empirical data of science, Hume implicitly set the task of explaining the data by subsuming them under laws, that is, under empirically well-confirmed regularities and sequences. This suggested a perfect analogy between the epistemological problems and methodology of the natural sciences, on the one hand, and, first, psychology but later sociology, on the other. The premise of this paradigmatic, conceptual result is especially noteworthy: it involved replacing an intentional self-understanding of action which retained its relevance to practice with the standpoint of theoretical observation even in regard to one's own actions.

In my view, the humanities or Geisteswissenschaften could develop a fundamentally different epistemology only from the traditional orientation of European humanism toward the problem of practical reason. Given this orientation, one that is fundamental for historians, there was little plausibility in a theoretically directed analysis that dissolved the intelligibility of actions into the datum of conscious willing, on the one hand, and the data of observable movements, on the other; for such a dissolution disregards the intentional presuppositions that already underlie the multiplicity of action descriptions.[9] In the humanist tradition the cognitive interest in comprehending and describing empirical data normally was bound to the teleological horizon of understanding. This meant that, in contrast to the empirical metatheory of natural scientific experience, one absolutely could not return to the standpoint in which the relation between subject and object took a theoretical form; rather, such a return abandoned the reciprocity between practical self-understanding and the understanding of the actions of other human beings, a reciprocity presupposed in every action and linguistic communication, as well as in the philological-historical mediation of tradition.

Thus the difference between the problem situation of the Geisteswissenschaften and that of the natural sciences was suggested, above all, by the fact that, in contrast to the latter, the former retained an ambivalent relation to the traditional Aristotelian separation of theoretical and practical reason, and particularly to its Kantian reformulation.[10] A reminder of this separation is patent in Mill's use of the term *moral sciences* and in its German translation as the *Geisteswissenschaften*. Indeed, both Mill's terminology and the key English words "the humanities" and "literary criticism" demonstrate that even within the traditional domain of empiricism and positivism, the nonscientistic Aristotelian and humanistic aspect of these sciences could never be eliminated. It was Kant's paradoxical treatment of the distinction between theoretical and practical reason, however, that revealed the philosopical depth of the problem of the Geisteswissenschaften and thus indirectly initiated its discussion.

In *The Critique of Pure Reason*, Kant critically restricts the scope of the constitution of the objects of experience. Hence one could—and can—draw from it only the methodological consequence of a radical scientism. It limits the idea of knowledge to modern natural science and, at best, to a quasi-natural science, the categories of which have been reduced accordingly. Kant did not rescind this restriction later in defining teleology as a "regulative idea" for reflectively judging the quasi-organic connection between experiences; instead, by emphasizing the nonconstitutive character of teleological judgment, he confirmed the Galilean elimination of an "internal" understanding from the concept of the object of scientific experience. The introduction of teleology as a regulative idea may have offered an adequate basis for the biological analysis of system functions (although this can be doubted in light of modern systems theory). Nevertheless, for the human sciences it must remain deeply unsatisfying that, in contrast to natural events, their basic, empirically given phenomena — intentional actions, as well as speech acts and texts — were not even recognized by Kant as themes in the sense of the constitution of the empirical world.

In the case of human actions — or, indeed, the speech acts that occur in the framework of the dialogic encounter between the I and the thou — what is unsatisfying is not only this exclusion from the sphere of an empirical world that can be constituted in the form of objects. It must be almost more irritating to us that Kant rejected their constitution in the sense of mere objects of the world of appearance. Kant wanted to ban the freedom of the will from the world of experience, first, by distinguishing between things-in-themselves and appearances, then, by confirming freedom in the sense of "intelligible" freedom. In interacting with other human beings, however, we can experience freedom as the practical freedom of action that belongs both to the other and to ourselves. This is an experience that is as certain as the "intelligible freedom" that Kant thinks can and must be "thought." At least in this respect, then, the entire systematic starting point of transcendental idealism, including the distinction between phenomena and noumena, becomes questionable.[11] In a certain sense, Kant seems to confirm precisely this point in his philosophy of practical reason. There, the experience of the social-historical world of practical freedom in action and its interpretation in human communication is neither scientistically nor phenomenally reduced; rather, it is implicitly — and unavoidably — rehabilitated.[12]

Today this paradoxical resolution to the problem reminds us of Wittgenstein's distinction in the *Tractatus Logico-Philosophicus*, between that which can be meaningfully described (the facts of natural science) and that which cannot be said (the higher things that nonetheless exist). In any case, from the problem situation that Kant left behind, the theory of science could draw only two kinds of consequences. Either the theory had to view a critical revision of the Kantian epistemology as the presupposition for grounding the Geisteswissenschaften (this was the conclusion that Dilthey reached in his program of a "critique of historical reason"), or it had to make the promotion of the Geisteswissenschaften to the status of science contingent on the possibility of reducing its categories to those of a theoretical science in Kant's sense—or, in other words, the conceptual language of causal-analytic, nomological natural science.[13] This was the consequence that, mutatis mutandis, positivism, and especially modern logical positivism, drew.

As these reflections indicate, a central issue in the E-V controversy seems to involve the fundamentally different attitudes assumed by the two sides with regard to the relation between theoretical and practical reason. Put more precisely, the issue involves the different extensions of the concept of science each side presupposed in connection with this relation. The scientistic view is oriented toward the concept of "science" as it has developed along the paradigmatic lines of no-mological and explanatory natural science.[14] At a deeper level of pre-supposition, this means that a theoretical ideal of objectivity is maintained, which can be guaranteed only on the basis of a cognitive relation that is value-free, free of interpretation and involving a pure "subject-object-differentiation." Over the long term, its program involves promoting the human sciences, if possible, as well to the status of sciences capable of progress under the limiting conditions of this scientistic ideal of objectivity. At issue here are, one, psychology and sociology (the concerns of Mill and Comte, with different accents), two, "real" history, and three, if it all, philology and the histories of art, literature, science, and philosophy. Conversely, the protagonists of the special status of the Geisteswissenschaften are prepared to hold their concept of science open, in view of the peculiar problems of practical and perhaps even aesthetic reason. They are ready to adapt methodology to new and different problems rather than to validate the rigid demands of scientific methodology and thereby restrict the area of problems that can be investigated. If at first only unclearly and one-sidedly, they nonetheless recognize that historical-social reality represents a novel phenomenal and problem situation that, in contrast to nature, its components exhibit a fundamentally different relation to human beings themselves, to what Dilthey calls the "feeling, willing and knowing subject" of scientific knowledge.

## 2.3 The Post-Hegelian Problem of a Hermeneutic Mediation of the Subject and Subject-Object of the Geisteswissenschaften

Philosophically, a reflection that had gone through Hegel could not overlook the fact that, with regard to its substance, the object of the Geisteswissenschaften, or social sciences, is also the subject of the science. (Put in a way that has fewer presuppositions but which is less suggestive and less informative philosophically: for the first time, humankind is concerned with itself.) To be sure, from a formal-logical perspective, it is clear that the empirical object of the cognitive relation never coincides with the subject, since the psychological process of reflection leads to an infinite regress. This circumstance is not relevant here, however. On the level of generality proper to Hegel's philosophical reflection, it is easy to see that a science of history and society is inadequate to its own theme unless it can make human beings the object of its knowledge as subjects of both culture and science. It seems to me that the confrontation with this novel phenomenon or problem had to present the philosophy of science with fundamental problems of two different kinds, neither of which can be united with the scientistic ideal of objectivity.

First, the historical and social sciences had to question the epistemological and (despite Kant and positivism or phenomenalism) even the ontological presuppositions of the scientistic account of the relation between subject and object. They could not avoid at least implicitly returning to the mediation of the difference between subject and object that Schelling and Hegel had developed in their philosophies of identity. It was—and is—misleading for historians, for example, to view the identity of their objects (persons, groups, societies, cultures, epochs) in Kant's sense simply as the cognitive subject's constitutive act in synthesizing merely sensuous data. It is just as impossible to replace an epistemological consideration of the self-identification of the subject-object of knowledge with the pure identification of objects in space and time as it is, for example, to replace the "object-constitutive" rules that human subject-objects follow with the intentions and rules that guide a knowing subject's synthetic acts of understanding. Instead, it was (and still is) necessary to see that the constitution of the identity of the cognitive subject is itself mediated by an interpretive identification with the subject-object of knowledge. On the prescientific level, it is possible to see human self-consciousness as the product of communication with others, as the result of putting oneself in the position of another and, at the same time, seeing oneself from the other's perspective. But if that is so, it suggests that the knowledge of the Geisteswissenschaften (hermeneutic understanding) is to be understood as the controlled, methodical continuation of communicative identification with others, for example, in terms of a reciprocal understanding with foreign cultures and peoples or as an interpretive appropriation of one's own culture. We can retain the concept of a transcendental subject as the condition of the possibility of knowledge under these altered premises; but we must never conceive of it as the "finished" subject corresponding to the split between subject and object (that is, to the determination of the not-I by the I). Rather, we must understand it as mediated by interpretive identification with others and as always to be mediated in its definitive constitution.

In the nineteenth century those attempting to ground the Geisteswissenschaften could refer, above all, to Hegel's philosophy of spirit for similar conclusions. Of course, if these sciences were to be founded as empirical disciplines (according to the paradigm of the so-called Historical school[15]), then the self-recognition of humankind in its own history could not claim the total mediation of the difference between subject and object which, in Hegel's speculative system, was to be accomplished in a "knowledge of knowledge." For this reason, Dilthey did not consider founding the Geisteswissenschaften on Hegel's sublation (*Aufhebung*) of the concept of empirical science in the speculative idea of philosophical science; instead, he followed Kant's critique of reason, seeing his task as a "critique of historical reason" that ultimately retained the Kantian assumption of a transcendental distinction between particular individual sciences related to objects and philosophical reflection on the theory of knowledge. Therefore, for Dilthey, the fundamental epistemological problem consisted in retaining the quasi-transcendental, philosophical foundation of objectively valid knowledge (which presupposed the separation of subject and object) while providing the possibility, in principle, of an empirical-hermeneutic mediation between subject and object based on an interpretive rediscovery of one's self in the other. *Verstehen*, in the sense of the methodical "hermeneutic circle" between "subjective" preunderstandings and their "objective" amendment on the basis of the sensuous data, took the place of Hegel's totally speculative mediation. Thus, it seems to me that this basic epistemological and methodological figure expresses both the connection and the difference between hermeneutics as the methodology of empirical understanding and dialectics.[16]

Second, the circumstance that the human subject of science in the Geisteswissenschaften is concerned with itself has a practical side, one that opposes every attempt to objectify man theoretically. Thus it contradicts not only the value-free, scientistically conceived relation between subject and object, but Hegel's demand for a dialectical mediation of their difference in reflection as well. As subject-objects of science, human beings are always already cosubjects of practice for the subjects of the science; they are partners in the sense that they can either cooperate (and cooperate in the science) or not cooperate (again in science, for example, by thwarting prediction and objectification by scientific procedures). To understand them as "objects— that is, understand the "social-historical world"—never means merely to grasp a "settled," factually given entity; neither does it imply only the extrapolation of future trends from objectively considered processes. Prior to both, it always already derives from an ethically relevant projection of a common human future. It means to apply to the reality to be reconstructed interpretive perspectives that involve interpretive identification (or distantiation even in the sense of failing to make something a theme). The young Hegelians already recognized the impossibility in principle of absorbing historical reality into a definitive ex post facto reflection as Hegel suggested. From this insight they derived the postulate of the mediation of theory and practice, a postulate to which the young Karl Marx gave the sense of transforming reality by sublating and realizing philosophy, and Kierkegaard, the sense of realizing the individual's existence.[17]

The attempt to ground the Geisteswissenschaften, then, could not reinvoke the teleological understanding of human actions in Hegel's sense. For Hegel, the "goal-directed activity" of world-spirit mediates itself with itself through the "subjective" goals that historical agents posit and the methods they use to achieve these goals. For those attempting to ground the Geisteswissenschaften, however, the issue could not be to once again counterpose the Galilean tradition of natural-scientific causal explanation to the Aristotelian tradition of teleological explanation; neither could they be concerned with thereby contrasting the objective, nomological explanation of phenomena that refers to "efficient causation" with a speculative explanation of world history viewing goals as "final causes" realized through appropriate means. As Max Weber's concept of purposive-rational understanding indicates, the philosophy of the Geisteswissenschaften had to employ a formal concept of means-ends rationality, in terms of which it could show the intelligibility of human action by investigating both the subjective goals that historical agents project and their beliefs as to the means of reaching them.

Therefore, the attempt to ground the philosophy of the Geisteswissenschaften was led to explore the form in which Kant's assertion of the primacy of practical reason could be rationally legitimated as the a priori of all historical-hermeneutic perspectives for reconstruction and interpretation. Should one begin from a notion of the progress of the human species in realizing its destiny, even if that destiny could no longer be metaphysically guaranteed but only ethically authorized, as it is in Kant's work? It seems to me that something like this was the tendency of a reconstructive philosophy of historical progress that furthered the Enlightenment and sought to instruct by means of a normative ethics. Certainly, as a material philosophy of history in Hegel's or the Marxist sense, this tendency did not avoid ontological dogmatization. Or should one begin from Herder's aperçu that "every folk has the center of its blessedness in itself," or, as Ranke put it, that "every epoch is immediate to God"? This position suggested the development of a philosophy of value which, on the one hand, conceived "value relation" (*Wertbeziehung*) as the condition of the possibility of interpretively evaluating individuals and which, on the other, viewed the "individualizing method" in history as that empirical-hermeneutic means of access to eternal values or to God that is open to us.

As an instance of this kind of reciprocal relationship, Franz Meineke's combination of Rickert's neo-Kantianism with Ranke's heritage resulted in a "historicism" in the positive sense.[18] Dilthey, and to an even greater extent Troeltsch, perceived both the danger of relativism contained in a hermeneutically individualizing historicism and the corresponding loss of a moral or practical orientation; but ultimately neither could find a convincing solution. Weber so relativized the notions of the relationship that values have to the individual situation that the result was the avowedly irrational position of the "polytheism of values." As has already been mentioned, for this reason he held a strict value freedom to be necessary in the social sciences.

The ideological constellation involved here is at the base of the contemporary Western complementarity system of scientism and existentialism. At this point I can only begin to indicate the horizon of problems it entails. Weber's conception of the process of rationalization—and especially the idea that his postulate of value-freedom presupposes, namely, that science progresses toward truth—both imply an ultimate "valuative" premise, as well as a total interpretation of history which itself is not value-free. Post-Weberian theory of science— for example, Popper's critical rationalism—admits this but interprets it to mean the necessity of an ultimate value decision. In this way, the complementarity system of scientism and existentialism remains unaffected. The ultimate presupposition in question here, however, includes an ethic involving the communication community of seekers of truth; hence, it is not a prerational decision, as Popper and Weber believe. Rather, it forms precisely the premise necessary to the scientistic demand for value-free objectivity. The significance of this claim becomes clear when two points are considered: (1) not only the decision in favor of science but all meaningful argumentation presupposes the ultimate value of rationality and the progress of truth in history, and (2) argumentation presupposes that it represents the moment of criticism and legitimation with regard to all disputed questions within human interaction—if the latter is not to collapse as communicative interaction or as a process of developing possibilities of mutual understanding.[19]

Perhaps the demand for value-free objectivity in the historical and social sciences is to be restricted to specific cognitive acts, for example, establishing facts or the historical relations between facts. As the considerations above make clear, however, precisely this demand is capable of disclosing a dimension of ultimate norms that must be recognized not only in science but in virtually all communication that is open to argumentation. The recognition of these ultimate norms of reason already implies a normative perspective for interpreting history, one that views history as rationalization, not only in Weber's but in another sense as well, namely, that of the hermeneutic and ethical rationality that is presupposed in all mutual understanding (*Verständigung*) about purposive rationality and objectivity. This is the rationality involved in reaching understanding (*Verständigung*) within the human communication-community. These reflections now give rise to the question whether a normatively grounded interpretation of history as a whole does not, and must not, also provide the hermeneutic sciences with a standard for critically interpreting all individual cultural achievements. In this case, we would have to give up the scientistically oriented distinction between a preunderstanding of the world that is not value-free and which is responsible for the selection and accentuation of scientific themes, on the one hand, and the value-free cognitive acts of explanatory science, on the other. It would have to be replaced with the conception of a "continuum of understanding," or, more precisely, of a "hermeneutic circle" formally derived from the ultimate normative foundation and involving the revision of our preunderstanding of rules and meanings on the basis of an empirical understandng of concrete rules and meanings.

Wherever one may stand on these problems in the historical-hermeneutic grounding of the special status of the Geisteswissenschaften, it seems clear that the issues are not pure phantasm. They are real problems that arise from the nature of something perceived for the first time. It need not be denied that expanding the concept of science was and still is dangerous, including as it does the dangers of methods that are inaccessible to rational control, the dangers of excessively speculative claims, of a quick transition from human *sciences* to professions of world view (*weltanschauliche Konfessionsliteratur*) and ideological agitation. To these dangers, however, we must contrast those that were and are connected to the scientistic restriction itself.

We should first note the danger of reductionistically violating the phenomena at issue and the resulting paradox in which a consistent scientistic position results. From the perspective of "rationality," what is one to say to the self-contradiction in which a behaviorist such as Skinner in ensnared when he attempts to employ *comprehensible* reasons to convince his fellow human beings that they must allow responsible scientists to *condition* them by reinforcing desired behavioral dispositions, thereby allowing an optimal augmentation of forms of behavior adapted to modern conditions?[20] Either one takes Skinner's naturalistic position seriously (in this case, the self-contradiction involves the unanswerability of the question as to who conditions the conditioners, in the sense of Skinner's demands), or one emphasizes his appeal to the rational insight and moral responsibility of experts and, possibly, politicians. In this case the suspicion arises that, from the start, behavioristic "reductionism" is to be applied only to part of humanity for whose happiness the others—those who can act and understand one another in terms of reasons—bear the responsibility, in the style of Dostoevski's Grand Inquisitor. This alternative way of understanding Skinner reveals the second danger associated with the scientistic position.

Whoever holds the social sciences up to the model of the nomological and experimental natural sciences, and considers only those forms of social science legitimate, will be inclined to consider social technology and social engineering as constituting the only possible connection between the social sciences and practice. This person will also not recognize a problem that is highly topical in modern industrial democracies, namely, the conflict between experimentally controlled planning on the basis of a quasi-natural scientific subject-object relation, on the one hand, and the much more complicated and exacting "dialogical planning," on the other.[21] A third danger in the scientistic restriction consists simply in that limiting the idea of science to the paradigm of value-free natural science (or, more precisely, to that of empirical natural sciences and logical-mathematical formal sciences) involves a corresponding restriction of the idea of rationality. This restriction is commonly understood as a sign of liberal tolerance with regard to the domain of individual freedom in moral, religious, and ethical decisions. As such, it is defended against the—unavoidable?— dogmatism of the claims of a reason that has not been scientistically or technologically abridged. From a philosophical point of view, however, the flip side of this apparent tolerance and modesty is a resignation of reason; both the entire domain of evaluative and normative meaning-orientation and the critical-hermeneutic reconstruction of the historical situation of action are surrendered to private discretion. In the vacuum of orientation which thereby arises, there develops a potential for an ideological, pseudoreligious, and dogmatic world view.

That is all I want to say about the complex of problems surrounding the Geisteswissenschaften's claim to autonomy as it forms the background of the first phase of the E-V controversy. I think it suffices to illuminate the unnecessary and misleading character of attempts to explain the controversy externally—for instance, in terms of the resistance that a nationally tinged, romantic irrationalism or a conservative theological apologetics raises against the Western tradition of Enlightenment.[22] To the extent that motives of this kind have shared in determining the real historical course of events (something I would not dispute), they are the theme of the critique of ideology. Such treatment, however, does not explain away the substantive issues; rather, it serves to liberate the essential core of the debate from the obscurities surrounding it. In what follows I try as far as possible to ignore these secondary and historically accidental aspects of the controversy. Nevertheless, in the interest of concentrating on matters open to rational argumentation, it is important to make clear the characteristic horizon of preunderstanding and inquiry. For this reason, having sketched the background of the first phase of the controversy, I would now like to develop some broad perspectives for a possible confrontation with the second.

# 3

# On the Second Phase of the Controversy: The Neopositivist Account of Scientific Explanation

From what I have said thus far, it seems to me that two questions arise: Is it actually the case, as it is often claimed, that the reductionist concept of unified science represents the tradition of the Enlightenment? Isn't this tradition better served by a theory of science that is differentiated according to prescientific life relations (Dilthey) to the objects of inquiry? These questions derive from the assumption that in the theory of science enlightenment has something to do with a constant radicalization of transcendental reflection (in Kant's sense) on the conditions of the possibility of science. To this (undoubtedly ambiguous) philosophical program, the modern logic of science, as it was grounded in the categories of logical positivism, adapted a characteristically ambivalent attitude. On the basis of the same suspicion of psychologism that the neo-Kantians had already leveled at Dilthey, logical positivism banned from philosophy qua logic of science not only the empirical problem of reflecting on the subjective conditions of the possibility of thought or knowledge, but the transcendental problem in Kant's sense or that of the later Husserl.[1] Thus, de facto, it retracted the step from formal to transcendental logic that Kant had taken beyond Leibniz and Hume, in other words, the step from a logic founding propositions about propositions to a logic concerned with the synthetic constitution of objects and with synthetic cognitive acts. The Kantian problem, as to the conditions of the possibility of objectively valid knowledge, was excluded from the very "context of justification" that Kant himself was the first to elucidate in criticizing the empirical psychology of knowledge. Instead, it was relegated to a "context of discovery" that was relevant only to empirical genetic studies.[2] In place of the Kantian and neo-Kantian distinction between an epistemology based on transcendental logic and the empirical psychology of knowledge, the modern logic of science applied a semiotically founded distinction based on the work of Carnap and Charles Morris. On the one hand, it refered to the logic of scientific sentences or systems of sentences that could be syntactically formulated and semantically interpreted; on the other, it pointed to the pragmatics of empirical contextual conditions, in the sense of the subjective-psychological or historical, social-psychological genesis and practical application of knowledge.

To a certain extent, this new orientation is comprehensible, given the philosophical paradigm of exact mathematical logic and the possibility of formalizing scientific languages associated with it. It is also understandable in view of the unclear position of transcendental logic precisely with regard to the demand that it broaden its formulation in the interest of providing a transcendental foundation for the Geisteswissenschaften or social sciences. Nevertheless, in view of the aporias into which the neopositivist logic of science can be seen to have fallen today, the question must be raised as to the cost of thus restricting the concept of philosophical logic. It appears to be similar to the price paid for positivistically restricting the concept of science, a price involving the dubious curtailment of responsibility for philosophical reflection on the conditions of the possibility of the intersubjective validity of science or the sciences. Precisely at a time when the successive development of new sciences required nonpsychologistic reflection on the constitution of possible areas of scientific inquiry and the objects corresponding to them, the entire problem complex of traditional epistemology was jettisoned from the domain of the theory of science. Thrown into the "wastepaper basket" of pragmatics were: (1) the problem of a nonpsychologistic reflection[3] on consciousness or on the subject of knowledge; (2) the problem of the cognitive relation of subject and object; not to mention (3) the possibility of expanding this problem complex to include a nonpsychologistic reflection on the constitution of forms of inquiry based on life relations or internal "knowledge-constitutive" interests.

In the meantime, this step has been in no way revised; at best, it is sometimes forgotten. I think the seriousness of its consequences has emerged particularly with regard to the once hopeful explication of the meaning of "scientific systematizations," in terms of formal languages.[4] With this remark, however, I have returned to the issue of the E-V controversy. In the following I shall attempt somewhat better to illuminate certain presuppositions that belong to the background of the subsumption-theoretic account of explanation, that is, the formal reduction of all scientific explanation to the model of Popper, Hempel, and Oppenheim.

As I have mentioned, the claim of unified science in Hempel's concept of motivational explanation depends on separating the understanding of motives from the methodological context of hermeneutics, itself not seriously considered as part of the logic of science. Hempel reduces the understanding of motives to the sensuous moment of empathy; he then establishes it as a prescientific factor that aids in the construction of hypotheses but is only heuristically and psychologically relevant in the context of the causal explanation of human behavior. Already we can see here a characteristic result of restricting the idea of the logic of science and the context of justification connected to it. In the light of a hermeneutically expanded logic of transcendental knowledge, one could define Hempel's procedure more exactly as follows: First, he ignores the specific validity claim of hermeneutic understanding as a synthetic act of knowledge referring to the particular class of data that express meaning or "meaning-intentions." Second, he misconceives the sensuous moment of empathy specifically related to the data of expression. Although, within the epistemologically relevant context of the hermeneutic synthesis, this moment operates together with the moment of understanding, Hempel equates it with the operation of understanding, or *Verstehen*, as a whole. Third, he separates the cognitive potential of empathetic understanding from the categorial inquiries and methodological claims that belong to it and attaches this potential to the heuristically relevant, cognitive act of hypothesis construction in the service of causal explanation.[5]

One could now suppose that this strategy permits the reduction (whether legitimate or illegitimate) of motivational understanding qua act of knowledge to that cognitive act of causal explanation that is methodologically confirmed in the natural sciences. This supposition could be supported by certain indisputable facts: (a) that the neopositivist reductionistic program of unified science was oriented from the start toward the paradigm of the natural sciences, and (b) that a least at the beginning, the demand for a material reduction in the sense of

the "physicalism" of scientific languages stood behind the demand of
the Hempel-Oppenheim model for a formal reduction. The proponents
of the methodological autonomy of the Geisteswissenschaften were
able to draw the consequences of this supposition. They had only to
show that the Hempel-Oppenheim model, which they were happy to
regard as an adequate explication of the sense of causal explanation
in the natural sciences, missed the specific meaning of the hermeneutic
understanding of rules and norms, for example, or of motives qua
reasons for actions, not to mention the symbolically mediated meaning
of speech acts.

The second phase of the E-V controversy labored under this presupposition for a long time, and our own confrontation with the third
phase will show how difficult a premise it is to avoid. In specific
circumstances it may be admissible to associate the dispute primarily
with the explicandum indicated by the Hempel-Oppenheim model,
in other words, with explanation from causal laws and antecedents
or "boundary-conditions." In this case, however, one ignores the pe-
culiarity and inadequacy of the explicatum provided by the Hempel-
Oppenheim model insofar as it interprets causal explanation in syntactic-semantic terms, that is, in terms of a formal langauge. In contrast,
my attempt to reconstruct the philosophical premises of the E-V controversy must question even this presupposition; for, if one begins
from a Kantian formulation of the epistemological question, one must,
I think, doubt the capacity of such a model to explicate the sense of
causal explanation as a synthetic cognitive act. In what follows I intend
to indicate the grounds for this assessment. I find myself faced with
the necessity of prefacing the customary debate between the philosophy
of the Geisteswissenschaften and the reductionist claims of the neopositivist theory of the natural sciences with a criticism of the latter
as a theory of the natural sciences. At this level of exposition it will
become evident that the philosophical assumptions that dominate the
second phase of the E-V controversy must be transcended in the
direction of those of the third phase. Thus, by inquiring more deeply
into the conditions of the possibility of causal explanation in the natural
sciences, it should be possible to provide the foundations for a critical
reconstruction of the neo-Wittgensteinian position and thus for a resolution to the problem of the E-V controversy.

## 3.1 The Aporia in the Logico-semantic Explication of Causal Explanation

Restriction of the logic of science to a (re-)constructive semantics dispensed with the Kantian question concerning the conditions of the possibility of an intersubjectively valid cognitive act, a possibility Kant grounded on a transcendental synthetic constitution of the objects of experience. This question was replaced with the question whether it is possible to explicate the meaning of specific structures of argument, or "systematizations," within formal logic in terms of semantically interpretable formal languages. With regard to causal explanation, this replacement meant that Kant's account of the nomological necessity of connections between events or circumstances in the experienceable world was abandoned. The necessity—which, in his view, could be claimed neither on the basis of empirical experience nor metaphysically in terms of pure concepts—was now represented *syntactically* as a deductive relation between sentences (the explanans and the explanandum). Moreover, the possibility of this relationship was *semantically* grounded on the empirical and hypothetical premise regarding the lawlike character of the universal sentence or sentences that formed part of the explanans. This syntactic and semantic reinterpretation had already implicitly dispensed with the Kantian distinction between the causes or empirical grounds of events that can be experienced and the grounds for holding sentences to be true within the framework of discursive argumentation. In the deductive-nomological model the categorial (synthetic a priori) claim of causal necessity or of the necessary conjunction of cause and effect is reduced to the Leibnizian claim as to the ratio sufficiens for argumentative statements, on the one hand, and to Hume's interpretation of causal laws as well-confirmed regularities in experience, on the other. The moment Kant found decisive involved the cognitive synthesis of the data of experience on the basis of the categorial significance of the question as to the causal necessity of the temporal conjunction of events. This now seems to be exposed as the subjective premise of the empirical genesis of explanatory hypotheses and, as such, only psychologically interesting. The account of causal explanation as a synthetic cognitive act in Kant's sense is replaced practically with the explication of an argumentative foundation for assumptions or convictions with regard to the world of experience. Popper states: "To give a causal explanation of an event means to deduce a sentence which describes it, using as premises of the deduction one or more universal laws together with certain singular statements, the initial conditions."[6] This formulation is prejudicial: in the "context of justification," the synthetic cognitive act that discovers the causes of an unexpected empirical phenomenon is equated with an operation providing logical foundations that can be identical with the derivation of consequences on the basis of a previously accomplished causal-nomological explanation (or simply on the basis of generalizing symptoms).

What happens to the attempt in the theory of science to preserve the account of causal explanation as a synthetic cognitive act when it is thus reduced to the structure of an empirically supported logical foundation? I believe the negative consequences of the neo-Leibnizian and neo-Humean premises of the Popper–Hempel–Oppenheim model as an explication of causal explanation have been revealed by the wearisome aporia that has since arisen.[7] Here I shall try to recapitulate only its most important points.

(1) Thus far, no satisfactory syntactic or semantic criteria have been delineated to account for the lawlike character of the general sentences that figure as premises in the explanans of the D-N model. This means, for one thing, that no syntactic or semantic criteria have been offered that could distinguish general sentences referring only to a finite number of cases (for example, cases restricted to temporally or spatially limited object-domains) from universally valid general sentences. Thus the following argument cannot be excluded as an example of D-N explanation:

All apples in this basket are red.
This apple comes out of this basket.

This apple is red.

(2) Likewise, satisfactory syntactic or semantic criteria have yet to be produced to distinguish between laws generally—that is, between regularities that obtain universally—and causal laws in such a way that one could show that the syntactic-semantic model of D-N explanation is an adequate account of the latter. To this extent, the neo-Humean attempt to explicate the concept of causality in logico-systematic terms by means of a hypothetical-deductive model seems to have failed.

The following example by Carnap should serve to make the problem of specifying causal laws intuitively clear, since it formulates two "if-then sentences," both of which seem to satisfy the syntactic and semantic criteria of universality:

(A) Whenever iron is heated, the earth moves.
(B) Whenever iron is heated, it expands.

The meaning of sentences of the second type seems, intuitively at least, to indicate a causal connection. As Charles Peirce first pointed out, however, it cannot be explicated sufficiently as an if-then relation in the sense of material implication, that is, in the sense of an extensional truth-functional logic. The if-then relation refers, rather, to irreal, "contrary to fact-conditionals" or "counterfactuals," thus to sentences of the type:

If the iron were heated, then it would expand.

or

If the iron had been heated, it would have expanded.

But under the purely logical conditions of general implication presupposed by the D-N model—that is, in the absence of a consideration of the difference between logical and real (causal) conditions, the special modal sense of this kind of sentence could not be explicated in an unparadoxical manner.[8]

(3) The above fact mirrors a conclusion Stegmüller reached at the end of his monumental reconstruction of the attempt to explicate the meaning of *explanation*. Referring to Käsbauer, he writes: "What he attempted to explicate were not scientific explanations at all, but the comprehensive class of scientific justifications understood in the sense of adequate answers to why-questions."[9] According to Stegmüller, however, this entailed the failure "to explicate the intuitive distinction between causes and reasoned grounds [*Vernunftgründen*]."[10] The significance of this conclusion becomes clear when Stegmüller claims that in three different cases of deductive-nomological systematizations the antecedent conditions express not real grounds but only grounds of knowledge. These are:

(a) D-N arguments that employ laws referring to symptoms or indicators (for example, the inference from a fall in the barometer to the expectation of rain).[11]

(b) D-N arguments employing laws about information (for example, predictions on the basis of the law that "whenever competent astronomers predict an event in the cosmos, this event will occur").

(c) D-N laws employing laws of physical geometry as lawlike premises.[12]

Given the perspective suggested above, this result cannot be surprising. It emerges as a consequence of the failure to maintain the Kantian distinction between a transcendental logic of categories, on the one hand, and formal logic, on the other. Whereas the former provides the questions and viewpoints guiding both knowledge and the corresponding cognitive acts, the latter refers to possible systematization in argument.

Stegmüller continues to conceive of the class of "explanations" as a subclass of "reasons," hence, as a possible "special problem" in the explication of scientific systematizations in Hempel's sense. In contrast, one could draw the more radical conclusion that even those D-N systematizations he considers "explanations" are to be distinguished in principle from synthetic acts of knowledge. This result would signal the impossibility of resolving either the categorial problem of explanation qua synthetic cognitive act on the level of the formal (syntactical-semantic) explication of meaning, or the problem of causality as the categorial condition of the possibility of causal explanation.[13]

Such a conclusion need not entail the impossibility of any relationship between causal explanation and D-N systematizations. With Kant we would rather presuppose the relationship between the experienceable world of connections between objects, states, or events and the world of facts represented in argumentative discourse by logical relations between sentences and propositions.[14] As a regulative principle we would therefore assume that the casual necessity of connections among events (the necessity that causal explanation qua synthetic knowledge must transcendentally presuppose) must reduce to a deductive relation between "sentential facts" in Hempel's sense on the discursive and theoretical level.[15] Even under this assumption, however, the account of causal explanation itself as a "deduction of the explanandum from the explanans" remains a category mistake. This is true even, and precisely, if one intends to use the account to reconstruct causal explanation normatively as a valid cognitive act. Such a reconstruction may never lose sight of the specificity of explanation qua knowledge, that is, of the possibility of an informative expansion of knowledge; but Hempel's D-N model is not equal to the task. Insofar as it reconstructs causal explanation in terms of the grounds of judgment, it fails even to express the distinction between innovative causal explanations in science and predictions that are derived from previously known causal laws. Hence its incapacity to distinguish between causal explanation and the completely heterogeneous grounding of judgments (as the inference from consequences or symptoms) seems almost self-evident.

Using Peirce's normative logic of synthetic inferences, one can comprehend causal explanation as an abductive inference from the explanandum to the explanans and see as ideal the case in which one discovers an explanans from which one can deduce the explanandum.[16] From this perspective certain distinctions become intelligible. For instance, we can distinguish between (1) an everyday explanation such as Hempel's example of an automobile radiator cracking, (2) a scientifically relevant causal explanation which presupposes that the pertinent natural laws are already known, and (3) an innovative causal explanation involving the discovery of previously unknown natural laws in the framework of a new theory.

The first case actually contains no synthetic abductive inference in the sense of Peirce's logic of synthetic cognitive acts. Here, the discovery of the explanans rests only on a psychologically relevant act of recalling the scientific knowledge at one's disposal. For this reason one can reduce the reconstruction of the logical structure of this kind of explanation to Hempel's and Popper's "deduction of the explanandum from the explanans."

The second case presents an abductive, synthetic inference of a kind that Peirce was the first to see as a form it might be possible to derive from the Aristotelian syllogism.[17] The unknown cause is inferred from the presence of the "result" and the general nomological premise as the instance of a deductive syllogism. This kind of inference is synthetic—first, because it is not apodictically necessary but rather hypothetical, and second, because the knowledge it provides may have to be augmented ad hoc by additional information. Neither the inference nor the causal explanation it makes possible, however, is innovative in the sense used above, since the hypothesis about the possible cause emerges from a law that is already known. Still, it is precisely in this case of a simple abductive inference that one can speak of a pure causal explanation in the sense of the synthetic logic of inquiry.

With regard to the theory of science or, more exactly, to the logic of inquiry, the third case is the interesting one (the one Peirce later claimed was the paradigmatic case of abductive, hypothetical inference in the sense of the logic of conjecture).[18] In this case one must infer a possible law from a pregiven result in such a way that, by presupposing the law one can think of a discoverable instance that could serve as the cause of the phenomenon present, viewed as a result. The practical necessity for this kind of explanation arises whenever a phenomenon occurs (for example, in the process of falsifying a theory) that is new to science, a phenomenon that represents the "determinate negation," so to speak, of the level the science has attained. In such cases it is often necessary to devise a new theory and reinterpret the phenomenon as an explanandum in light of the theory. Only through such a rein-terpretation (and therefore not without the intervention of a herme-neutically relevant agreement about meaning among scientists) are the conditions created in the third case for a "pure" causal explanation in the sense of the second.

I believe Peirce's conception of the abductive inference does in fact permit an account of the structure of causal explanation that is relevant to both epistemology and the logic of inquiry. It at least accommodates the distinction between the formal-logical systematizations of knowl-edge, in Hempel's sense, and synthetic acts of knowledge. However, even this conception does not yet sufficiently explicate the *differentia specifica* separating causal explanation from other kinds of synthetic cognitive acts. Hence, I do not think one can avoid re-posing the Kantian question concerning the function of causality as a categorial condition of the possibility of intersubjectively valid experience. Under the premises of the language-analytic logic of science, this means rescuing from the wastepaper basket of empirical pragmatics at least part of those transcendental-logical conditions if knowledge that Frege, Russell, Wittgenstein, and Carnap discarded on the suspicion of psychologism.

Nevertheless, it follows from this claim that Hempel's formal-lin-guistic, syntactical-semantic, or "logically systematic" model of ex-plication cannot simply be replaced with a colloquial-pragmatic model. Hempel appears to be correct in suggesting that the explanations that are relevant to science cannot be equated with the everyday answers that would satisfy the why-questions of specific individuals under the premises of specific empirical situations.[19] In particular, if a scientifically valid explanation is to be conceived as the answer to a concrete question, it is illegitimate to suppose that it is to overcome astonishment or misgiving by reducing a surprising phenomenon to the familiar or unusual. Such a conception would, at best, characterize the psychological-anthropological mechanism—in scientists as well—to which the need for, and possibility of, explanations are connected. It would not, however, resolve the Kantian question concerning the conditions of the possibility of an intersubjectively valid, and hence scientific, explanation. The concept of scientific explanation that must be explicated is not, in fact, an empirical-pragmatic conception in the sense of "explaining something to a specific individual in a specific situation." This is already shown by the fact that in the age of science, if we want to explain something to someone (whether schoolchild, student, or lay person), we usually presuppose a scientifically valid explanation. Thus the typical examples of explanation do not involve scientific explanation but, at best, their application. This is true for the everyday explanations of ordinary-language philosophers and for Hempel's famous example of the automobile radiator that cracks on a cold night.[20]

Can we therefore infer from this circumstance that explanation in the sense of the reconstructive theory of science merely involves a two-place relation (x explains y), a relation that can abstract from both the subject who asks or answers questions through cognitive acts and the contextual assumptions involved in asking and answering (for example, the preunderstanding, problem situation, and stage of science)? The logical empiricists did draw this conclusion; indeed, because the premise of their philosophical paradigm represents a complete disjunction of formal-logical and empirical problems, this conclusion seems impossible to avoid. In fact, an alternative to the disjunction of formal-logical (syntactic-semantic) and empirical-pragmatic accounts of explanation can be conceived of only under two conditions. First, in whatever form, one must redemonstrate the validity of the idea of the transcendental subject of knowledge, and second, one must repose the question about the subjective conditions of the possibility of intersubjectively valid knowledge. From a fear of psychologism or metaphysics, one can attempt to avoid both steps at any cost and reduce to a two-place relation the essentially three-place relation of explanation (qua knowledge that, in principle, is to be valid for every knowing subject). In this case, however, one commits an "abstractive fallacy"[21] that seems to me to be the *proton pseudos* of restricting epistemology or the transcendental logic of knowledge to the logic of science as a (re-)constructive semantic.

In the present situation of philosophy, however, how can we illuminate the problematic of a transcendental subject in an appropriate form? In our analysis of the problem of explicating causal explanation qua synthetic cognitive act, we established the necessity of renewing the inquiry into the constitution of the meaning of causality as the categorial condition for the possibility of experience. Furthermore, we suggested that one can abstract from the context of the empirical conditions of explanation insofar as this context involves answering the questions of a knowing subject. If the meaning of explanation is to find a satisfactory explication, however, this abstraction does not entail the possibility of neglecting such contextual conditions altogether. The connection of these two claims seems to require that the functional meaning of causality as a category of thought be conceived as a non-fortuitous question addressed by the subject of knowledge to nature; this means the meaning of causality must be grasped in terms of the context—but not in the sense of empirical pragmatics—of the formulation of the question under study. To this extent, the rehabilitation of the pragmatic context in question represents a task for *transcendental* reflection by the subject of knowledge on the subjective conditions of the constitution of objects.

Thus the return of transcendental reflection to the pragmatic context of causal inquiry involves a return to the subjective conditions of the constitution of the meaning of causality. Obviously this means more than merely the return to acts of understanding qua functions of a pure consciousness. Rather, transcendental reflection goes behind the abstract meaning of the concept of causality that is the theme of semantics, to illuminate the "language game" to which causality belongs, the one involving causal why-questions and causal explanations as replies to them. Hence, transcendental reflection must have as its theme the paradigmatic relation between causal inquiries, on the one hand, and the actions through which they are imposed on nature (as well as the linguistically interpretable experiences one can have in this context), on the other. It seems to me that these nontrivial assumptions in reflecting on what is called "conceptual analysis" provide the possibility of reconstructing Kant's transcendental problem complex under the conditions of post-Wittgensteinian philosophy.[22]

Before entering into the system of transcendental idealism proper, Kant himself offers a clue to the transcendental investigation required here in explaining the motive behind the Copernican revolution in thought. In the preface to the second edition of *The Critique of Pure Reason*, he starts from the pragmatic context of the "experimental method" in order to make clear that the investigation of nature "must approach nature," "constraining nature to give answer to questions of reason's own determining." Of course, he comes at once to the principles of reason as the conditions of this investigation of nature. Nevertheless, the context suggests that, under his premises, transcendental idealism is unable sufficiently to clarify the character of categories as questions, hence, as the conditions of the possibility of experiment. In other words, he is not actually able to show that, as he puts it:

Reason, holding in one hand its principles according to which alone concordant appearances can be admitted as equivalent to laws, and in the other hand the experiment which it has devised in conformity with these principles must approach nature in order to be taught by it. It must not however do so in the character of a pupil who listens to everything the teacher chooses to say, but of an appointed judge who compels the witness to answer questions which he himself has formulated.[23]

If this position represents the actual motive for the Copernican turn, then it seems to mean the following: The problem of constituting the meaning of the categories and, in connection with our problem, particularly the meaning of the category of causality, must be resolved from the perspective of the interrogation of nature in experimental action.[24] Unless one presupposes this transcendental life relation (Dilthey) on the part of the subject of knowledge, one can understand neither how the meaning of causality for example can be constituted for us nor how the principle of causality could prove to be objectively valid as the a priori of every possible experiment irrespective of its empirical result.[25]

It is also necessary to explicate the linguistic and communicative presuppositions of the Kantian problem complex with regard to the constitution of meaning and the intersubjective validity of knowledge. In connection with the constitution of the meaning of the categories, this means: Kant's reference to their metaphysical deduction from the table of judgments and to the functional necessity of the transcendental unity of apperception achieved with their help can be regarded as indicating a task that is at best still unresolved. For, even if the categories provide the basis for the possibility of meaningful inquiry, whether and how they are contained in the table of judgments would first have to be clarified within a transcendental philosophy of language. (One might, for example, refer to the depth structure of language in the sense of a universal or transcendental grammar.[26]) On the other hand, the transcendental unity of apperception is to be presupposed in any possible transcendental grounding of knowledge as the postulate of the possibility of knowledge. Despite Kant's suggestion, however, it cannot really guarantee the possibility of the intersubjective validity of the meaning and truth of linguistically formulated cognitive arguments; rather, it guarantees only something like the subjective certainty of knowledge for any consciousness whatever. At most, in connection with the Kantian notion of a functional apparatus of categories already lying in consciousness, it can illuminate a prelinguistic, precommunicative validity on the part of the cognitive schemata at the base of synthetic a priori judgments.[27] This would, however, imply the assumption that the constitution of the publicly explicable meaning of the categories—and hence, of the validity of synthetic a priori judgments as fundamental principles—could not be conceived adequately without presupposing language as a condition of the possibility of the intersubjective validity of meaning.

Husserl's attempt to reduce the constitution of meaning to the intentional acts of a transcendental consciousness leads to a similar difficulty. That a pure ego consciousness cannot be considered the sufficient transcendental basis of the constitution of meaning is, I think, made indirectly clear in his quasi-categorial use of the *epoché*, that is, in bracketing the existing world, including both others' and one's own empirical ego in the interest of methodically isolating the "I think" which then appears as the "primordial sphere' of the transcendental constitution of the world. To anyone who presupposes the public character and linguistic mediation of meaning—something Husserl himself must presuppose in inviting the reader to participate in his transcendental thought experiment—it is clear that the meaning of the "I think" is itself sublated with the conscious sublation of language and the life relations that connect the ego to both the external and the social world (*Mitwelt*) in the sense of the "thou" and others as communication partners.

These reflections suggest that one should attempt to validate the standpoint of transcendental logic not in the medium of the philosophy of consciousness (whether within transcendental idealism or methodical solipsism) but rather under the premises of the new post-Wittgensteinian paradigm of language-analytic philosophy. I have noted my objection to the current disjunction of formal-logical (syntactic-semantic) and empirical-pragmatic dimensions of the explication of meaning. It seems to me that we must attempt to distinguish between a transcendental-pragmatic domain in which the meaning of categories is constituted in terms of the subjective conditions of the possibility of explanation and the empirical-pragmatic, contextual conditions of explanation. Through an analysis of language, such a distinction would have to uncover both the conditions in consciousness and the general conditions in practical life relations of the constitution of the meaning of why-questions. Moreover, it would have to show the legitimacy of the latter as the epistemological basis both for the analysis of categories and for the explication of synthetic cognitive acts. This foundation will be illuminated more clearly in connection with the example of causal explanation and its relation to the understanding of action.

## 3.2 An Explication of Causal Explanation in the Light of a Transcendental Pragmatics of Language

I would like first to recapitulate the basic reasons for the inability of (1) constructive semantics, (2) the empirical pragmatic analysis of contextual conditions, or (3) Kant's transcendental logic to resolve the problem of explicating the meaning of causal explanation.

1. The first mode of treatment appears to be inadequate because it fails to distinguish between the *grounding* of judgments on regularities (whether prognostically relevant or irrelevant) and *explanations* that refer to genuine causal laws.[28]

2. In the sense of ordinary linguistic usage, the second mode of treatment can distinguish satisfactorily between those answers to why-questions that are relevant to the particular context and those that are not. The mode, however, is unable to differentiate between those answers to causal questions that are scientifically relevant (or, more precisely, that are relevant to the progress of science) and those that

can be relevant and valid explanations only "before" of "after" science, that is, under empirical and subjective conditions such as those analyzed by psychology, pedagogy, and cultural anthropology.

3. The third mode of treatment helps correct these inadequacies insofar as it points to transcendental conditions from the start, to the conditions under which a causal-nomological explanation can finally be conceived of as a synthetic, intersubjectively valid act of knowledge, hence, as the possible answer to a scientifically relevant question. It owes this ability, first, to its distinction between rational grounds for inductively or deductively deriving or successfully predicting the explanandum, grounds that can be represented semantically and syntactically, and the true causes or real grounds of the explanandum in the sense of the nomologically necessary conjunction of events. It owes the ability, second, to its premise that in the sense of the transcendentally necessary and categorial question as to the law-governed cause of events, "the existence of things insofar as they form a law-governed connection" is implicated as the condition of the possibility of discovering intersubjectively valid causal laws in the framework of theories.

Even the third mode of treatment, however, cannot ground or clarify the extent to which the meaning of the transcendentally necessary question as to the law-governed cause is constituted for us, and hence, the extent to which the discovery of causal laws is a priori guaranteed for us. (Kant's reference to the "hypothetical judgments" of logic is incapable of distinguishing among them those that are relevant to causal analysis and those that are not—for example, if-then propositions in the sense of material implication. At this point, just like the D-N model of causal explanation, he already presupposes the ungrounded special meaning of causal-nomological necessity.) Even if Kant had established the transcendental foundation of the necessity of presupposing a law-governed connection among events in the experienceable world, this foundation would still leave unclear the extent to which epistemologically contingent (or empirically verifiable, causal laws) are possible. (Kant himself poses the latter question in the "Metaphysical Foundation of Natural Science" and the "Opus Postumum" when he raises the question of the possibility of the transcendental deduction of the particular laws of Newtonian physics.[29]) In short, under the premises of the idealist notion of transcendental consciousness, Kant's defense of causality as a category of the understanding is unable to illuminate the extent to which we can presuppose and verify the conformity of natural occurrences to causal laws in an experimental science.

I take the last proposition to offer a decisive indication for the way in which a transcendental pragmatics might resolve the problem of causality and causal explanation. It would not only have to consider causality a category of the understanding; it would also have to consider the meaning of this category as it is presupposed in experimental science. As the basis for the Copernican turn in his philosophy, Kant claims the old topos of Cusanus, Hobbes, and Vico that we can only "correctly understand what we could also have made if the material were given to us."[30] In the case of the experimental natural sciences, however, this "ability to make" (Machen-Können) means that through bodily intervention in nature (which we interpret in light of our theories), we can produce the initial conditions of those material processes nature itself completes in confirming our causal-nomological hypotheses. It is on the basis of this ability to produce natural effects—which, we must assume, would not have come about without our bodily intervention—that I think our categorial concept of causality is constituted.[31]

In this way, our transcendental-pragmatic reconstruction and transformation of Kant converges with neo-Wittgensteinian themes, or, more precisely, with von Wright's account of causality from the viewpoint of experimental intervention and action. In what follows, I shall attempt to integrate von Wright's concept of interventionist causality into the transcendental-pragmatic approach. This integration should provide a deeper understanding of von Wright's contribution to resolving the E-V controversy.

Clearly, the concept of interventionist causality just illustrated with regard to natural scientific experiment must also be presupposed in prescientific experimental interactions with nature, for example, in handicraft, as a necessary moment in understanding our capacity to make or produce things. I think, however, that one can claim the necessity of presupposing the same concept of causality in interpreting natural phenomena that are inaccessible to us—for example, in grasping regularities in the domain of astronomy or astrophysics to be governed by causal laws. In this case, it is completely clear that only the transcendental-pragmatic presupposition of interventionist causality allows us to conceive of constant relations between events passively observed in terms of the causal necessity of their conjunction, hence, not only in Hume's sense of empirically well-confirmed regularities but in Kant's sense of nomological necessity. We must always already interpret every constant conjunction of events in light of a thought experiment according to which the necessity of the events rests on causal factors that an action can, in principle, manipulate. That is, we must consciously reduce observed constancies of conjunction to necessary conjunctions of events in systems sufficiently isolated from external influences, the initial states of which we could, in principle, have produced or hindered. (That celestial phenomena involve such systems is a fortunate, contingent circumstance which made possible the rise of the mathematical natural sciences and particularly the foundation of physics as the causal explanation of sublunar and translunar spheres.)

It could be objected that, in understanding causality not as a category of the pure understanding in Kant's sense but as an implication of the concept of interventionist action, such a transformation of transcendental philosophy annihilates itself as a theory of the a priori presuppositions of experimental science. To understand the interventionist causality of actions, the theory must already presuppose the very notion of the causal necessity of a conjunction of events, but it is the transcendental necessity of constituting this notion that is at issue. This objection rests on untenable premises, since, with Hume, it assumes that one could apply the same type of objective observation and causal analysis to interpret an interventionist action as is applied to a natural process. As long as we are concerned to understand the action in its meaning as action, however, this is impossible. If we wish to understand an experimental interventionist action as such, we cannot objectify it as an observable nexus of events in the external world. If we could, we would of course again confront the Humean problem, and would be unable to infer a causal necessity from the conjunction of phenomena observed. Nevertheless, from a transcendental-pragmatic perspective, we must assume that precisely this necessity obtains in the objectifiable external world (that is, its meaning constitutes itself in relation to the external world) when we reexecute our own interventionist action or that of others in a reflective, interpretive way.[32]

We can check this argument by separating two phases of the idea of action as the experimental or technical production of natural effects through manipulative intervention in nature. The phases are: (1) the interventionist action itself, and (2) the natural process thereby initiated.[33] The latter, of course, can be observed as an objective succession of events or states, and indeed as a connection the causal necessity of which can be presumed only in light of its possible integration in our creation or production of an effect. However, the first phase that is thereby presupposed—that is, the bodily and goal-oriented intervention in nature which we must assume initiates, hinders, or interrupts a causally determined natural process—is the first phase of the entire experimental or technical action. In principle, it can no longer be observationally objectified as a conjunction of events, on pain of no longer understanding the intention of the action. In other words, it is, in principle, impossible for me to observe the cause of my action; I cannot observe the neurophysiological cause of my intention that is presupposed by the materialist theory of "central states."[34] Neither can I follow a nonreductionist theory of dependence that postulates the dependence of successful actions on the simultaneous quasi-instrumental efficacy of natural objects.[35] That is, I cannot observe the neurophysiological cause of my action as a bodily action that already, as such (as a self-movement of the body) interferes in nature. Still, to the extent it is understood as the first phase of the production of a natural effect, precisely this spontaneous act of intervention, which can be neither objectified nor analyzed in causal analytic terms, is the condition of the possibility of interpreting objectifiable connections between events, and especially constant conjunctions as causally necessary ones. In short, understanding the causal necessity of natural conjunctions presupposes understanding the freedom of action in the sense of the possibility of initiating or preventing natural processes.

It must be added here that understanding the real freedom of action itself rests on assuming causally necessary processes in macro-nature. This assumption seems to be implied in the idea of the capacity to act and in the relation between means and ends. If everything were possible, if natural laws placed no conditions on the realization of actions, it would make no sense to discuss what one *can* do. The concept of the ends-means rationality of action seems to include the a priori postulate that it is theoretically possible to transform knowledge about nomological relations between cause and effect into technological if-then propositions about the necessary and/or sufficient conditions of the instrumental realization of goals. To this extent, the categorial framework of instrumental action implies the categorial concept of experimental action, hence, the categorial concept of causal necessity that guides our abductive discovery of the hypotheses for causal explanation. It also implies the notion of the generality of repeatability of scientific results that serves as the foundation of our idea that general laws are inductively confirmed by individual cases.[36]

We cannot assume the "subject-object distance" of pure observation toward both the world and our active "being-in-the-world," in the sense of the empirical metatheory of scientific logic that Hume bequeathed. The moment we do so, we destroy the transcendental-pragmatic context (*Zusammenhang*) of a priori valid constitutions of meaning that makes experimental research possible. By means of pure observation, plus formal logic, it is impossible to perceive the necessity of either a causal conjunction among events or the validity of confirming inductive inferences "in the long run" (Peirce). The world must now assume an alien character for us, in view of which it can offer neither categorial viewpoints nor truth criteria for the confirmation of explanatory hypotheses.

This consideration also affects Popper's theory of falsification despite its logical superiority to the theory of inductive confirmation. Even it still presumes that we can identify phenomenal criteria as reasons for accepting basic sentences—and not, as Popper also suggests, as causal motivations for "explaining" basic decisions.[37] This means that the theory stands or falls with the possibility of grounding induction in transcendental-pragmatic terms.

The standard aporias under which the modern theory of science has suffered since the time of Hume can now be clarified in terms of a single comprehensive philosophical standpoint: The process of renouncing understanding, which has served as the foundation of explanatory causal science since the Renaissance, now proves to be part of a developmental process which, from Hume on, has abandoned those transcendental-pragmatic premises of understanding meaning that are indispensable as the conditions of the possibility of the experimental natural sciences. If, as the premise of all critical philosophizing, the empiricist and positivist tradition brackets every categorial preunderstanding of the world in favor of purely empirical studies, and if it makes this the starting point of the logic of the social sciences, such bracketing now reveals itself as the transition to a quasi-worldless limit case of Heidegger's "being-in-the-world": the merely present-at-hand can no longer exhibit any relation to the structure of involvements. At this point in our reflections, the question arises whether the standard aporias of the modern logic of the natural sciences can be solved if and only if those categories of knowledge (such as the concept of teleology) that had to be abandoned as conditions of the possibility of understanding nature are grasped as conditions of the possibility of understanding action, and hence, indirectly of understanding causal explanation as well. Instead of postulating a reduction of the teleological understanding of action to the causal explanation of natural events, we would have to conceive of the former as the epistemological presupposition of the latter.

This transcendental-pragmatic analysis of the conditions of possibility of the meaning of causal necessity has already opened up a fundamental insight into the original relationship between causal explanation and the understanding of action. The possibility of understanding interventionist action as such cannot itself be objectified as a theme for causal analysis, but rather is the condition of the possibility of a real causal explanation of objectifiable natural processes. With regard to the difference in their conceptual interpretation, the phenomenal realms of causally explicable processes of events, on the one hand, and of intelligible actions, on the other, apparently presuppose one another; that is, they *exclude* one another to the extent that their conceptual interpretations must supplement one another. One could well speak of a complementary relation here in Niels Bohr's sense, considering it the legitimate foundation of the "methodological dualism" of explanation and understanding in Dilthey's sense. The conception of complementarity also seems to dissolve the stubborn prejudice of scientism, according to which the epistemological or methodological dichotomy of explanation and understanding tears asunder phenomenal realms and the sciences attached to them. Instead, the antireductionist crux of the dichotomy consists in recognizing that (a) precisely in the case of the self-understanding of the experimental natural sciences, the sharpest distinction between the two domains of explanation and understanding is required, and (b) this distinction serves the interest of their reciprocal supplementation.

The plausibility of this view increases when one remembers that the two phenomenal realms—those of causally explicable natural processes and of the understandable experimental actions thereby already presupposed—are merely components of larger phenomenal domains which stand in a complementary relation as well. Processes that can be explained causally belong to the total domain of a nature that can be objectified as the "existence of things insofar as they form a law-governed connection." (To this domain also belong the phenomena that can be explained only in terms of statistical or inductive probabilities and the "systems" of organic nature that, to a certain extent, can be objectified in functional explanations.) The objectifiability of this entire domain, however, presupposes that human action can be understood; it presupposes the comprehensibility of both purposive-rational actions (including the experimental productions of repeatable natural effects in the service of verifying law-hypotheses) and rule-guided interactions between human beings. Above all, it presupposes the comprehensibility of linguistically mediated communicative actions, only in light of which we can explicate the comprehensible meaning of all other actions and, in particular, human explanations as acts of understanding with regard to the nature we have objectified.

The entire conception of complementarity can now be seen as a transcendental-pragmatic transformation not only of Kant's transcendental-idealist premises in *The Critique of Pure Reason* but of his notion of the relation between theoretical and practical reason as well. It affirms the "primacy of practical reason" proclaimed by Kant but does so independently of his transcendental-idealist premise with regard to the still metaphysical distinction between a knowable, objectifiable, causally explicable world of natural phenomena and an unknowable world containing the intelligible freedom of our morally relevant actions.

We can now reconstrue the critical point of transcendental reflection on the subjective conditions of the possibility of an objectively valid knowledge of nature: We must abandon the aspiration of knowing "things-in-themselves," that is, knowing things that, in principle, cannot be the objects of possible experience. We must abandon the attempt to lift ourselves in cognition to a position outside the world from which its structure can be grasped in purely theoretical, ontological terms, that is, apart from practical, bodily (*leibhaft*) engagement in the sense of categorial lines of questioning. Overcoming the precritical attitude of theoretic or dogmatic ontology, however, does not imply renouncing the knowledge of things as they are in themselves in favor of the knowledge of mere appearances. Rather, it means that one ceases to orient the meaning of knowledge toward a paradigm of knowledge that is not possible for us. In transcendental-pragmatic reflection, one attains a radically new conception of possible knowledge and of the real, possible objects of knowledge. Instead of "things-in-themselves" conceived without reflection on the subjective conditions of their possibility, but nonetheless considered objects of knowledge, we have the concept of natural things as objects of possible experience occurring, in principle, under the conditions of subjective experience and knowable in themselves. Instead of an ontological knowledge *sub specie aeternitatis*, which is conceived independently of engagement (*Theoria*, in Aristotle's sense), we have a theoretical knowledge of nature which, as experience, is fundamentally connected to meaning-constitutive bodily and practical engagement (although it remains open to hermeneutic and transcendental reflection). This is nature as the existence of things insofar as they are objects of why-questions understood in causal analytic terms.

These results have the following implications for causal explanation and the subjective conditions of its possibility: In the first place, one must abandon the precritical attitude that Hume still retains, according to which something like causal necessity could be conceived under ontological-theoretical premises and hence established as the possible object of passive observation. As Hume and the neo-Humeans or neopositivists have shown, under such premises the categorial concept of causal necessity and causal law presupposed in natural scientific experiment can be neither philosophically confirmed nor explicated. The transcendental-pragmatic significance of this insight becomes clear only when it is generalized to all categorial constitutions of objects and relations: under the assumption of a purely passive or observational distance to the world—that is, apart from the standpoints that arise from a practical engagement in it (standpoints underlying the inquiry into and understanding of something *as* something *in* relation to)— we can acquire no preconception as to knowledge of an a priori necessary structure of the world of experience.

In light of the world engagement presupposed here as the necessary condition of the constitution of meaning, the Kantian position of transcendental idealism must be seen as a residue of theoretical ontology. More precisely, it has to be understood as an ontological-metaphysical residue of Cartesian dualism and be transcendentally-pragmatically superseded. The philosopher wishing to comprehend the possibility of causal necessity cannot raise himself above the real world in his interpretive acts and interrogative viewpoints in such a way that he is forced to conceive of the subjective conditions of a possible experience of nature, not as acts of experimental interference but as the objectifiability of nature and its openness to explanation through causal laws. In so doing, he delivers up the real world, including the "phenomenal" aspects of human action within the real world, to causal nomological determinism, so that the freedom of morally responsible action must be derived from a cause outside or behind the world—that is, from an intelligible will of which it has to be presupposed: (1) that it can begin a series of successive things or states, and (2) that it can alter nothing in the world of appearance, for such a capacity would confuse and disconnect everything, thus making impossible nature as the object of causal explanation.[38]

The philosopher who wishes to grasp the possibility of causal necessity must assume the standpoint of transcendental-pragmatic reflection. That is, the philosopher must recognize that the subjective conditions of action are not components of the objectifiable world (which can be observed and explained in theoretical, causal-analytic terms) but still belong to the comprehensible real world. In this way he will achieve the position Kant describes in analyzing the thesis of freedom in the antinomy of freedom and causal determinism: "to admit within the course of the world different series as capable in their causality of beginning of themselves," that is, "attribute to their substances a power of acting from freedom." Under this premise, as the subjective condition of experimental action, causal necessity can be postulated as the relation between successive phenomena or states within closed systems of which one can, in principle, suppose they could be set in motion by experimenters through manipulatively producing their initial conditions. Again, in the sense of the thesis of freedom in Kant's antinomy, one can claim of such systems that their initiation "does not form part of the succession of purely natural effects" as "the mere continuation of them." Rather, "in regard of its happening, natural causes exercise over it no determining influence whatsoever."[39] In experiment we must, in fact, assume that without our active interference no already existent state of nature changes into the initial state of the system we set in motion.

Determinism thus proves to reflect an illegitimate totalization of the structure of an objectifiable fragment of the world of experience, an extrapolation that presupposes the freedom of action in experiment. This means, however, that determinism, as a metaphysical absolutization of causal necessity, is a "pretranscendental-pragmatic" product of metaphysical theory—whether in the sense of a pre-Kantian ontology that does not reflect on the subjective conditions of the possibility of experimental experience, as in the case of Laplace, or in that of Kant's transcendental idealism, which, in a quasi-Cartesian manner, divides the conditions within consciousness of the categories and their graphic schematization from the corresponding conditions of bodily action.

If transcendental-pragmatic reflection thus overcomes the premise of an ontological metaphysics that intends to explain the world theoretically, entirely in terms of a position outside it, then the prospect emerges of simplifying Kant's architectonic with regard to problems of transcendental philosophy. In distinguishing between (1) the merely phenomenal domain of knowable natural processes, (2) the transcendental domain of acts of understanding that can only be formally reflected upon, the acts of the "I" in the sense of transcendental apperception, and (3) the unknowable but intelligible domain of free actions which are also the theme of ethics, Kant's complicated architectonic is scarcely compatible with his own critical intentions. In place of this architectonic, the position of transcendental pragmatics emphasizes the fundamental difference between that which can be explained and that which can be understood. It thereby opens the possibility of establishing a relation between knowledge of the world governed by natural laws and the different knowledge of the world of practical reason and morality.

Within the comprehensible world of intentional action, of course, we would still have to distinguish between the ideal-typical domain of technical rationality and the genuinely moral domain of practical reason in Kant's more limited sense. The domain of technical rationality involves actions that can be understood in purposive-rational terms to the extent that, as instrumentally mediated actions, they are bound to causally explicable natural processes, or to the extent that, as strategic interactions among people, they can be understood in terms of the rationality of decision or game theory. The domain of practical reason involves positing goals on the basis of conventional (institutional) norms or on the basis of subjective maxims of action subsumed under ideal norms or laws of ethics. The knowledge of the comprehensible world of intentional actions and their rule or meaning complexes (technologies, institutions, works, etc.) represents an empirical-hermeneutic task for the social sciences qua cultural sciences or Geisteswissenschaften. Such a task would have to be distinguished from the transcendental-pragmatic or transcendental-hermeneutic reflection of philosophy on the complementary relation between the world that can be explained and the world that can be empirically hermeneutically understood.[40] In this sense, then, transcendental reflection in philosophy legitimately takes the place of the traditional claims of the theoretical and metaphysical explanation of the world from a position outside it. In replacing metaphysical-theoretical objectivism by transcendental reflection, we would overcome both dogmatic metaphysics in the pre-Kantian sense and the reductionistic scientism that forms the basis of the positivist and neopositivist idea of the unity of science.[41]

# The Neo-Wittgensteinian
# Renewal of the Claim of the
# Interpretive Social Sciences to
# Methodological Autonomy

In the previous chapter I developed the idea of a transcendental-pragmatic transformation of Kant by criticizing both neopositivism qua neo-Humeanism and Kant's transcendental idealism. I think this conception also provides the horizon within which the neo-Wittgensteinian approach, and thus the reconstruction of the most recent (third) phase of the E-V controversy, is to be understood. In the next chapter I would like first to consider the post-Wittgensteinian position in analytic philosophy as a new answer to the nineteenth century's question concerning the special status of the Geisteswissenschaften or social sciences. Adopting the perspective of a transcendental pragmatics of language, I would then like to re-pose certain questions raised by the traditional philosophy of the Geisteswissenschaften but which this new approach leaves unanswered. I shall leave a critical discussion of the neo-Wittgensteinian analysis until Part Two, where I focus on the work of Georg Henrik von Wright.

## 4.1 The Language Game of Events and Their Causes Versus the Language Game of Actions and Their Reasons

In 1965 Charles Landesman criticized the neo-Wittgensteinian distinction between two language games as a "New Dualism in the Philosophy of Mind."[1] Landesman sees the distinction as an attempt to replace the Cartesian duality in substances, as an alternative to physicalism, with a language-analytic distinction between two mutually exclusive categorial frameworks. In this way the crux of the position is preserved, whereas the hypostatization of a "ghost in the machine" that Gilbert Ryle criticized is avoided. I do not intend to argue against Landesman's criticism; instead, I would like to point to a different historical analogy in order to illuminate the relation of the neo-Wittgensteinian approach to the problem complex of the nineteenth century.

As already noted, the neo-Wittgensteinians distinguish between, on the one hand, the language game in which one can talk of things, events, and causes subsumable under laws and, on the other hand, the vastly different language game in which one can talk of persons, actions, action intentions, reasons, goals, and rules or norms. This distinction is comparable to the dualism in the Kantian system already elucidated; that is, it conforms to the distinction between the categorial framework for the constitution of the objects of natural scientific experience in the "critique of pure (theoretical) reason," and the conceivability of free intelligible action, a conceivability not presupposed in the constitution of theoretical experience, but which is nonetheless required to orient practical reason. If one attempts to work out this comparison in detail, however, one quickly realizes that the neo-Wittgensteinian dualism in language games conforms more closely to our transcendental-pragmatic transformation of Kant's transcendental idealism than to his own architectonic. Kant's distinction between the world of theoretical experience and the merely intelligible world, the conceivability of which founds a world of practical experience, remains metaphysical. In the neo-Wittgensteinian approach it is reduced to one fundamental distinction that is grounded both phenomenologically and language-analytically, and hence, seems to be strikingly similar to the concept of complementarity elucidated above. Whether one can interpret the neo-Wittgensteinian position as a transcendental-pragmatic transformation of the Kantian program might be open to question, but I do not want to discuss that here. Rather, I wish, first, to characterize the main arguments by which the neo-Wittgensteinian approach permits reconstruction and rehabilitation of the claim to the epistemological-methodological autonomy of the hermeneutical Geisteswissenschaften.

## 4.2 The Logical Connection Argument against Reducing the Understanding of Action to Causal Explanation

The neo-Wittgensteinians criticize the attempt by logical positivism to reduce all types of explanation—including those it admits are heuristically mediated by the understanding of reasons, motives, or goals—to the deductive-monological model of causal analysis or to a weaker inductive or probabilistic version of the same. From the neo-Wittgensteinian perspective, this kind of reduction represents a category confusion that can be exposed by what has come to be called the "Logical Connection argument" (LC argument).

The reductionistic thesis involves the supposition that intentions as to goals, and assessments of the situation related to these intentions (in particular, assumptions as to appropriate means), can be considered volitional-cognitive complexes within the D-N model of causal explanation. The neo-Wittgensteinians deny this by pointing to a categorial distinction.[2] The relation between the "volitional-cognitive complex" and the action to be explained is not a contingent one; it does not refer to a connection between two natural events conjoined by causal laws, as Hume supposed; neither is the appearance of necessity in this connection the result of a law hypothesis imposed externally. Rather, the relation between the meaning of a goal intention, the meaning of the situation assessment, and the meaning of the action to be explained is an internal, conceptual-analytic, even logical relation. According to the neo-Wittgensteinian argument, one cannot understand the action in the sense appropriate to it unless one already understands the meaning of the goal projections and situation assessments preceding it, while conversely, the constitution of the "volitional-cognitive complex" requires prior knowledge that a person possessing such goal intentions and situational assessments will act in ways compatible with these intentions and assessments (barring the intrusion of external or internal obstructions, which it would be especially important to identify).

The neo-Wittgensteinian argument concerning the logical implication of the supposed "cause" in the explanandum can be illustrated by the following example. The event in which A has murdered B is to be explained by assuming the volitional-cognitive complex, "A, the nephew of B, wanted to be his uncle's heir and believed that he could achieve this goal only by murdering B." Here, even to describe the action to be explained, one must establish that A actually killed B with the knowledge that B was his uncle and the intention of murdering him—in other words, that A did not kill B as a stranger, for example, or out of self-defense. Without this reinterpretation of the facts of the case in light of the volitional-cognitive complex already presupposed, the explanandum cannot even be identified as such in the sense of the explanation proposed. Now, in the case of the natural sciences, it may generally be necessary as well to subject the explanandum to a reinterpretation in light of the explanatory theory. In that case, however, reinterpretation will show that the relation between the explanandum and its presumed cause is a logically contingent one which rests on subsuming both events under an empirical law connecting cause and effect.[3]

The following example may serve to illustrate the logical implication of the supposed causal effect in the explanans. Someone claims that he intends (that is, he does not simply *wish* but has *decided*) to visit his grandmother that day, no matter what the cost. He further believes he can accomplish this purpose by taking the six o'clock train from X to Y, and by no other means. If, without apparent obstruction or alteration of his intention, he nevertheless neglects to make the trip, we have grounds for doubting either his sincerity or the adequacy of his own understanding of his goal intentions and situation assessments. This means that the explanans itself must be thrown into question as a fact if the would-be causal sequence does not occur. Put in general terms: If human beings acted as a rule in the way we have depicted— that is, if, without obvious reasons, they did not act according to the sense of their announced intentions and assessments of the situation, (in other words, if they did not act in accordance with the conceptual-analytic, internal relation between the meaning of the intentions and situation assessments, on the one hand, and the meaning of the action, on the other), we would have to draw the consequence to which Wittgenstein pointed; children would be unable to learn a language or internalize the rules of action and experience associated with the rules of that language or, therefore, the rules for acquiring intersubjectively valid knowledge.

The argument about the logical necessity of the connection between the volitional-cognitive complex and the action to be explained through it can be explicated in terms of the structure of a teleological system.[4] We can view the goal intentions and associated assumptions as to the necessary and sufficient means of achieving the goals as the constitutive elements of such a system. Then the fulfillment of the goal intentions by the corresponding event—that is, by the action to be explained (which the agent considers the means to the achievement of the goal)—is not the logically contingent, successful effect of a volitional-cognitive causal complex. Given normal conditions, it is, rather, the logically necessary component of the teleological system initiated by the volitional-cognitive complex. If the action does not succeed in fulfilling the goal intentions, we need not speak of falsification of the prediction made on the basis of the volitional-cognitive causal complex. Instead, we can say that the normal conditions under which the teleological system stands could not be fulfilled.[5] These remarks indicate the importance of deciding whether motivational explanations—that is, explanations in terms of a volitional-cognitive complex—must be seen as teleological explanations, or whether they can be interpreted as causal explanations as well. In this connection, the Wittgensteinian argument with regard to a child learning a language seems to speak decisively in favor of the Logical Connection argument as a form of teleological explanation. Children would be unable to learn the language of goal intentions, and assumptions about means and their conjunction in the volitional-cognitive complex, if the appropriate actions were not performed under normal conditions. In this view, the occurrence of the action to be explained by presupposing the volitional-cognitive complex is not an empirical confirmation of the prediction corresponding to a causal explanation; rather, it is the logical criterion for establishing the volitional-cognitive complex itself.

This central neo-Wittgensteinian LC argument already seems to demonstrate the impossibility of reducing to pure causal explanation motivational explanations mediated by the understanding of reasons. Moreover, if one realizes that the cognitive grasp of an internal conceptual connection involves the empirically correct grasp of a meaning connection (*Sinnzusammenhang*) that is, in itself, a priori evident, a positive reconstruction of the insights of traditional hermeneutics seems to come into view, namely, a reconstruction of the hermeneutic talk of meaning convictions that are understandable from inside, according to intuitive evidence, and empirically disclosed in the reciprocal play of vague preunderstandings and their revision within the "hermeneutic circle." Finally, if understanding the teleological connection between the meaning of goal intention, means cognition, and action makes possible a motivational explanation of action, this procedure seems to be a reconstruction of Weber's notion of the "purposive-rational understanding" of "purposive-rational action," which he considered the ideal type of rational comprehensibility. The neo-Wittgensteinian version of this procedure, of course, seems to cast doubt on Weber's intention to extend the use of "interpretive understanding" to "interpretive (causal) explanation."

## 4.3 The Distinction between Institutional Rules and Natural Laws as a Renewal of the Dialectical-Hermeneutic Idea of "Objective Spirit"

Another focus in the neo-Wittgensteinian reconstruction of the essential motivations of traditional hermeneutics and the philosophy of the Geisteswissenschaften emerged from the concept of rules (of language games and the institutions or "forms of life" interwoven with them).[6] Unified science talked of observing, describing, and explaining facts in light of the regularities or laws that structurally determine them, but neither its ontological nor its epistemological premises were compatible with the concepts of de facto rules (or institutional facts) or with the conditions of the possibility of their knowledge. Ontologically, a sharp distincton emerged between natural laws that hold without exception and rules that can be followed or, in case of exceptions, not followed. Epistemologically, a similar distinction arose: on the one hand, the use of observation to confirm or deny observational facts and hypotheses about laws and regularities, and on the other, the grasp of rule-facts. In the latter case, adequate knowledge depends on an understanding of rules that must, in principle, be able to prove its adequacy through successful participation in the rule game to be understood (strictly speaking, in the common language game belonging to it).

The ontological and epistemological point of a theory of rule-facts and rule-understandings can be seen as a reconstruction of Dilthey's renewal of the Hegelian concept of objective spirit. (It has affinities as well with the conception of an interpretive sociology of objective spirit or institutions as elaborated by H. Freyer and A. Gehlen.[7]) In German Idealism, objective spirit belongs neither to the domain of what the individual can experience through psychological introspection nor to the external natural world. Instead, its mode of being is seen as the expression of something "inner" and thus as the externalization of subject spirit (for example as the spirit of a people [*Volksgeist*] or a time [*Zeitgeist*]). In the neo-Wittgensteinian formulation this objective spirit is interpreted as a context of rules or norms that are more or less dependent on institutions and conventions. This means that the function of objective spirit can be viewed as a regulation or normative determination of human actions not motivated by individual psychology, as a determination in the sense of actions bound to institutional rules or customs and procedures dependent on ritual, tradition, or style. Not least, it can be seen as an institutional regulation or the organization of productive labor and the exchange or distribution of goods.

Thus knowledge of the hermeneutic Geisteswissenschaften, a knowledge mediated by interpretive empathy, finds its reconstructive counterpart in the linguistic-communicative mediation of the cognitive language game of the subject of knowledge and the rule-guided actions of the human object of knowledge. It seems essential to this reconstruction, first, that the mediation of the subject-object difference formulated by Hegel's philosophy of identity (a mediation, in principle, still presupposed by the notion of hermeneutic understanding) is incompatible with the concept of objectivity central to natural scientific knowledge, and second, that it corresponds to the postulated communicative mediation between two rule systems. Indeed, according to the neo-Wittgensteinians, in the cognitively relevant description of social facts, it is, in principle, inadmissible for the social scientist to ignore the rules in terms of which human subject-objects orient themselves in favor of the regularities imposed by the social scientist's own language of observation. It is also inadmissible to describe social rule-facts in a language the subject-objects could not, in principle, use to reconstruct their linguistic self-understanding.[8]

The renewed dialectical-hermeneutic point of this epistemological and methodological principle becomes clear if it is not limited to refuting the empiricist-positivistic or neopositivistic concept of unified science, but is also compared to the basic postulate of (at least the early) Popper's critical-rationalist "unified methodology," itself inspired by Kant.[9] In this comparison it immediately becomes evident that the problem of the valid understanding of rules involves a special problem, one that is resolved neither by the distinction between "the context of discovery" and "the context of justification" nor by the assumption that all "facts" and "data" can be described only in light of theories or linguistic frameworks of belief. Rather, it consists in the fact that linguistic frameworks of belief (and perhaps even theories) mediate the constitution of social facts or data in a double way—as the linguistic framework and theories of the scientists and as those of the acting subject-objects in their interpretation of their institutions and situations. Precisely in the context of justification, the particular task of the Geisteswissenschaften or social sciences lies in mediating the hypothetical approach to rules immanent in the theories and rules according to which subject-objects orient themselves.

In the case of the quasi-natural scientific behavioral sciences, this mediation may approximate the paradigm of experimental intervention and observation by using interviews and questionnaires. In the case of a typical Geisteswissenschaft—for example, the study of literature or, more recently, the history of science—this mediation emerges as *the* crucial methodological problem. It has led to a dispute about the direction of such sciences, about whether they involve an objectivistic-immanent hermeneutic of "identical reproduction" or a critical-reflective understanding that goes beyond the self-understanding of the original. Even the latter would remain tied to a conceptual language that subject-objects could, in principle, employ—or could have employed—in reconstructing their rule-guided self-understanding.

In connection with this sketch of the main dimensions of the post-Wittgensteinian reconstruction of hermeneutic positions, two additional problems should be clarified, to which the neo-Wittgensteinians give insufficient consideration and to which perhaps sufficient consideration cannot be given.

## 4.4 Open Problems

1. The first problem concerns the similarity of and difference between understanding the purposive rationality of actions and understanding the conventional systems of rules and norms constitutive of social institutions and cultural traditions. The question is whether only the second case involves rules, or whether we can speak of rules in another sense with regard to the first case as well. Can we speak of rules of purposive rationality that are not mediated by social conventions? Can we speak of rules that as such are no more "private' in Wittgenstein's sense than conventionally mediated rules but which, in contrast to the latter, do not represent a problem for interpersonal and intercultural

processes of coming to an understanding, which instead represent an a priori standard for the rationality of individual actions? In other words, do the rules for the purposive rationality of action in the widest sense (including conceptual strategies for action and argumentation) constitute a standard for action and understanding action which, while it does arise historically, is nonetheless intercultuarally valid from the beginning, insofar as it cannot be relativized as a convention? Max Weber seems to move in this direction in viewing both the ideal type of purposive-rational action and the concept of rationality connected to it as keys to understanding cultural development (at least in the West).

We can also ask whether, in addition to the rules of purposive rationality, there are not, or must not be, other nonconventional—thus, universally valid—rules which are therefore presupposed in all hermeneutic understanding. In my view, a second problem which thus far has not become a theme points in this direction: that of reconstructing the dialectical-hermeneutic tradition in the medium of a philosophy of rule-understanding.

2. This sketch of a possible reconstruction of the philosophy of objective spirit raises the question: What is the significance of Hegel's conception of absolute spirit, and why is it revived by neither Dilthey nor the interpretive sociologists Freyer and Gehlen? Is this conception to be considered merely the hybrid speculation of dialectical idealism, and does it thus pose no reconstructive problems for a critical philosophy of rule-understanding?

A negative answer to this question is indicated by the inability of Dilthey, the interpretive sociologists, or the neo-Wittgensteinians to resolve the problem of relativism in values, rules, or norms.[10] Put differently: These philosophers were no longer in a position to redeem the validity claims of their own statements or the possibilities of intersubjective consensus formation that they presuppose as possible accomplishments of rule-guided action even within the framework of their social and historical understanding. They could not show these validity claims to be possible in principle—for a reason that can be easily understood. Any scientific statement involving a truth claim must draw on the intersubjective validity of the rules of argumentation it presupposes, as well as on the validity of the corresponding rules of interpersonal communication and interaction. Only in this way can it enter into public discourse as a process of reaching understanding about meaning and building consensus about norms. This validity cannot be reduced to the social validity of rules and norms described objectivistically, however, without encountering relativistic aporias. Hegel depicted just this problem in distinguishing between an explicitly self-antagonistic objective spirit qua form of the history of spirit and the absolute spirit that mediates itself through the truth claims of art, religion, and philosophy. Even if we can no longer accept the form of absolute knowledge Hegel associated with absolute spirit (that is, the idea that has come to itself in the otherness of reality), there can be no doubt that a mere descriptive understanding of spirit, a mere descriptive understanding of the systems of rules that depend on human institutions, conventions, and forms of life can neither reconstruct Hegel's problem nor resolve it.[11]

At this point the question arises whether a normative, transcendental-pragmatic or universal-pragmatic transformation of the philosophy of rule-understanding is possible and whether it is necessary. At issue is the transcendental-reflective consideration of the implicit rules, the validity of which is presupposed in all communication and especially in argumentative discourse as the ultimate (*nicht hintergehbaren*) reflective moment of legitimation for all human communication.[12] In this case we would have to reckon with a third type of rule: the universally valid rules of human communication and interaction (for example, morality). These would have to be distinguished from (a) the universally valid rules of purposive-rational action (or, perhaps better, the rules of technical rationality) and (b) the rules of communication and inter-action that depend on conventions and institutions (for example, mores).

The relation of the universally valid rules of communication and interaction to (a) is suggested by the following point. Not only *should* human beings not reciprocally degrade one another to mere means in the service of purposive-rational manipulation, as Kant demanded; although such a mutual relationship may be possible and even un-avoidable in particular cases, in principle, it *cannot* be made the standard for interaction. If it were, the self-understanding of the acting ego already presupposed in all projection of goals would be impossible; as both Hegel and George Herbert Mead pointed out, this self-under-standing rests on the reciprocity of communicative recognition and agreement (*Verständigung*). From a transcendental-pragmatic viewpoint, this could mean that the universal rules of technical action, in the widest sense, already presuppose the universally valid rules of ethically relevant communication and interaction.

Perhaps the relation of these rules to (b) can be characterized in terms of two complementary relations. First, in terms of the principle of historical concretization, the universal rules of communication and interaction must be realized conventionally (in the sense of objective spirit) in social institutions, for example, in specific languages. Second, as universally valid rules, they also represent the normative conditions of the possibility and validity of all explicit conventions (for example, the validity of contracts). The latter would have to be shown by means of a transcendental-pragmatic reflection on the conditions of the possibility of agreement. From this, it would follow that norms resting on the internalization of conventional rules (for example, of morals) cannot be reduced only to rationalization in the sense of the Enlightenment. That is, they would not be subsumed only under the rules of purposive rationality in the utilitarian or Weberian sense. It would be decisive that they could be grounded or legitimated in practical discourse on those norms that can be shown from the transcendental-pragmatic perspective to form the conditions of the possibility of intersubjectively valid conventions (for instance, explicit agreements in the process of forming a consensus).

In the next section I do not intend to focus on the entire scope of possibilities we have examined for reconstructing the philosophy of the Geisteswissenschaften or social sciences. Ours was an ideal-typical reconstruction of the possibilities opened up by the neo-Wittgensteinians in light of a transcendental-pragmatic. It was meant to provide only a sufficiently wide horizon for examining the main issue in the renewed E-V controversy, namely, the neo-Wittgensteinian arguments against Hempel's reduction of motivational explanation or purposive-rational understanding to the causal explanation of volitional-cognitive causal complexes that can be encompassed within the D-N model. The most advanced stage of this argument is represented in von Wright's book *Explanation and Understanding* and the discussion related to it.[13] In the following, major part of the present work I want to address myself to this topic.

**II**

# On the Present Status of the Explanation-Understanding Controversy

# 1

## The Importance of von Wright's Interventionist Theory of Causality in the Context of the Explanation-Understanding Controversy

Georg Henrik von Wright's book, *Explanation and Understanding*, seems both paradigmatic for the post-Wittgensteinian reconstruction of the E-V controversy and to contribute to its resolution—for two reasons. First, the distinction between two language games—between speaking of intentionally understandable modes of action, on the one hand, and causally explicable movements or modes of behavior, on the other, is explicitly related to the problem of methodology. The second reason, however, is more important, in view of the epistemological implications of the neo-Wittgensteinian position. In von Wright's book the distinction between language games or conceptual networks not only is used, as it usually is in the discussion, to defend the claim of the interpretive social sciences to autonomy against the reductionist claim of the Hempelian D-N model of causal explanation. The distinction is also used to effect a critical revision of the neo-Humean presuppositions of Hempel's model itself, more precisely, of the presupposition that the notion of a causal law is adequately comprehended by the notion of regularity. The same concept of intentional action that in Chapter III of the book serves as the presupposition for a theory of intentional understanding and teleological explanation is seen in Chapter II to form the presupposition for the concept of causal-nomological necessity; for here, the concept of intentional action is one of experimental action that can interfere in the course of nature.

This conception perhaps represents von Wright's most original contribution not only to problems in the theory of science but also to the traditional problem of the compatibility of freedom and determinism.[1] I think, however, that it also involves a complex of problems that goes beyond the mere differentiation of language games or conceptual frameworks. The question arises as to the ground for both the distinction and the connection between language games. In this regard, von Wright fails to clarify fully the relation between chapters II and III of his book. In Chapter II he argues that the concept of action—and, implicitly, of understanding action—forms the presupposition for the concept of causality and, implicitly, of causal explanation; whereas, in Chapter III he focuses not only on intentional understanding but on the motivational or teleological explanation of action as well. It is precisely the connection between these two, however, that is important to a critical evaluation of von Wright's contribution to the E-V controversy. For this reason, the following remarks are restricted to von Wright's explication of causality and causal explanation. Von Wright makes ingenious use of the apparatus of propositional modal logic and the "onto-logic" of logical atomism, in order to go beyond an analysis of the necessary and sufficient conditions of world states and elaborate the notion of a "closed" causal system that can be set in motion experimentally.[2] In my reflections I shall refer only to the philosophical dimensions of this elaboration.

## 1.1 The Transcendental-Pragmatic Reconstruction of von Wright's Thesis

In my attempt to transform the Kantian system along transcendental-pragmatic lines, I have already anticipated both the essence of von Wright's conception of causality and the supersession of metaphysical determinism that it involves. I must emphasize that von Wright's account of an experimentalist or interventionist concept of causality seems to be the first to allow a satisfactory transformation of transcendental philosophy with regard to the decisive point as to the subjective conditions of the possibility of experimental experience.[3] At the same time, I think it important to contrast this interpretation (which may sound speculative) with his own self-understanding. In this connection, it is noteworthy that von Wright does not refer to Kant, but, instead, seems to ground the reflexive self-understanding of experimental action empirically, in terms of the certainty of the capacity to intervene in the natural process.

Thus von Wright asks for the source of our certainty "that certain states of affairs will stay unchanged (or will change in a certain way) unless we interfere productively or preventively with the course of nature." He answers: "obviously from experience." Hence, for him, "the notion of action is rooted in our familiarity with empirical regularities."[4] Here, von Wright appears to return to a Humean position. This is confirmed by his admission that the view of causality which he defends agrees "in a certain sense" with Hobart's "defense of the Humean 'passivist' regular sequence view of causality and natural law" in which Hobart claims that "the mere sequence of events themselves generates necessity in them as characterized by us."[5] Von Wright explicates the extent to which he can agree with Hobart:

The idea of natural necessity, as I see it, is rooted in the idea that we can bring about things by doing other things. Our knowledge that our doing certain things "brings about" other things rests, however, on observations of regular sequences. To say that things "bring about" other things is therefore misleading: this "bringing about" is nothing but regular sequence.[6]

Here, von Wright's position seems, prima facie, paradoxical. On the one hand, it is supposed to overcome the Humean (and neo-Humean, i.e., neopositivist) "passivist" conception of causation and natural law. The notion of empirical (contingent), exceptionless (universal) uniformity and regularity is to be replaced with a concept of natural necessity that coordinates with the concept of action. On the other hand, the concept of action that is presupposed for all experience of natural necessity—the certainty of being able to intervene in nature and bring something about—itself rests on the evidently passivist observation of regular sequences of events.

Now, to a certain extent, the appearance of a contradiction, circle, or infinite regress that arises here can be resolved. For, although the constitution of the concept of action presupposes observation of regularities, it does not exclude the necessity of this concept for the constitution of the concept of natural necessity. Von Wright interprets this hierarchy of presuppositions in quasi-Wittgensteinian terms as a hierarchy of language games that we have learned or can learn. Given the empirical regularity of sequences of events, which corresponds to our bringing something about by doing something else, we can learn to act and form a concept of action. On the basis of this concept, we can then form the concept of natural necessity and on its basis discover and empirically verify causal laws. "One could say that we can be as certain of the truth of causal laws as we can be of our abilities to do and bring about things."[7]

From a pragmatic perspective, the degree of certainty here is very high, involving as it does a measure of certainty that differs as qualitatively from the certainty of contingent life experiences as the concept of these experiences differs from the concept of our capacity for action. This qualitative difference attains transcendental-pragmatic status, however, through a further Wittgensteinian consideration: The language game comprising the theoretical and experimental investigation of nature—i.e., the search for natural laws and their verification by testing—presupposes as its "paradigm" the pragmatic certainties implied in the concepts of action and causal necessity. That means these certainties can no longer be treated as mere certainties of experience. Rather, they must be seen as a priori standards establishing possible certainty and possible doubt, and that means as the subjective-intersubjective conditions of the possibility of experience.[8]

Of course, one could object that even an interpretation of von Wright's analysis which sees it in terms of the Wittgensteinian concept of paradigms does not neutralize the difference between von Wright's quasi-empiricist self-understanding and my attempt at a transcendental-pragmatic interpretation. Even if one grants the compatibility between von Wright's quasi-empiricism and Wittgensteinian's quasi-transcendentalism with regard to paradigms of language games, the following difference seems to persist: In the foregoing, I used the opposition between a "passivist" and an "experimentalist-interventionist" conception of causality to extrapolate a "paradigm" for the opposition between the external standpoint of a "theoretical ontology," or "metaphysic," and a transcendental-pragmatic philosophy. For the latter the concept of an objectifiable nature that can be observed and explained theoretically can, in principle, be conceived of only under the presupposition of a reflection on the subjective conditions of the possibility of experience, that is, only as the complementary concept to the concept of reflexively intelligible, intentional actions. Now, this conception seems incompatible with von Wright's interpretation of the experimentalist conception of causality. To be sure, von Wright seems to say that the constitution of the objective-theoretical concept of causal necessity presupposes as its subjective condition the reflexive concept of (the certainty of) the capacity to act. He further says, however, that the latter depends on an objective observation of regularity and that, as experience, the possibility of this observation itself does not presuppose subjective conditions. Hence, ultimately the correlation or complementarity between objective experience and reflexive understanding of action is dissolved; a passivist conception of empirical experience retains the final word (thus, also, a theoretic-objectivistic-ontological conception of philosophy that either does not reflect in principle upon the subjective conditions of the possibility of experience, or, ultimately, objectifies these conditions from an external standpoint as merely empirical).

Nevertheless, I am not certain whether these consequences are or must be entailed by von Wright's position. In itself, it does not seem impossible, a priori, to bring von Wright's quasi-empiricist view that our certainty with regard to our capacities for interventionist action is rooted "in our familiarity with empirical regularities" (thus the evolutionary thesis of Hobart and even Peirce, that "the mere sequence in events itself generates necessity in them as characterized by us") in harmony with the transcendental-pragmatic perspective. It is necessary only that this quasi-empiricism be interpreted in light of a conception of the mutual dependence of experience and the subjective conditions of the possibility of experience. This mutual dependence rises through levels; and at no level is experience conceived without reflection on the subjective conditions of its possibility. Von Wright's mention of "familiarity with empirical regularities" as the basis for the concept of action seems open to such interpretation; for, it seems to me, "familiarity with empirical regularities" means something different from the "observation of regular sequences." The latter may be the basis of our knowledge that "things done" by us—i.e., the initial conditions of closed systems—"bring about other things"—i.e., they have results. In contrast, experience, in the sense of "familiarity," can be called the foundation of our certainty that we can bring something about by doing something else if and only if, in addition to the objective observation of regularity, a reflexive-intentional understanding of action is presupposed. The latter case must already include the subjective conditions of the possibility of the experience of mere regularity, subjective conditions that, under the impression of experience, can in different ways form categories and paradigms for language games.

From an evolutionary perspective I believe this reflection has the following consequence. It means that, to comprehend the beginning and further growth of human learning processes, one must "subjectively" assume a certain creative spontaneity in the sense of both Kant's "synthesis of apperception" and the bodily practical world engagement that belongs to it. Empirical development of this a priori of spontaneity cannot be conceived apart from a biological, psychological programming or, in other words, from innate schemata. To this extent, however, the transcendental-philosophical viewpoint of the subjective conditions of the possibility of experience is valid even in the empirical-genetic consideration of the evolution of human knowledge. (This is the source of the Kantianism of the evolutionary theories of knowledge elaborated by Popper, Lorenz, and possibly Chomsky—a Kantianism, as it were, without transcendental philosophy.[9])

For an epistemology and logic of experimental science, however, both the certainty of the active capacity to alter natural sequences by interfering with the course of nature and the certainty of the objective validity of causal laws that is grounded on this capacity represent a transcendental-pragmatic a priori. To be sure, in a thought experiment, philosophical reflection can imagine a different human environment in which the empirical conditions of successful, controlled action do not hold, nor, therefore, do the conditions of causal explanation.[10] In this case we would be unable to isolate, for example, the closed causal systems which, in principle, can be set in motion by our interference with nature. To that extent, philosophy can question or empirically relativize the transcendental-pragmatic a priori. At the same time, however, by means of this thought experiment, it eliminates the possibility and the rise of experimental science itself. Thus it confirms the relativized a priori in its transcendental-pragmatic function. We can distinguish this function from that of empirical (inductive or falsifying) cognitions with appropriate sharpness if we consider that all scientifically valid confirmation and falsification already presuppose the possibility of repeatable scientific experimentation, hence, the transcendental-pragmatic framework of the capacity to act that von Wright shows to be conceptually presupposed for the constitution of the concept of causality.[11]

I can specify what this means more precisely by referring to Popper's "logic of inquiry," which states that individual causal laws in natural science cannot be verified definitively, but instead must reckon with the constant possibility of falsification. Even if that is true, however, the case of falsification itself presupposes the conceptual framework of experimental action and thus of causality—qua why-question and the assumption it contains as to the causal-nomological necessity of connections in nature. This presupposition is a categorial one; that is, it refers to the transcendental-pragmatic condition of natural science and not simply to general empirical concepts within natural science. Hence, the conceptual framework at issue here would be brought into question only if, as a rule, empirical causal laws could no longer be confirmed or corroborated; for, in this case, the transcendental-pragmatic framework itself would prove dependent on contingent facts of nature. In view of the confirmability of empirical causal laws, however, we must at least modify Popper's devaluation of empirical induction, a devaluation motivated by purely logical considerations. As long as there are causal laws that are confirmed, von Wright's thesis holds:

That such a test is successful (with a view to the truth of the law) means that we learn how to do things by doing other things (which we already know how to do), that our technical mastery of nature is increased. One could say that we can be as certain of the truth of causal laws as we can be of our abilities to do and bring about things.[12]

We can also agree with C. S. Peirce that, "in the long run," we can be as certain of the methodological validity of the inductive verification of causal laws as we can be of our increasing ability to master nature in the practical and technical manner implied in the transcendental-pragmatic framework of experimental action.[13] To precisely this extent, then, I consider my transcedental-pragmatic transformation of Kant to be a reasonable interpretation of von Wright's theory of causality.

Indeed, it seems to me that the transcendental-pragmatic perspective presents a stronger claim for certain consequences of von Wright's approach than the claim he himself makes. According to von Wright, the concept of causal determination presupposes the concept of the freedom of action as the ability to bring about an alteration in the world by doing something. If this is correct, then the notion of universal causal determinism amounts to a demonstration that the subjective conditions of the possibility of establishing causal determination are illusions. Von Wright's approach, however, allows us to see that the introduction of such a "metaphysic" (in the pre-Kantian sense) constitutes an illegitimate totalization of the causal determination operative in isolatable systems—indeed, that this determination is meaningful only in relation to the world that we can objectify and regulate experimentally. In other words, this "metaphysic" assumes that, from a position outside the world, one could pose the question whether all alterations within the world are causally determined, i.e., that one could pose the question without having to reflect on the subjective conditions (in the sense of the bodily, practical world engagement of the knowing subject) of the possibility of the constitution of concepts.

In comparison with this thesis, I find von Wright's conclusion in *Causality and Determinism* too weak. He states that "the validity of the deterministic thesis for the whole world must remain an open question," and grounds this, among other ways, as follows:

Action, however, cannot rightly be said to presuppose the existence of ontic alternatives in nature, i.e., the truth of some form of indeterminism. What action presupposes is only the epistemic certainty which, as long as it is not undermined, entails the belief in the ontic contingency of some changes and this takes for granted a certain margin of indeterminism in the world.[14]

Previously, however, von Wright showed that "undermining" the presupposed "certainty" that he considers possible, in principle (i.e., conceptually), would itself again presuppose the same certainty. Under these circumstances, it seems to me that his proviso with regard to the ontological truth of epistemic certainty amounts to holding open—and therefore undecidable—the question how the world acts "in itself," i.e., independently of any possible experience of it. From a transcendental-pragmatic standpoint (which I also understand as a critical standpoint), I would respond that the question concerning the role of causal determination in the world "in itself" cannot even be raised in an intelligible way. This is precisely what is stated by the complementarity of the conceptual knowledge of causal necessity and the freedom of action.

Von Wright's quasi-empiricist proviso recalls Stroud's objection to the significance of transcendental arguments.[15] Stroud assumes that it might be possible to specify the necessary presuppositions for meaningful discourse—for example, those for the existence of language.

He claims that one would have to prove to a skeptic only that the persons arguing must believe in the existence of the language, but not that the language actually exists. Consequently, that the language actually exists would have to be demonstrated with the help of a version of the verification principle according to which the belief of the arguers in the language can be intelligible only if it is, in principle, possible to specify criteria for establishing the existence of language. Thus, Stroud concludes that the possibility of answering the question as to the existence of language depends not on the validity of transcendental arguments but on the validity of a version of the verification principle.

Now, to me, the converse seems to be the case: the version of the verification principle to which Stroud refers already depends on the validity of "transcendental arguments"—if they are correctly understood—for two reasons. First, if the language does not exist in the sense that all arguing presupposes it, then (a) no version of the verification principle can be formulated, and (b) no criteria can be used to establish the existence of language. Just this insight is generalized in the transcendental-pragmatic argument: in the case under discussion the existence of language must be presumed if the argument before or against a given assumption is to be meaningful. Second, in view of this result, to demand that one prove the existence of language independently of the transcendental argument is to demand that one establish what the state of the existence of language would be in itself, i.e., independently of the possibility of an intersubjectively valid identification. I find this a meaningless demand. Thus it is clear that we cannot "go behind" the transcendental argument; rather, it remains the foundation of every critical argumentation about meaning and even grounds the meaning-critical thrust of Stroud's version of the verification principle as well.

With regard to von Wright's discussion of the certainty of the margin of freedom in experimental action, we cannot, of course, secure the certainty of a transcendental-pragmatic reflection that has the same quality of not-being-able-to-be-gone-behind, as we can in the case of the existence of language. Von Wright has shown that, from the standpoint of our reflective thought (which, as argumentation, already presupposes language) the possibility of experimental action is a contingent fact which we can "go behind." The world could have been created in such a way that our action would have been able to find no ontical correlate in causal systems that were sufficiently closed to disturbances. In this case, our concept of action would have to be very different—something we may find difficult to imagine but which nonetheless is, in principle, not as impossible as conceiving of the concept of a different form of thought.

Through reflective thought (which has formed its language game in the discourse of philosophy since philosophy is freed from the constraints of action), we can, in fact, distance ourselves from every specific, practical world engagement, together with its corresponding experimental a priori, even if this is identical with the evolutionary programming of "apparati of cognition" (Konrad Lorenz). In principle, we can enter into another world engagement qua a response to a different possible world. This possibility seems to have played a role in the formation of nonclassical theory in physics—for example, qua a response not to the immediately measured human environment but to the spheres of the largest and smallest. Nevertheless, the relativization of the Kantian a priori of experience that is possible here remains related to the "methodical a priori" of "protophysics." Moreover, it in no way alters two conditions. First, as the condition of the possibility of every conceivable experience or of the construction of any empirically confirmable theory, we must presuppose subjective conditions of some kind. Second, these conditions correspond to a practical meaning-constitutive world engagement on which we can reflect and hence are not related to a world-in-itself. Therefore, if on the level of a transcendental pragmatic it is clear that we can go behind Kant's specific a priori of experience, the thought of the a priori of experience in general remains one we cannot go behind. Finally, again on the level of a transcendental pragmatic, the a priori of reflective, critical, or question-raising thought—thus, the a priori of argumentation—cannot be gone behind even as a specific a priori; for, although it must be further elaborated, it must prove itself to form the condition of the possibility of any conceivable questioning and hence of any doubt and self-criticism that is supposed to be intersubjectively valid.

## 1.2 The A Priori of Action, the A Priori of the "Lived Body," and the Compatibility of Freedom and Determinism

If the interpretation given above of von Wright's theory of causality is sound, then it has the following consequence. It is true that I have presupposed the post-Wittgensteinian distinction between language games—between the language game of series of events that can be causally explained and that of actions that can be intentionally understood. I also presuppose, however, an internal relation between these language games, a relation which seems suited to overcoming a difficulty with regard to understanding the freedom of action introduced by the mere separation of language games.

The difficulty I refer to is that, in differentiating language games, the "New Dualism" does not exclude the fact that the event interpreted as an intentional action is also determined by a natural cause. In fact, this refusal to preclude the causal explanation of the event corresponding to the action seems to constitute the merit of New Dualism; for, given the present level of science, we cannot imagine any action that manifests itself as a sensuously perceptible event without postulating a physiological cause for it. At the same time, the idea that I perform an action obviously is incompatible with the notion that the corresponding event was sufficiently determined causally, irrespective of my action. If, however, one understands the New Dualism as a mere differentiation of language games, it does not, in fact, exclude this possibility.

Von Wright's elaboration of the neo-Wittgensteinian conception is different in that he argues that the concept of causal determinism presupposes that of interventionist or interfering action. Of course, he retains the merit of New Dualism insofar as he assumes the fundamental compatibility between understanding actions and explaining the corresponding events causally.[16] If, however, the meaning of the concept of causal determinism presupposes the meaning of the concept of action, we can be certain that, in the normal case, the event that corresponds to the action as its result—for example, the arm rising when one raises one's arm—does not occur independently of performance of the action. This does not mean that the action itself must or may be conceived as a cause in the sense of the natural scientific concept of causal determination. This inference would destroy the distinction in language games and thus the advantage involved in seeing the fundamental compatibility between the freedom of action and causal determination. Further, the notion of an immediate causal determination of natural events by the human will would amount to animism.[17] Nevertheless, the dependence of the meaning of the former concept on the meaning of the latter does affect the causal determination that can come under consideration with regard to "basic actions." It must be a priori related to those bodily movements that correspond in the same way to the action to be performed as the event to be determined corresponds to the result of the action.

In my view, this argument is based on the circumstance that the possibility or necessity of "basic actions" is bound to the existence and special status of the actor's own physical body (*Körper*) as the body lived in (*Leib*). It would not be enough to argue that the natural cause of the event corresponding to, or resulting from, the action must belong to the physical body of the actor.[18] In the case of raising my arm, for example, this notion of my own action would not exclude the possibility that my brain stimulated the corresponding movement on the basis of external stimulation by a neurologist. But a process in the brain can be considered the natural cause of the event corresponding to the action only insofar as it is part of my "lived" body and, as its conceptual determination in Merleau-Ponty's phenomenology shows, this is a process that the actor cannot objectify insofar as the lived body forms the perspective from which one has the world.[19]

As far as I can see, von Wright does not focus directly on this correspondence between actions and bodily movements. Nevertheless, in what follows I would like to show that it results from his analysis of the structural interrelation between causally explicable natural processes and experimental actions appropriate to them. With the help of the concept of action, this structural interrelation allows one to distinguish between cause and effect in the sphere of natural events. As von Wright puts it: "$P$ is a cause relative to $q$, and $q$ an effect relative to $p$, if and only if by doing $p$, we could bring about $q$ or by suppressing $p$ we could remove $q$ or prevent it from happening."[20]

In view of this structural interrelation, what we are supposed to understand as cause and effect in nature (with regard to both their possibility and their reality) is, at the same time, that which we can do or bring about by acting. Thus, by opening the window ($p$), we can bring air into the room ($q$), and hence, assume as a fact the causal necessity of the relation between the window being opened qua natural phenomenon ($p$) and the subsequent event of air circulating ($q$). (In cases where we cannot actually do $p$, the assumption of a causally necessary relation in the regular succession of $p$ and $q$ must remain an undecidable hypothesis.) With regard to nature, this structural interrelation means that we can set a causal system in motion through repeatable actions and isolate it sufficiently as a system closed in a relevant aspect. According to von Wright,

In the terminology of "systems," the performance of an action . . . means the transition from a state preceding the initial state of a system to this initial state. . . . The idea that man, through his action, can bring about things is founded on the idea that sequences of events form closed systems, if not absolutely, then at least relative to some conditionship relation between their states. The identification and isolation of systems again rests on the idea that man can do things, as distinct from bringing them about, through direct interference with the course of events (nature).[21]

Given this structural interrelation of causally explicable natural processes and intentionally understandable action, we can now understand the transition to the analysis of the teleological structure of action undertaken by von Wright in Chapter III of his book in distinguishing between the inner and outer aspects of action. The outer aspect of action consists in the causally conjoined phases of a natural process (of an isolatable system) that are integrated in the action of bringing something about by doing something else, or that, as von Wright says, can be subsumed under the same intention.[22] The inner aspect consists in the teleological intention to bring something about by doing something else.

In the phases of the outer aspect of an action, von Wright includes the intentional object qua result of doing something and the intended effect or consequence in the sense of bringing something about. Notably, however, he includes as well "causal antecedents" or "conditions" of doing something.[23] In this respect he follows Anscombe's account of the unlimited possibilities for intentional descriptions of complex actions; this shows that highly complex chains may be integrated within a single action, causal chains which, as antecedents of the intended result, actually precede the initial state of the system set in motion by the action.[24] Are the antecedents of the initial state of the system set in motion by our action now also set in motion? And is this the case even though, as natural events, they are the causal conditions of the initial state of the system set in motion? This apparently is von Wright's position; as long as the complex actions can, for their part, be understood as bringing things about by doing things, this position poses no difficulties. Perhaps one can say that the operations required to open a window are also set in motion with the action of airing a room, since the latter action can be conceived of as the effect of opening the window or the effect of turning a handle. Yet, what about the case of "basic actions" which no longer can be dissected into the phases of doing and bringing about?

To understand this question we need a more precise explication of the notion of basic action. As von Wright demonstrates against Danto, the division of actions into basic actions and nonbasic actions refers only to individual, not generic, actions.[25] Nevertheless, one can postulate that for each human being there must be actions that cannot be further analyzed and that the human being therefore performs as basic actions. I think this postulate can be grounded in the distinction between nature as the physical body's external world and action as the lived-bodily intervention in nature. Thus it is immediately clear that, in principle, it is impossible ever to consider one's own lived body (the presupposition of action) entirely as the physical body's external world, in other words, as objectifiable nature. Every possible attempt to replace a basic action with an indirect production of its results—for example, replacing the raising of the arm directly with a technically mediated procedure—must refer to another possibility of direct bodily intervention in the physical body's external world (with regard to a paralytic, to the possibility of stimulating the membrane). Hence, individual differences notwithstanding, the concept of basic action can be explicated in transcendental-pragmatic terms as a consequence of conceiving of the lived body as the subjective condition of the possibility of action (and thus of experimental experience).

Now, having thus defined basic actions, we can raise the question: Must we reckon with the possibility that there are causal antecedents or conditions of the results of such basic actions that the latter also set in motion? Given von Wright's starting point, we must answer this question in the affirmative. If the capacity to actively interfere with the course of nature is the subjective condition for the possibility of the causal-analytic account of natural processes—or, more precisely, if one must assume that the initial state of a closed system can be set in motion by our lived-bodily intervention in such a way that this would not occur without it, and if, conversely, we acknowledge that with regard to their outer aspect, lived-bodily actions always presuppose objectifiable natural causes, for example, the stimulation of muscles by the brain—then we must accept the following: Whenever basic actions set closed systems in motion, there are causes in the physical human body (for example, in the brain as a component of the material world) that, as a rule, do not become effective apart from our intentional actions. Now, it follows from the concept of irreducible basic actions that, in principle, these causes cannot be the intentional object of our acting qua setting systems in motion. Hence, under von Wright's premises, if the material causes of basic actions are set in motion as well, this can be seen only as a "bringing about" that is mediated by the basic action itself—that is, in principle, nothing but the bringing about of the intended results of the basic action.

It seems to me that this interpolation clarifies why von Wright develops the remarkable theory of the possibility of "retroactive causality."[26] According to this theory, a basic action (normally represented by the example of raising an arm) allows us to bring about an event, for example, in our brain, that can temporally precede the action—if not its beginning, then its result! In view of our present problem complex, this theory is significant because it seems to represent an extreme consequence and illustration of the thesis that action represents the subjective condition of the possibility of definitely establishing causal relations in the objectifiable world of experience. As we have seen, every experimenter must assume that the result of his interventionist action would not come about without it. From this necessary assumption it follows, in fact, with the same necessity that the material causes of the result of the experimenter's action (causes integrated within the bodily interference) are normally coproduced by this action itself. For von Wright, this consequence constitutes solid proof of the possibility of the freedom of action, since the conceptual possibility of coproducing the material causes of the result of action shows "why the existence of causes of the results of our actions does not necessarily make action an illusion."[27]

## 1.3 Transition to the Problem of the E-V Controversy: Three Perspectives

From what has been said about the structural interrelation of experimental action—as the possibility of bringing something about by doing something else—and causal connections between natural events, it seems to follow that we cannot conceive of action qua action that can be understood in intentional terms (in the sense elaborated thus far) as itself causally explicable (also in the sense elaborated thus far).

The phenomenal domains of intentionally understandable actions and causally explicable natural processes apparently are complementary in the sense already elucidated, a sense that seems to correspond to the neo-Wittgensteinian differentiation of language games. It appears that this complementarity already provides the most basic foundation for arguing against the reduction of intentional-teleological explanation to causal explanation. Nevertheless, in Chapter III of his book, von Wright treats this problem in a relatively autonomous discussion of the "subsumption-theoretic" conception of causalistic reduction deriving from Hempel; for the most part, the critics of his teleological conception also refer to this discussion.[28] Before we look at it, I would like to introduce two perspectives from which we can see the difference between its presuppositions and those illuminated so far.

First, it is to be noted that bringing something about by doing something else—as in the case of a successful experimental verification of a causal hypothesis or in the case of the technical, instrumental action allowed by this confirmation—represents only a special, if ontologically eminent, case of actions that can be understood as intentional-teleological or purposive-rational in the formal sense. Specifically, it indicates that case in which the actor's assumption that his action is suited to bringing about the state which is his end is fully confirmed by the causal system set in motion.

Under von Wright's premises, the action must also prove itself suited to bringing about the material causes of the intended result. In the case of a sudden paralysis that does not allow one to raise one's arm as intended, one must say that the causal system consisting of the stimulation of muscles by the brain—a system whose activity the actor does not set in motion directly but which the action itself can also bring about—has failed as a quasi-means of action. Exactly the same obtains for the miscarry of a difficult athletic feat.

In contrast, the understanding of actions in light of the schema of intentional teleology or formal purposive rationality is concerned with all cases in which it can merely be assumed that the actor could have acted consistently, given his assumptions as to the means appropriate to reaching his goal, assumptions that could be true or false. In the first, special case of teleologically intelligible actions, the objective causal necessity of natural processes is integrated without rupture, so to speak, into the subjective (intentional) teleology of action. This is a consequence of the structural interrelation between successful actions qua interventions into nature and causal relations that can be established factually. Moreover, this integration is of such a kind that it seems equivalent to, or continuous with, the integration of the causal mechanism into the "objective teleology" of functional biological systems, for example, of the organism.[29]

Here again, bringing about physical-bodily causality by basic actions possesses a peculiar, intermediate position, or transitional function. In this case, only the goal, and nothing like the choice of means, is entrusted to the freedom of the intentional actor. Nevertheless, there could be no choice of means, and hence, no explicit intentional-teleological action, unless the human being could, in principle, trust that his physical body would function as a nonselectable means for achieving the goals of basic actions. As I have already clarified, even in the abnormal case in which the body fails to function in this way— as, for example, in paralysis—the technically mediated ersatz action derives from a basic action and thus from an unintended function of the physical body. Still, in the case of explicitly instrumental-teleological action—for example, using a tool—the highest degree of reliability is attained if the function of the instrument no longer needs to be the intentional goal of acting but, rather, is integrated into the intentional, lived-bodily action in such a way that the goal of the action—setting a causal system in motion—can be advanced. In precisely this integration, the function of the a priori of the "lived body" proves itself the presupposition of all action.[30]

In contrast to the special case described above, the subjective teleology of human actions in general covers a vast field. Here, understanding the intentional teleology or formal purposive-rationality no longer is bound to the structural interrelation between the "bringing about" of things through acting and the known (or, in the case of one's own body, assumed) causal laws of nature. Hence, the rational key to translating the means-end relation in action into a law-governed, cause-effect relation—for example, one that can be presupposed in functional systems analysis—is missing. Precisely this situation, however, seems to necessitate a formal, purposive-rational understanding of human action as such, that is, the understanding of human action characteristic of the Geisteswissenschaften or cultural sciences. Here, the point is no longer to grasp the teleological structure of intentional purposive-rationality as the transparent content of the structure of our successful instrumental-technical ability to act (as it has accumulated in the technical knowledge of millennia). Neither are we concerned with the correspondence of this structure with the law-governed structure of a nature that can be investigated in experiments and technically mastered. Rather, we are concerned with the variety of culturally determined modes of human behavior, especially the more or less unprecedented nature of historically relevant actions, and in neither of these cases can we assume that the teleology of action and natural causality correspond. The point, then, is to achieve an understanding of good—that is, rationally justifiable reasons—so that one can see the correspondence between an actor's goal intentions and the actor's assumptions as to the appropriate means. This achievement, however, presupposes the possibility of discovering and understanding the goal intentions and assumptions as to the appropriate means human beings have, independent of insight into the substantive correspondence between natural causality and the teleology of action.

Now, this possibility, for its part, requires the heuristic assumption that a hermeneutic imagination allows insight into the domain of needs, values, norms, and maxims that lies behind goal intentions as well as the domain of opinions lying behind assumptions about means. These domains, however, can be constituted as the object of cognitive efforts only by the Geisteswissenschaften, cultural or social sciences. Hence, it is clear, I think, that, if the intentional teleology of human actions is to possess more than a purely formal rationality, it must establish its rationality on two sides, so to speak. Its technical-instrumental realizability depends on insight into the causal nomological structure of nature (and, as I still must show, of human, social quasi-nature); but precisely because of the positing of goals, its rationality as intentional teleology depends on ethical, hermeneutic insights into what is demanded by the historical situation of human beings or what corresponds to their true interests. At this point, I can go no deeper into the problems involved. I merely wish to point to the new dimension of understanding that opens up if one considers the intentional teleology of actions; for that cannot be understood always to correspond to the structure of causal laws, and, therefore, neither can its substantive rationality be understood in these terms alone. The new dimension of understanding, rather, refers to understanding the reasons for acting and thus concerns the goals that human beings have posited as worthy of their aspirations, as well as the ways or means they regard as suited to attaining them.

Nevertheless, if the structure of motivations for human actions is not to be analyzed in terms of its correspondence to a technically mastered natural causality, it is still possible to understand the interest in explaining action very differently. Here, the point is not to understand the action as rationally justifiable, given its subjective teleological principles. Rather, by presupposing certain "motives," one attempts to explain causally its occurrence as an event, that is, an event that had to happen and could be expected or even predicted. This leads me to the second perspective mentioned above, under which the premises of the discussion between von Wright and his critics can be seen to depart from arguments that view the understanding of actions as the ground of causal explanation.

Thus far, we have generally considered actions that can be understood from one of two perspectives: that of a transcendental-pragmatic reflection on the subjective conditions of the possibility of the concept of causality, and therefore of causal explanation; or from that of the interest in understanding the formal, purposive-rationality of human actions. In order to confront the representatives of the "causalist" attempt to explain actions in terms of motives, we must, it seems to me, introduce another perspective: Actions to be "explained" are now to be viewed neither as subjective conditions of the possibility of causal explanation nor as actions that can be understood to be potentially purposive-rational; rather, they are to be seen as objects of theoretical, causal explanation on analogy with natural events.

Thus, with regard to talk of "explaining" and "understanding" actions, the following questions arise: Is the term *explanation* to designate only a methodologically relevant explication of "purposive-rational" understanding, in Max Weber's sense, as William Dray suggests with his notion of rational explanation? Or is the conjunction of both terms (as we actually find it in Weber) to indicate that purposive-rational understanding can be employed for a theoretical explanation that answers the same why-question as does a natural scientific explanation? Weber precluded Hempel's answer to the latter question in advance, namely, that understanding is nothing but a heuristic accomplishment prior to causal explanation. Weber, of course, never argues that understanding is not a heuristic accomplishment prior to causal explanation. Nevertheless, with the neo-Kantians, Windelband and Rickert, he views the understanding of both individual meaning and the purposive rationality of actions that presupposes it in the light of possible (for example, religious, ethical, aesthetic, political, economic) value relations. Thus he sees this kind of understanding as the appropriate task of the cultural sciences and of "interpretive sociology." In criticizing Dray's theory of "rational explanation," however, Hempel assumes that this explanation is an explanation in his sense. He then refutes this claim by arguing that demonstrating "good reasons" for an action by itself (that is, independent of the statement of a law that informs us of the causal efficacy of these reasons) represents no explanation and thus no answer to the question why the occurrence of the action was to be expected or why the scientist would have good reasons "for the assumption that $x$ actually occurred."[31]

## 1.4 On the Terminology of the E-V Controversy

As I have already indicated, the aggravating feature of this entire phase of the E-V controversy consists in the fact that both sides begin with different concepts of explanation, concepts that are supposed to answer different why-questions. In essence, Hempel begins from the old dichotomy between causal explanation and understanding, permitting only the former to count as an answer to any methodologically relevant question. In contrast, with the concept of rational explanation, Dray wants to provide not an alternative answer to the Hempelian why-question but an answer to the question he considers characteristic of historical science, namely, why given circumstances make the performance of a certain action appropriate and reasonable.[32] To this extent, Dray actually revalidates the Weberian problem complex of "purposive-rational understanding," a complex Weber considered methodologically relevant to the Geisteswissenschaften or social sciences alone, in complete independence of the problem of explanation.

The terminological confusion that arises here is characteristic of attempts to relate the post-Wittgensteinian explanation of action based on the framework of a language-analytic theory of action back to the two older phases of the E-V controversy. Hence, I think it advisable before entering the last round of the discussion set off by von Wright to reflect on the possibilities of linguistic usage that are relevant to the debate. We can, I think, distinguish three typical strategies, all of which have hitherto functioned less explicitly than as unclarified *petitiones principii* within the discussion.

1. The first strategy can rely, in all innocence, on both English and German linguistic usage. It begins from the premise that *to understand* belongs etymologically with *understanding*, that is, with the linguistically expressible apprehension of data *as something* while *to explain* belongs etymologically with *to make clear* and thus means an additional, perhaps methodical and scientific, act necessitated by difficulties in understanding. To this extent, it can refer to natural, lawlike connections between events, as well as to the meaning of linguistic assertions, for example (as in the explanation of words, sentences, or texts). Naturally, no objection can be raised against such linguistic usage, in itself; it is just as clear, however, that it makes the terminological language used by the founders of the philosophy of the Geisteswissenschaften incomprehensible, and indeed, unjustified. This strategy, then, is best suited to those who wish either to disavow the problems constituting the E-V controversy or to downplay their significance.

2. As far as I can see, the second strategy is characteristic of both language-analytic philosophy and, in a certain sense, the hermeneutic phenomenology or philosophical hermeneutics that began with Heidegger. This strategy takes up the linguistic usage explicated in the preceding paragraph, starting from the premise that understanding and explanation refer, respectively, to the prescientific apprehension of data and the methodological, scientific systematizations of knowledge. It then emphasizes that the understanding of the world accomplished in the prescientific apprehension of data (either in the paradigmatic experience determined by a language game or in the constitution of meaning or disclosure of the world in the sense of the original hermeneutic synthesis of something as something) is philosophically refined insofar as it represents a preunderstanding of the world that is also epistemologically relevant. This strategy will be further open to a differentiation of methodological, scientific systematizations of knowledge in terms of different types of explanation. This seems to me to be the strategy that lies at the heart of the neo-Wittgensteinian theory of action. Its assumptions permit one not only to question the methodology of "unified science" but also to see the extent to which post-Wittgensteinian linguistic analysis and hermeneutic phenomenology approach each other. Still, as the discussion between Hempel and Dray shows, it does not yet allow one to reconstruct or validate the actual crux of the E-V controversy, that is, to reconstruct either the methodologically relevant concept of *Verstehen* characteristic of the first

phase of the E-V controversy or the Hempelian concept of explaining events. The crux of the E-V controversy is confronted only in the third terminological strategy, sketched briefly below.

3. The first step in this strategy is the transcendental-pragmatic sharpening of the fundamental distinction already elucidated between objectifying and reflective-communicative life relations or modes of being-in-the-world, a distinction indicated in Heidegger's *Being and Time*, as well as in Royce's transcendental-hermeneutic use of Peircean semiotics.[33] This sharpening makes it clear that the prescientific pre-understanding of the world includes a systematically reconstructable presupposition that demonstrates the possibility of explanatory arguments on the level of a methodology that can be made normatively precise; it shows these explanatory arguments to be systematizations of objectifiable knowledge (that is, of technically utilizable knowledge) and specifies this form of knowledge as one refering to the primary subject-object relation. But it also indicates the possibility of arguments complementary to this knowledge, which represent a methodologically relevant (hermeneutic) elaboration of the intersubjective, communicative understanding of meaning intentions and reasons, an understanding that refers to co-subjects of conviction and action who must constitute themselves as "subject-objects" of knowledge on a level of secondary objectification.

We can now understand the actual hermeneutic accomplishment of the Geisteswissenschaften of the nineteenth century; it now appears not as a competitive alternative to the theoretical-objectifying explanation of events but, rather, as a methodologically relevant elaboration of the prescientific achievement of understanding with a practical intent (including the transmission of tradition). In this dimension of the hermeneutic-methodological elaboration (restoration or improvement) of understanding, prescientific understanding differs from the objectifying preunderstanding of the world, in that it is not replaced by a scientific explanation that presupposes a fixed or semantically explicated understanding of data. Rather, this prescientific understanding—of actions, works, institutions, epochs, even history as a whole—can continue to function explicatively within hermeneutic-methodological understanding in such a way that, in the "hermeneutic circle," prescientific presuppositions are both methodically renewed and methodically corrected in view of the data. In short, the emphatic concept of understanding characteristic of the first phase of the E-V controversy can be reconstrued as a methodologically relevant counter or complementary concept to the theoretical-objectifying explanation of nature. We can also, however, now finally and fully appreciate the thrust of Hempel's or unified science's concept of the subsumption-theoretic, causal explanation of both spatio-temporal events in nature and actions objectified as nature. We can raise the question whether its claim must conflict with the argument for the methodological autonomy of the hermeneutic, interpretive Geisteswissenschaften or social sciences.

Relying on this third terminological strategy, I shall attempt to present a critical reconstruction of the latest phase of the E-V controversy and show how this reconstruction opens up the possibility of resolving the debate.

# 2

## Von Wright and His Critics: Questions for the Third Round of the Controversy

In the third chapter of *Explanation and Understanding*, von Wright justifies his neo-Wittgensteinian approach in explicating a model of "intentional" or "teleological explanation." He views this model as at least a partial resolution of the E-V controversy, insofar as it offers the social sciences a "definite alternative to the subsumption-theoretic covering law model."[1] As noted, von Wright's book can be seen as the highest point of the neo-Wittgensteinian theory of action (with regard to the LC argument and the differentiation of the two language games of action understanding and causal explanation). Furthermore, in his introduction von Wright's explicitly places his approach in the historical context of the E-V controversy, a controversy he understands as a confrontation between the Galilean and the Aristotelian points of view. In view of these two considerations, it may be appropriate to raise certain questions that follow from the perspective of the older phase of the E-V controversy and transfer them to his book and its subsequent discussion. These questions are:

1. Can von Wright's neo-Wittgensteinian approach be regarded as an ideal defense of the interests and motives of the traditional philosophy of "hermeneutic understanding" at the present level of philosophical argumentation?

2. Can one say that the neo-Wittgensteinian distinction between language games and its conceptual (onto-semantic) consequences clearly have overcome the reductionism of methodological unity associated

with Hempel's model? Indeed, can one say that the distinction has overcome the reductionism in such a way that one can speak of a definite solution to (or linguistic dissolution of) the problem of the E-V controversy?

In this main section of my investigation I try to obtain an answer to both questions. To facilitate understanding and confirmation of my argument, however, I want to anticipate the results of the investigation in the form of theses. (That way, my strategy follows the unavoidable "circle in understanding," since the theses stated here can be fully understood only after the argument has been developed more fully.) I can give a clear, affirmative answer to neither question. Instead, I have concluded that epistemological inquiry requires a new, methodologically differentiated beginning. It is not sufficient solely to distinguish between the language game of explaining (natural) events and explaining actions, as an onto-semantic New Dualism tries to do; for this distinction does not always and necessarily correspond to the older distinction between causal explanation and hermeneutic understanding that is grounded in the pragmatic difference in types of inquiry or interests of knowledge. To be sure, the older distinction implies, on the one hand, the possibility of a differentiation within the social-scientific account of actions that partially conforms to the neo-Wittgensteinian distinction in language games, while, on the other hand, demonstrating the inevitable theoretical relevance of an analogy between the causal explanation of natural events and the motivational explanation of actions as events.

Because of the formal analogy in possible answers to why-questions in terms of causal explanation, Hempel's reductionistic argument for the validity of the subsumption-theoretic model retains a certain limited justification within the social sciences. Of course, we must also acknowledge the methodological relevance of the distinction between explanation and understanding that Hempel and the reductionist conception of unified science dispute—not only with respect to the difference between natural science and Geisteswissenschaft but also with regard to the difference between a causal-analytic "quasi-natural science" and a hermeneutic Geisteswissenschaft *within* the social sciences. Nevertheless, the validity of post-Wittgensteinian New Dualism appears indisputable only if one assumes the possibility of equating two distinctions: (a) the onto-semantically determined distinction between natural events and actions, and (b) the transcendentally-pragmatically determined distinction between the question of causal explanation and the question of understanding reasons.

Now, with regard to von Wright's book, this claim means we cannot confirm the thesis that there is a clear alternative between subsumption-theoretic causal explanation and the teleological explanation of action (Chapter III, *Explanation and Understanding*). In making this argument von Wright must assume (and partially intend) the thesis that the explanation of natural events, in the sense of causal necessity, pre-supposes the teleological understanding of action. In my view, the latter thesis constitutes the crucial kernel of truth in the book insofar as it allows one to ground the reciprocal supplementation and exclusion (or, in Niels Bohr's sense, the complementarity) of the language games of understanding and explanation in both onto-semantic and tran-scendental-pragmatic terms. In contrast, the concept of "teleological explanation" von Wright pursues proves systematically ambiguous:

1. To the extent that, as Hempel always assumes, "teleological ex-planation" is supposed to offer an answer to the question why or on basis of what effective conditions an action occurs, perhaps one can speak of a motivational explanation, i.e., a teleologically mediated quasi-explanation. In this case, one can ignore the fact that the logical cogency of the explanation is mediated by the understanding of a "practical inference" that refers to the reasons (goal intentions and beliefs about appropriate means) for a given action being rational; for the logical cogency that is demanded cannot, in principle, be guaranteed by the schema of the "practical inference" alone. As Tuomela, in particular, has shown, to the extent that a logically conclusive expla-nation is possible at all in this case, it can rest only on the expansion of von Wright's schema of the "practical inference," to include the subsumption-theoretic schema of causal explanation. Hence, I think, the methodological conception of a quasi-nomological explanation of action is partially justified. Its limits, however, emerge when one con-siders the occurrence of actions that are historically relevant.

2. But "teleological explanation" is not always supposed to offer an answer to the why-question elucidated above. Rather, it is used as well to answer the question: Why (in the sense of "for what reason") was it purposively rational for someone to act as he acted in a particular situation? In this case, von Wright's schema of "practical inference"

is sufficient to guarantee the logical cogency of our knowledge, since this cogency does not warrant predictions of actions as events. Here, the knowledge one acquires does not represent an "explanation" in the sense assumed by Hempel. Rather it represents something which, with reference to Max Weber, we should call the "purposive-rational understanding of action."

Purposive-rational understanding is both necessary and, in principle, not reducible to causal or inductive and statistical explanation. Therefore, it represents a hermeneutic alternative to explanation in the human sciences, although by no means the entire alternative. Ultimately, these claims issue from the complementarity of causal explanation and the understanding of action.

3. Von Wright's most prominent intention seems to be to use "teleological explanation" to answer the question why a historically relevant action occurs. In ths case, it must consist in understanding an action *ex post actu* as rational and causally necessary. That is, here, understanding refers to an action that actually occurs; hence, if understanding is to be empirically correct, the good reasons attributed to the agent must not only be present as grounds for the action's rationality, they must actually have become causally effective.

By considering these three different applications of teleological explanation, we arrive at a resolution of the E-V controversy. The basis of this resolution lies in the transcendental-pragmatic analysis of different kinds of inquiry—or, more precisely, of the different interests in knowledge that serve as conditions of both the constitution of the meaning of different inquiries and the corresponding domains of possible scientific knowledge.

This new methical approach reveals two further domains of questions at which my investigation thus far could only hint:

1. Within the methodology and theory of science the question arises: Should the transcendental-pragmatic reflection on meaning-constitutive questions—in other words, on knowledge-constitutive interests—be pursued further; indeed, should it be completed in a system of human cognitive interests? In this case, it is to be expected that precisely in the domain of the social sciences (although, also, in natural sciences which, at least onto-semantically, are to be distinguished by referring to physics and biology), the methodological differentiation of "scientific

systematizations" (Hempel) that emerges from the combination of onto-semantic and transcendental-pragmatic distinctions will produce a still more complicated picture than the "architectonic" of methodologically relevant distinctions developed here to resolve the E-V controversy.

2. If the E-V controversy is resolved by distinguishing between and combining onto-semantic and transcendental-pragmatic viewpoints, viewpoints which perhaps are to be completed in a system of human cognitive interests, then a fundamental, philosophically significant consequence can be drawn. If the epistemologically and methodologically relevant differentiation of the foundations of scientific theory is based on neither onto-semantic nor transcendental-pragmatic distinctions alone, if, rather, it is based on a distinction and combination of both,[2] then the following question arises: How are we to conceive of the fundamental relation between ontology or onto-semantics and a transcendental epistemology related to practical reason by means of pragmatically distinguished cognitive interests? In my view, this question poses the question of first philosophy anew, now transformed into language-analytic or semiotic terms.

# 3

## The Ambiguity in von Wright's Neo-Wittgensteinian Strategy

By applying the neo-Wittgensteinian perspective to the theory of science in a new model of teleological explanation, von Wright, it seems to me, entangles himself in an ambiguous form of argumentation, one that allows his critics to rehabilitate the subsumption-theoretic model of (causal) explanation for which the teleological model of explanation was supposed to provide the social scientific alternative. This ambiguity is expressed in von Wright's programatic introduction of the practical syllogism or practical inference, which he takes from Anscombe's reconstruction of Aristotle and uses to ground the model of teleological explanation:

Practical reasoning is of great importance to the *explanation and understanding* of action. It is a tenet of the present work that the practical syllogism provides the sciences of man with something long missing from their methodology: an explanation model in its own right which is a definite alternative to the subsumption-theoretic, covering law model. Broadly speaking, what the subsumption-theoretic model is to causal explanation and explanation in the natural sciences, the practical syllogism is to teleological explanation and explanation in history and the social sciences.[1]

The methodological ambiguity of this position is expressed in the symptomatic discussion of "explanation and understanding" often encountered in von Wright's book (even in the title), as in Dray's *Laws and Explanation in History*. Those acquainted with the language-analytic theory of action and its characteristic, casual retrospective on the problem of hermeneutic "understanding" will be inclined to offer the following defense: Talk of "explanation and understanding" does not express a methodological ambiguity but, at worst, the intention to connect two aspects of a methodological claim that belong together; these aspects are explicated in a logically binding way in a new model of explanation, the teleological model, for which the logically expressible structure of the "practical inference" alone is suited. They could add that, if the "understanding" to which the tradition appeals is at all methodologically relevant, at best, it can be seen as the prescientific proto-form of a new type of "explanation." This objection is connected to the distinction between the "context of justification," which is supposed to be explicated in logical-semantic terms, and the merely empirically and pragmatically relevant "context of discovery." Given the present state of the discussion, the objection is both intelligible and plausible. Nevertheless, in an analytic confrontation with neopositivism, it is necessary to exhibit the alternative to an empathetic notion of understanding, an alternative that can be explicated in terms of a logical inference and hence evade the attempt of Neurath, Hempel, and others to reduce it to a description of the psychologically heuristic function of a cup of coffee (see Part One, Chap. 1).

In what follows I would like to show that the standard presuppositions of the analytic logic of science make it impossible to show the validity of the structure and function of the "practical inference" that von Wright correctly sees as the methodologically relevant alternative to the subsumption-theoretic model of explanation. More precisely, I wish to make two points. First, in von Wright's account, the model of teleological-intentional explanation substantiates two absolutely opposed claims. On the one hand, it attempts to offer a logically satisfactory explication of purposive-rational understanding in Weber's sense (here, I think the structure of the "practical inference" actually can be applied); on the other, as is suggested by von Wright's explicit inference schema, the model of teleological-intentional explanation claims to represent a way to explain the occurrence of actions that competes with Hempel's model. Hence, it can be shown that, despite contradictions in the text, von Wright does not explicitly preclude the claim of a theoretical-explanatory argument to explain actions as events in a logically conclusive way. Second, von Wright provides his critics with the possibility of rehabilitating the subsumption-theoretic model of the causal explanation of actions in restricted form.

By means of a textual analysis of *Explanation and Understanding*, I shall try to expose the polar tension, or implicit contradiction, in the methodological claims that the model of teleological explanation involves. I shall then explore criticisms of von Wright and the neo-Wittgensteinian approach generally, to show that the conception of the "practical inference" suggested by von Wright's model of teleological explanation does lead to restitution of the subsumption-theoretic model of explanation. Finally, I shall demonstrate that this restitution does not do justice to von Wright's actual interest or to the basic thrust of the neo-Wittgensteinian position, and, therefore, that it cannot be used to rehabilitate the reductionist conception of unified science.

## 3.1 The Fundamental Ambiguity in von Wright's Model: Understanding in the Light of Purposive-Rationality or the Explanation of Events?

I begin with the textual analysis. I think the "scientistically" oriented reader who accepts Hempel's preconception of theoretical explanation will understand von Wright's claim as follows: A model of teleological explanation is proposed for the sciences of action that represents a definite alternative to the subsumption-theoretic covering law model. Here, the premise is that a teleological explanation that explains actions in terms of reasons or motives can function as the answer to the same why-question Hempel claims must be answered by a subsumption-theoretic model of explanation. That is, it answers the question why an action occurs or must occur as an event at a specific time and place, and thus why it is to be predicted under similar circumstances. (In this context one could substitute "why an action . . . was to be expected," since, in the case of the assumed knowledge of motives, one can ignore the fact that answering a prognostic question alone does not require a true motivational or causal explanation. Under certain circumstances, as in the case of seismology, inductive extrapolation from symptoms is enough.

This version of von Wright's model conforms poorly or not at all to the many points at which he elucidates the unique logical structure of the "practical inference" and insists that, for conceptual reasons, the structure is incompatible with the structure of causality in Hume's sense. Moreover, it is particularly incompatible with those points where von Wright disputes the predictive power of his notion of teleological explanation. Before we examine these statements in more detail, however, we must show reasons for arguing that the standard explication of the inference schema, as a schema of explanation, justifies the "scientistic" interpretation.

The first version of the inference schema runs as follows:

(P1) A intends to bring about *p*.
A believes that he cannot bring about *p* unless he does *a*.
Therefore A sets himself to do *a*.[2]

One can read this formulation in the same way the analytic logic of science normally does: as a schema for theoretical explanation, in other words, as the formulation of an inference that the objectifying scientist is justified in making about a human action. In this case, the form of the conclusion that von Wright chooses seems to suggest that the new schema of explanation claims to explicate the possibility of answering the Hempelian question why an action actually occurs. Here, the question immediately arises, whether the schema is conclusive or whether it requires supplementation to be conclusive. The latter possibility becomes clearer in the "final formulation" of von Wright's inference schema:

From now on, A intends to bring about *p* at time *t*.
From now on, A considers that, unless he does *a* no later than at time *t'*, he cannot bring about *p* at time *t*.
Therefore, no later than when he thinks time *t'* has arrived, A sets himself to do *a*, unless he forgets about the time or is prevented.[3]

As in the first version, this conclusion expresses the actual occurrence of an event, and now even its occurrence at a specific time. Hence, one is inclined to view the premises (which refer to the time at which the conditions are present) as antecedent conditions of a "theoretical explanation" in the sense already noted. The object seems to be to ascertain that, at the time of the event to be explained, the motives assumed by the teleological explanation are still present and effective, so that the event of action occurs or, indeed, must occur. Then, however, one wonders why no nomological premises are necessary for von Wright's conclusion. In addition, there is something curious about the two qualifications referring to possible internal or external obstacles to the action involved in the final version of the inference schema; these are not treated in the usual way, as antecedent conditions in the sense of a ceteris paribus clause and considered in the premises.

We shall return to the consequences of this "scientistic" version of the new model of explanation, but first I want to try to clarify the alternative conception that could be hidden in von Wright's schema of the "practical inference." In this context, I mean an alternative, not in the sense of a new form of explanation that would refer to the same why-question to which Hempel's subsumption-theoretic schema refers but in the sense of a schema of purposive-rational understanding that refers to a different why-question. In his book, von Wright himself indirectly indicates the form the conclusion of a practical syllogism must assume if we are concerned not with the schema for explaining the occurrence of an event but, rather, a schema for understanding the rationality of human actions—that is, if we are interested not in a theoretical proof of the necessity of the occurrence but in "practical reasoning." In a footnote, he writes:

The genuinely "practical" inference could also be called a commitment to action. It is an argument conducted in the first person. Its conclusion, when expressed in words, is "I shall do *a* (now)" or "I shall do *a* no later than at time *t*." The qualifications "unless I am prevented" or "unless I forget about the time" do not belong to the inference as a commitment. Should the commitment not be fulfilled, however, they may be offered as excuses. It is only when we look at the case from the point of view of a spectator ("third person") that the conclusion will have to be stated in the more guarded form of the agent's "setting himself" to do the action and will have to be subject to the qualifications about nonprevention and nonforgetfulness."

The first part of this passage—and, indeed, only the first part— gives adequate expression to the nontheoretical, nonexplanatory but rather practical-normative character of the cogency or bindingness of the "practical inference." Here, it becomes clear how von Wright can conceive of this inference schema as an alternative to the deductive- nomological inference schema of subsumption-theoretic causal expla- nation, for it answers a different why-question than the one Hempel presupposes. The inference with the conclusion, "I should do *a* (now)," provides an answer not to the odd but conceivable question, "Why has it come to pass that I am doing *a* now?", but, rather, the question, "Why should I do *a* now?". One would suppose, therefore, that in the third person the question would have to be expressed: "Why should A do *a* now?" and the conclusion as "A should do *a* now." Or better, because the "practical inference" is normatively binding (in the sense of purposive rationality alone and not, for example, in the sense of an ethical reason related to the positing of goals), the question would have to be: "Why is it (purposively) rational for A to do *a* now?", or "Is it (purposively) rational for A to do *a*?"

This analysis offers the best way to reconstrue not only Max Weber's idea of the "purposive-rational understanding" of actions but also Dray's idea of a rational explanation resting on an evaluative assessment of reasons. The "practical inference" helps answer the question why, from someone's own perspective, it was rational for him—for example, a historical agent—to act as he actually did act in a given situation. (This question does not presuppose that one already knows exactly how the agent acted; exact determination of the action can be the result of a deeper understanding of the action as a specific action, an understanding mediated by the "practical inference.") Thus the abstract schema of the "practical inference" must look something like this:

(PI′) A intends to bring about *p*.
A believes that he cannot bring about *p* unless he does *a*.
Therefore, it is (purposively) rational for A to do *a*.

By means of this inference—that is, by means of its definition in abstracto of situation-specific criteria of purposive rationality—we can achieve a purposive-rational understanding of a given action, i.e., a historically particular action on the part of a particular agent in a particular situation. The positive accomplishment of this form of knowledge does not lie in the "explanation" of why, under specific conditions; a specific action—i.e., an event at a specific time—*had* to occur (or, in the case of a how-possible explanation, *could* occur). Rather, it makes a specific action that actually did occur at a specific time intelligible from the inside, as it were, as an action suggesting itself to and binding on the knowing subject (under appropriate presuppositions with regard to will and belief).

As further elucidation, we can add that the interest in such knowledge does not obtain with regard to objects of knowledge one can observe only from outside and perhaps manipulate through one's actions; rather, it obtains solely with regard to objects of knowledge that are virtual co-subjects of knowledge and action and with whom one can and must come to an understanding about good and poor reasons for acting. Moreover, if we want to test the accuracy of the purposive-rational understanding of an action achieved through the "practical inference," an understanding that sees the action as a specific action (e.g., as an attempt at murder or as an act of self-defense), then we will not refer primarily to the fact that an action has occurred or will occur which could have been, or can be, predicted on the basis of the assumed understanding. The critical test of accuracy consists in the fact that we can apply understanding which employs a specific "rational inference" to the human behavior present as an event and in the fact that this application is empirically and hermeneutically correct.

This conclusion, of course, presents us with the difficult problem of providing empirical verification for methodical (hermeneutic) understanding, a problem that differs from scientism's standard problem of verifying explanatory hypotheses through observation. To my mind, the former problem has rarely been explicated in a suitable way. Nevertheless, to continue the textual analysis of von Wright's ambiguous strategy of argument, I must interrupt the attempt to develop a systematic alternative to the subsumption-theoretic model of explanation.

Here we find ourselves confronted by the following circumstance: On the one hand, the text confirms the interpretation of the "practical inference" I have proposed; this is still to be shown; on the other hand, in the passage cited above, this interpretation is disavowed. In the last part of the passage, von Wright does not draw the same consequence for the conclusion of the inference schema that I draw from the plea for a normative understanding of the "practical inference." Surprisingly, he again explicates it as an answer to the Hempelian why-question in the way I have characterized as explanatory and theoretical. He does this with the remarkable statement:

It is only when we look at the case from the point of view of a spectator ("third person") that the conclusion will have to be stated in the more guarded form of *the agent's "setting himself"* to do the action and will have to be subject to the qualifications about nonprevention and nonforgetfulness.[6]

I am inclined to understand this statement as follows: If we look at the case from the point of view of a spectator—i.e., that of a subject of knowledge interested not prmarily in the (purposive-rational) understanding of the action but in explaining its here-and-now occurrence— then indeed our reenactment of the "genuinely practical inference" has a merely heuristic value. It merely helps us construct a quasi-causal explanation that refers to motives or effective grounds of motion.

In this case, the conclusion in fact must take the form of "the agent's setting himself to do the action," and for von Wright, that apparently is a "more guarded" form than the normative conclusion, because its cogency does not depend on the internal cogency of the practical inference alone. It still depends also on the factual occurrence or nonoccurrence of obstacles at the time at which the motive is expected to become effective.[7] Here, again, a model of explanation is suggested which the causalist must view as a competitor to the subsumption-theoretic model. Indeed, the causalist would be inclined to give additional reasons for the view that the conclusion must now assume a "more guarded" form, possibly saying, "not only because obstacles may occur, but primarily because the "practical inference" can only postulate a normatively correct and therefore intelligible transfer of intentions, it cannot "explain" the occurrence of the action. In order to "explain" the occurrence of the action, the causalist might add, the intention that is correctly adduced for the decision to act must still somehow become causally effective. I now return to von Wright's text.

In my view, the transition von Wright describes from the "practical inference" in the first person to "the point of view of a spectator" is in no way identical with the *possible* transformation of the "practical inference" from the point of view of the "first person" into that of the "third," as he seems to suppose. The move to the "third person" need not make the person who executes, or has executed, the "practical inference" the object of a theoretical explanation "from the point of view of a spectator." It can also constitute the other as a virtual co-subject of possible action, even in the case in which one performs a certain quasi-objectification and speaks of the other as a "subject-object." In this case, the analysis will not take a merely indirect, heuristic interest in the other's reasons (or in his action as the conclusion of those reasons in the sense of the "practical inference"). That is, it will not focus on an explanation of the event or action, but instead will be directly interested in the other's reasons as the good or bad reasons of a co-subject with whom one can integrate oneself strategically or consensually, or into whose situation one can interject oneself. Clearly the move from first to second person need not result in the transformation of the schema of the "practical inference" into an explanation of an event. The same is true of the move from first to third person. Hence, as I have proposed, the conclusion of the inference runs as follows:

Therefore it is (or was) (purposively) rational for A to do *a*.

Thus, why, in this situation, does von Wright commit the "Metabasis eis allo Genos" that he seems to commit in the light of my interpretation?

It is instructive that, in an earlier footnote,[8] von Wright distinguishes the "practical inference" formulated in *Explanation and Understanding* from that studied in an earlier work, where he took the conclusion to be "a norm 'A must do *a*.' "[9] Also illuminating are his remarks about Dray's account of rational explanation:

To explain an action is, in Dray's view, to show that the action was the appropriate or rational thing to do on the occasion under consideration. . . . He thinks, quite rightly it seems to me, that this type of explanation has logical peculiarites of its own. But he obscures his own point unnecessarily by trying to find these peculiarities in an element of valuation rather than in a type of teleology.[10]

Von Wright, then, does not want to integrate the element of evaluative judgment into his model of teleological explanation. In view of what he himself says about the "practical inference" as a commitment, this is not only astounding but seems to indicate again that, despite statements to the contrary, his model is supposed to represent a theoretical explanation of what occurs or must occur.

This conclusion, however, does not contradict the reference to the normative character of the "practical inference" alone; it also contradicts those points at which von Wright explicitly focuses on teleological explanation as the explanation of an event. I refer primarily to an example which, I surmise from the literature, has caused problems for many readers. We can refer to it as the example of the assassin. Von Wright imagines that, at the decisive moment, an assassin does not shoot even though all the premises of the "practical inference" are fulfilled at this time (he was not prevented, did not forget the time, did not give up his intention, or the like) "It is characteristic," von Wright comments,

of the case which we were imagining that the agent should do literally nothing. . . . Thus, despite the truth of the Logical Connection argument, the premises of a practical inference do not with logical necessity entail behavior. They do not entail the existence of a conclusion to match them. The syllogism when leading up to action is "practical" and not a piece of logical demonstration.[11]

At this point von Wright adds the footnote on the character of commitment involved in the "practical inference."

To me, it seems possible to interpret these statements in a uniform, consistent way only if one alters the conclusion of the "practical inference" to conform either to Dray's formulation or to the version I have proposed: "Therefore it is (purposively) rational for A to do *a*." This version makes it clear that the existence of the conclusion—i.e., the action qua event—does not necessarily follow from the premises on conceptual grounds, no matter how improbable this may seem in the individual case. In contrast, if one retains von Wright's conclusion, "Therefore, A sets himself to do *a*," then, to demonstrate the possible cogency of the schema, one is forced to do precisely what von Wright considers dogmatic and logically unnecessary: "We turn the validity of the practical syllogism into a standard for interpreting the situation."[12] In other words, in the case in which a prediction based on the "practical inference" is not realized, one is forced to immunize the teleologically mediated causal explanation to falsification by insisting that one or some of its premises are not fulfilled. I shall return to this possibility, one von Wright admits "may be reasonable." In any case, because he nevertheless rejects the possibility as dogmatic and logically unnecessary, it offers no satisfactory answer to the question why he persists in the theoretical-explanatory form of the conclusion even while explicitly disputing its cogency.

## 3.2 Von Wright's Account of the Logical Connection Argument and the Interpretation of Intentional Explanation as Ex Post Actu Explanation

The key to answering the question just proposed may lie in von Wright's assumption of the "truth of the Logical Connection argument" at the core of neo-Wittgensteinian New Dualism. This argument can be understood as follows: Even, and precisely, when the "practical inference" is used to explain occurrences of action—that is, when the reasons seen as grounds of the action (goal intentions and the convictions about appropriate means) constitute the "volitional-cognitive causal complex" of a quasi-causal explanation—then the connection between this volitional-cognitive complex and the action to be explained is not a contingent one, but, rather, is logical or at least conceptual and analytic. Hence, a teleological explanation (one mediated by an understanding of goal-intentions) does not satisfy the presupposition Hume argued had to be postulated for any causal, nomological explanation— namely, the contingency of the connection between observable events that follow one another regularly. With regard to actions, then, we can conclude that there must be not only an understanding in terms of reasons but an explanation of the action as an event, an explanation mediated by such understanding and thus not conforming to the structure of subsumption-theoretical causal explanation.

I think the specific form of von Wright's interpretation or use of the Logical Connection argument confirms my conjecture about his decisive motivation. He begins by considering that version of the argument according to which one cannot define the intention of an action (as opposed to a spark of fire that causes an explosion) without referring to the intended action. With Stoutland, he argues that this version is not sufficient to ground a noncausal way of explaining events or occurrences, since "the logical dependence of the specific character of the will on the nature of its object is fully compatible with the logical independence of the occurrence of an act of will of this character from the realization of the object."[13] Therefore, to use the LC argument to ground a nonsubsumption-theoretic model of explanation, von Wright wants to show that, in the case of teleological understanding, not only the intention to be defined but the facts of the explanans and explanandum to be established are not logically independent of each other. In other words, he does not refer to a circularity in definition but, rather, to one in the verification of explanandum and explanans:

Let it be asked how, in a given case, one ascertains (verifies) whether an agent has a certain intention, "wills" a certain thing—and also how one finds out whether his behavior is of a kind which his intention or will is supposed to cause. Should it turn out that one cannot answer the one question without also answering the other, then the intention or will cannot be a (Humean) cause of his behavior. The facts which one tries to establish would not be logically independent of one another.[14]

Von Wright demonstrates this thesis by means of a series of subtle investigations of the problem of verification, and comes to the following result:

The verification of the conclusion of a practical argument presupposes that we can verify a correlated set of premises which entail logically that the behavior observed to have occurred is intentional under the description given to it in the conclusion. Then we can no longer affirm these premises and deny the conclusion, i.e., deny the correctness of the description given of the observed behavior.[15]

At this point von Wright adds: "But the set of verified premises need not, of course, be the same as the premises of the practical argument under discussion." Hence, it seems that verifying an analytic connection can itself yield an increase in knowledge. The practice of the hermeneutic explication of meaning always already surrendered this problem to the logicians. For von Wright, however, it accordingly holds:

The verification of the premises of a practical argument again presupposes that we can single out some recorded item of behavior as being intentional under the description accorded to it either by those premises themselves ("immediate" verification) or by some other set of premises which entail those of the argument under discussion ("external" verification).[16]

Thus the truth of the LC argument consists in the "mutual dependence of the verification of premises and the verification of conclusions in practical syllogisms."

To clarify these results, we can raise (and answer) two questions in a thought experiment:

On the basis of empirical-analytic (e.g., psychological and social psychological) research into behavioral motives, we can ask why we cannot establish the presence of both the volitional-cognitive complex and the action to be explained simply by asking the actors. One would think that, in practice, this would allow one to procure the facts necessary for verification in total independence of one another. Von Wright's answer is that, even supposing the information to be trustworthy, in principle, one cannot be certain that the agent who is asked about his intentions and beliefs will not alter them before performing the action to be inferred from them.[17] Thus one cannot know definitely whether the motivation to which the agent attests actually comes into question as the cause of the action to be explained. Conversely, unless the agent characterizes his action truthfully by referring to the motivation attributed to him (a circumstance that would contradict the presumption of a logically independent verification), one cannot preclude the possibility that the action identified as a specific action on the basis of the agent's information is not the result of certain intentions established earlier.

We can illustrate this answer with the help of an example I have already used. Suppose that on different occasions a man has declared that he wants to inherit his uncle's wealth at any cost and believes that he can achieve this goal only by murdering him. Suppose, further, that one day the nephew kills his uncle, that it is admitted and established that he has done so. Is it therefore proved that he murdered his uncle for the motives he asserted earlier? Obviously not. He can certainly have discarded the plan to murder his uncle long ago, but then had an argument with him one day and killed him, perhaps even in self-defense. Or perhaps the nephew retained his plan up until the time of his uncle's murder and simply did not know that the man he killed (for whatever reason) was his uncle because he had never met him.

To this extent, one must admit that von Wright is correct in pointing to the mutual verification of explanans and explanandum in the case of an intentional-teleological action. (Social scientists and historians will not be completely satisfied with his results. I shall return to this point momentarily.) One can ask whether this successful application of the LC argument does not prove something more and different than anything a proponent of theoretical explanation can welcome.

In his explanation schema von Wright accounts for the possibility of changes in the agent's intention by relating the premises that comprise the volitional-cognitive complex to duration of time: "From now on, A intends to bring about $p$ at time $t$. From now on, A considers that, unless he does $a$ no later than at time $t'$, he cannot bring about $p$ at time $t$." However, because of the version of the LC argument von Wright uses, one that precludes the possibility of the independent identification of an intention, it seems to me the following also holds: Verification of an intention, which must already presuppose verification of the action to be inferred, cannot, in principle, include certification of the length of the intention. Conversely, this certification cannot include verification of the action itself in light of the intention that constitutes it. Thus, under the premises of the LC argument, there is no point in determining the length of the intention or belief as a constituent of the volitional-cognitive complex in the explanation schema. It would make sense only if one assumed that the presence of the intention or belief at any point could be identified independently of the occurrence of the action. According to Hempel, one must assume this with regard to action intentions that were never abandoned but whose action correlate could never be verified because the action was prevented. This assumption contradicts the LC argument, however.

The assumption can be pursued only if one foregoes certifying that the imputed intention is the cause of an action to be established later. Behavioral scientists who think in causal terms are, in fact, ready for this methodical risk; they assume as a theoretical premise—and, I think, correctly—that empirically identifiable intentions (and corresponding behavioral dispositions) exist as possible causes of action even in cases where the intended action is not performed. This can be established by inquiring. Although the corresponding behavioral dispositions can be made theoretically accessible only through recourse to intentions that can be understood, they also assume—again, I think, correctly—that these dispositions possess a contingent relation to the spatio-temporal event that belongs to the action and that is disclosed by it. Hence, these dispositions can be considered causes in Hume's sense.

From this analysis, I draw the conclusion that, under the premises of the LC argument, one cannot explain actions as events by referring to the intentions that precede them. These premises, rather, permit only a here-and-now understanding of the intention in light of the action and of the existing action in light of the intention.

It appears that von Wright even confirms this point insofar as he states: "It is characteristic of these verification procedures that they presuppose the existence of some factual behavior upon which an intentionalist "interpretation" is then put."[18] As I have emphasized, however, the verification procedure qua interpretive procedure can be connected to an increase in knowledge. This suggests that the mutual dependence of the verification of explanans and explanandum in teleological explanation is to be understood as a special aspect of the "circle in understanding" with which the hermeneuticists are familiar. Such a conclusion would avert the otherwise trenchant, scientistic objection, according to which von Wright's verification of teleological explanation amounts to a *"circulus vitiosus."* With regard to the explanation of events in which previously fixed meanings are presupposed, the circle must be a vicious one in deduction. With regard to the understanding of meaning, however, it becomes a *"circulus fructuosus,"* a kind of spiral in the procedure of explicating analytic relations of significance. In this way it becomes possible for hermeneutic understanding to be an empirically informative process of knowledge.

This consequence of the LC argument means that von Wright's inclusion of the duration of the intention and belief in the inference schema is no longer justifiable; it seems to present an attempt to maintain the appearance of something like causally effective antecedent conditions in the interest of a model for explaining events. Actually, by including the duration of the intention and conviction in the inference schema, he can only mean to secure the validity of the conclusion, "therefore A sets himself. . . ." As his interpretation of the example of the assassin demonstrates, however, this conclusion is not justified. My own interpretation of von Wright's version of the LC argument shows that the logical or analytic connection between the explanans and the explanandum must be seen in terms of a temporally independent circle in understanding that refers to an existing action; hence, it shows that the connection cannot be seen as a logical connection between events. Now, this result does correspond to von Wright's interpretation of the example of the assassin; at the same time, it seems to vitiate the strength of the LC argument as an argument against the causalists. The latter will demand that the LC argument demonstrate that a "teleological" explanation of action as an event to be disclosed (in the sense of von Wright's schema) presupposes an analytic connection between explanans and explanandum rather than a subsumption-theoretic one.

To the extent that von Wright uses the Logical Connection argument as an argument for the possibility of a noncausal means of explaining actions as events or occurrences, we must raise another, more general question. We must ask where the cogency of the inference schema lies if, as has been inferred from the text thus far, it does not lie either in the logical deducibility of a prediction (as in the case of a theoretical, causal explanation) or simply in the deduction of a "commitment" (as in the case of a "practical inference in the first person").

The text offers an answer to this question, one we have not yet considered. A few lines after his claim that "despite the truth of the Logical Connection argument, the premises of a practical inference do not with logical necessity entail behavior," von Wright continues: "It is only when an action is already there and a practical argument is constructed to explain or justify it that we have a logically conclusive argument. The necessity of the practical inference schema is, one could say, a necessity conceived ex post actu."[19]

This statement seems to indicate a third possible way to understand cogency, in addition to the normative-practical and theoretical-demonstrative (or predictively testable) ways. The point of this new possibility apparently lies in the following circumstance: It is true that, insofar as the teleological or intentional explanation of action depends on the "practical inference," it cannot be verified through prediction, as can a theoretical, causal explanation. Nevertheless, it remains the explanation of an event, and thus exceeds the limits of an inference schema that is merely normatively relevant; for, if an action has already been performed, and if to understand it a normatively grounded practical inference can be applied with empirical validity, then, at the same time, the action is ex post actu explained as necessary. The question involved here goes behind the pure understanding of reasons, and asks whether the occurrence of the action as an event can be explained as necessary by the same means. Given the ex post perspective permitted by the fact that the action is present, this question necessarily is always already answered in the affirmative. Thus, if understanding in light of the "practical inference" is adequate (that is, if it can be empirically-hermeneutically verified), then, simultaneously, the action as an event is ex post actu conclusively explained. The possible objection that the practical inference presupposed by the agents could have led to a completely different action or to none at all (as in the case of the assassin) does not affect the point of the ex post actu "explanation" we are concerned with here. We are not concerned with a form of explanation that can be tested prognostically, but rather with one that, by definition, can always be claimed only ex post actu because its force consists only in the normatively necessary (i.e., conclusive in the sense of the "practical inference") understanding of an action actually present.

The attempt to explicate ex post actu "explanation" seems to come closest to the tenable intention behind von Wright's model of explanation. It also becomes clear now why we could analyze his interpretation of the LC argument in terms of the circle in understanding, and not reduce it to a too weak version according to which it claims only that the definitions (or explication) of explanans and explanandum presuppose one another. The difference between von Wright's version of the LC argument and the too weak one is that, in the case of teleological ex post actu "explanation," the hermeneutic circle between understanding intentions and understanding actions can refer to an action that necessarily always already exists. Understood this way, the model seems to represent a significant philosophical insight. Von Wright himself has made this clear by using the model to interpret Hegel's idea of the ex post understanding of historical necessity and by distinguishing it as an "intelligibility" type of determinism from the predictive type suggested by Marx's historical determinism or by what Popper calls historicism.[20]

Despite all this, we must question whether this third possible way of explicating von Wright's model of explanation can justify the inference schema or, in particular, its conclusion. Again, our answer must be negative. If my interpretation of ex post actu "explanation" as a third possible way of understanding cogency is correct, the structural element of this explanation by which it exceeds normative explanation consists in the fact that, in light of the cogency of the normative explanation, an action that is "already there" becomes intelligible. Therefore, its ex post actu "explanation" is itself conclusive. Precisely this and no more is confirmed by the following exemplar of the inference schema in which von Wright silently abandons his previous schema of the "practical syllogism" in order to match it with ex post "explanation":

A intended to make the bell ring.
A thought (knew) that unless he pressed the button, he could not make the bell ring.
Therefore, A pressed the button.[21]

In this schema substitution of the imperfect or past tense for the present tense of the standard schema is not insignificant. It is not the same as a corresponding transformation of the volitional-cognitive causal complex in the case of a subsumption-theoretic, causal explanation. In the latter case, the transformation is innocuous because, in both instances, the force of the inference rests on the same deductive-nomological cogency. In the case of the teleological explanation that von Wright discusses, the same apparently innocuous transformation implies the transition from the claim to a theoretical-explanatory, prognostically testable cogency which even von Wright considers untenable to a tenable claim—namely, the claim to cogency that is articulated only as an ex post claim referring to an ex post "explanation" supported by understanding of purposive rationality. Now, if one recalls what von Wright has said about the practical nature of the inference and the pure determinism in intelligibility of the explanation of action founded on it, one must see how inappropriate the definitive version of the inference schema is. Both the present-tense explication of the duration of the intention and belief and the present-tense explication of the event of action (to be expected?) appear to signal a model of explanation that competes with Hempel's schema. For this reason, they must also provoke the question whether they do not represent a shortened schema for subsumption-theoretic causal explanation.

### 3.3 The Causality of Intentions or Actions in Ex Post Actu Explanation: A Difficulty for the New Dualism

In order fully to clarify the problem of the ambiguity in von Wright's model of "explanation" or "understanding," I must draw attention to a structural element of the ex post actu explanation of action, an element I have not yet mentioned and one that may raise questions about von Wright's fundamental neo-Wittgensteinian conception. Here, I am not concerned with von Wright's taking too little account of the structural difference between the prognostically relevant causal explanation of events and the ex post explanation based on practical inferences; I am concerned, rather, that he also overestimates this difference and projects it upon two clearly distinct conceptual models.

To clarify what I mean, I must once again emphasize that ex post explanation differs from the pure understanding of the normative cogency of the "practical inference," in that, in addition it presupposes the actual occurrence of the action as a behavior identifiable in space and time. (If it cannot presuppose the occurrence, then an empirically and hermeneutically successful application of the "practical inference" to the action is not possible.) With this additional premise, however, the model of ex post explanation must go beyond understanding an agent's good reasons (i.e., the purposive rationality of the "practical inference") and incorporate their causal efficacy as well, no matter how this is to be grasped philosophically, given the dualism in language games. As with von Wright's account of the LC argument, this point can be clarified by the example of the nephew who wants to kill his uncle. As I have already explained, however, we are concerned not to show the plausibility of an insight of the neo-Wittgensteinians but to point to an apparently necessary limitation, one that almost justifies the causalists' use of the example as applied in Donald Davidson's famous essay "Actions, Reasons and Causes."[22]

We can make the same assumptions we made in first using the example, as well as raise the same question. The negative response to this question is still valid, for the original reason. This time, however, in analyzing this negative response, we must not focus on the possibility that the uncle's murder occurred not for the supposed good reasons (i.e., it may not have followed from these reasons in the sense of the pratical inference) but for other reasons. Instead, we must focus on the possibility that the act may not have followed from the *efficacy* of the supposed reasons, that it may have followed from the *efficacy* of other reasons. This time, what is demonstrated is neither the circularity in the hermeneutically mediated identification (or verification) of explanans and explanandum nor the necessity of a here-and-now understanding of the intention in light of the existing action and of the existing action in light of the relevant intention. Instead, what is demonstrated is the necessity of presupposing the intention as a causally antecedent condition for the occurrence of the existing action, no matter how the causality is to be grasped philosophically.

It seems, then, that in the case of the teleological-intentional ex post explanation of an action, one and the same example proves the correctness of both von Wright's version of the Logical Connection argument and its opposite, the causal interpretation of teleological-intentional explanation, in Davidson's sense. Naturally, for logical and conceptual reasons, this cannot mean that the Logical Connection argument about the relation between intention and action can be united with the subsumption-theoretic view of the causality of action intentions, since this follows Hume in presupposing the contingency of the relation between events. Thus we can conclude only that, in the case of an ex post explanation mediated by an understanding of reasons, or by the "practical inference," causality qua the efficacy of intentions must be presupposed in a way that does not imply a causal-nomological explanation in the sense of the subsumption-theoretic model. This is an insight which William Dray already reached.[23]

Von Wright also seems to take into account this conclusion, since, at certain points, he admits that we may talk of a "non-Humean causality" with regard to our intentions as long as we do not thereby confuse teleological-intentional explanation with causal explanation in the usual sense, i.e., the sense of the subsumption-theoretic model.[24] In admitting a non-Humean causality, however, von Wright obviously confronts inner difficulties, at least to the extent that it is not clear how, under his premises, such a causality is to be imagined. In my view, these difficulties are thoroughly intelligible in the context of the argument: Not only a fundamental and, in itself, entirely plausible conception of the post-Wittgensteinian New Dualism stands opposed to the discussion of a causality of intentions; it is also opposed by von Wright's own neo-Wittgensteinian-inspired theory, according to which object-related discussion of natural causality in the natural sciences (i.e., discussion of the causal necessity of alterations of state or of series of events) presupposes the concept of the free action of experimenting human beings (intervening in nature and bringing about new system states). This extraordinarily profound and fruitful theory can scarcely be contravened; on the contrary, it is to be made more precise in the way I attempt in Chapter 2 of Part One.

One solution to the difficulty might be seen in the discussion of the non-Humean causality of actions or their intentions. One could argue that this ensures a compatibility between the concept of the causality of action and the concept of natural causality that can be conceived of only under the presupposition of the concept of action. Hence, for example, it is not at all necessary that the causally effective actions or intentions themselves be considered effects of natural causality. That would not be compatible with the dualism—or, more precisely, the complementarity—of language games. (If one defends this possibility, as many try to do, the result is a race between the tortoise and the hare, between the "hasty" concept of action causation and the concept of free action that must constantly be presupposed so that the tortoise always wins.[25] Such arguments about compatibility, however, in no way make it clear how, under von Wright's post-Wittgensteinian premises, one can conceive of anything like the causal efficacy of action intentions with regard to action events that always include natural events as well. This difficulty is most distinctly expressed in the following note to the text:

What I have called "the counterfactual element in action" is . . . not that certain changes would not happen were it not for the agent's making them happen. The element of counterfactuality consists in that the agent confidently thinks that certain changes will not occur unless he acts. This confidence has an experiential basis. But this does not show that a causal tie exists between certain changes (the results of his action) and his acting. *Acting does not cause events in the world.* To think that it does would be "animism."[26]

Von Wright's point is clear enough, at least at the end of this note; it immediately discloses the force of the post-Wittgensteinian dualism in language games in its modern reformulation of the distinction between phenomena and noumena with which Kant solved the same problem (not to mention Cartesian dualism, which is still older and which ultimately serves to solve the same problem as well). In fact, if natural events are supposed to be caused, then, according to von Wright as well as Kant, one must posit natural events as causes (and so forth, ad infinitum). One cannot posit causation through an action or action intention in the same sense as direct casuation, as it were; to do so would be "animism," or the confusion of two language games or "conceptual frameworks."

In a certain sense, one can also deny any need to apply the category of "causation" to the sphere of actions or action intentions. In an experiential world objectified in the sense of Kant's account of causality, the possibility of intervening action and of experimental action that brings things about is constantly presupposed in a dimension which, in principle, cannot also be objectified. As von Wright puts it, "When I observe, I let things happen. When I act, I make them happen. It is a contradiction in terms both to let and to make the same thing happen on the same occasion. Therefore no man can observe the causes of the results of his own basic actions."[27] This contradiction—hence, the impossibility or nonsensical character of applying the category of causality to one's own action—would also arise if one could view foreign actions or one's own past actions and action intentions in the same way as one views natural events: as objects in the world of experience. This seems to constitute the incontrovertible truth of the neo-Wittgensteinian position.

In certain contexts, however, for example, in history and the social sciences, one can (and must), in a certain sense, objectify human actions and action intentions within the rubric of the experienced world. Therefore, one must, in addition, in a certain sense apply the category of causality to them. One need not inquire after a cause of action intentions. Intentions are, in principle, grounded; they are not caused even if they follow from "manipulation" or the "force" of circumstances. Here, naturalistic discussion of causation can always be replaced by the categorially more precise discussion of a reasoned response, however weak, to an experienced situation; but the situation is quite different with regard to the context in which the *causal efficacy* of action intentions is in question. Such a case arises with regard to an existing action (e.g., the murder of the uncle by his nephew), where the intention necessary for an understanding of the action (e.g., the well-grounded, purposive-rational intention of the nephew to inherit his uncle's estate by murdering him) is conceded beyond a doubt. In this case we must ask whether the existing intention was effective in bringing about the result of action. Indeed, because human actors are responsible for their actions, we cannot evade this question.

Thus, despite his differentiation of two worlds, the experienceable and the unknowable, even Kant had to raise the question of the causality of action, since the acting human being is a "citizen of two worlds."[28] He answered this question by introducing a "causality of freedom" in addition to natural causality. Moreover, he tried to adapt this answer to his "critical" differentiation of two worlds by, on the one hand, defining the "causality of freedom" as the "power of spontaneously beginning a series of successive things or states," and, on the other, reiterating its inability to alter anything in the phenomenal world.[29] For, if it could affect alteration, everything would become "confused and disconnected," and it would be impossible to make nature an object of causal explanation.

This Kantian solution to the problem is hardly satisfactory. It does not allow one to see how human beings can be responsible for the success of their actions in the world of historical events (which, as I have already indicated, are always connected to natural events). In fact, Kant's ethics has been called—correctly, I think—an ethics of pure intention, that is, an ethics in which the "good will" is certainly considered a will to be seriously effective but in which, for systematic reasons, it cannot be responsible for that which, given the universality of causal determinism, must happen in the world of experience.

Now, von Wright decisively undermines the notion of universal causal determinism which Kant, like Laplace, presumed to be self-evident. The concept of a causally determined series of events qua alterations of states in the world presupposes the idea of a closed system that can be set in motion by an experimenting agent. Hence, the idea of a universal determinism proves an illegitimate, metaphysical totalization extrapolated from the legitimate thought of a closed system always resting on the a priori of the possibility of human interference. In other words, it is the metaphysical absolutization of the transcendental framework of an objectifiable nature, which, as Kant says, is "the existence of things insofar as they form a law-governed connection." This assumption (the premise that the conceptual constitution of a causally determined system is made possible not only by the actions of the understanding [Kant] but by the actual interfering actions of actual experimenters) is no longer a transcendental-idealist presupposition; rather, it is a transcendental-pragmatic assumption that makes impossible any longer the avoidance of the concept of a "causal agency," or whatever one may call it, capable of effecting alterations in the experienced world of spatiotemporal events.

It now simply must be possible to distinguish between the case in which my bodily movements are effected by a cause outside the decisions of my will—e.g., by a physical cause outside my body or by a biopathological cause within my body and the case in which my bodily movements, and, where possible, motions outside of my own body mediated by them—are effected by a decision of my will. From a phenomenological point of view, my relation to my own body is different in the second case, which is assumed for experimentation, than it is in the first case. The second case does not involve my physical body (*Körper*), to which I can maintain the distance characteristic of the subject-object relation; rather, it involves my lived body (*Leib*), with which I must identify in acting. (In language-analytic terms, this point can be expressed thus: In the performative part of a speech act, e.g., in the sentence "I hereby declare that. . . ." the word *I* also includes my lived body and not simply my consciousness in the sense of the Cartesian *res cogitans*.) The question is: Can this distinction between the physical body to which I remain distant and the lived body in which I exist provide a key to understanding the causality of action? Insofar as this causality of action qua causality of the lived body is integrated within unobservable, subjectively relevant action, it neither can nor should be conceived of as causality. To this extent, the neo-Wittgensteinian view is confirmed. If, however, as in explaining the occurrence of an action, my body is objectified as the physical body—e.g., as the brain—the relation between it and my decision or intention to act must be viewed as a kind of causality.

From the perspective of causal agency, it appears that what von Wright says about the "counterfactual element in action" in the passage cited is unclear, if not misleading. It is, of course, evident that, under certain circumstances, certain changes in nature that we can bring about experimentally can also occur without our assistance; that is, we cannot exclude such a possibility. From this, however, it does not follow that we would not be justified in claiming that the world of action must, in principle, be so created that, ceteris paribus (and every-thing hinges on this), those changes that we can bring about exper-imentally would not also occur without our assistance. Hence, I think we can claim that, ceteris paribus, "certain changes would not happen were it not for the agent's making them happen," and that the thesis "the agent confidently thinks that certain changes will not occur unless he acts" is too weak.

In my view, another of von Wright's theses about the relation be-tween action and natural causality is also too weak. Suppose the ad-vocate of causal determinism demonstrates to the defender of the freedom of action that when the latter lifts his arm, an event has occurred in his brain, an event "we think is a sufficient condition of [his] arm's rising."[30] He cannot, as von Wright suggests, answer, "Well, I see my arm would have risen in any case." Von Wright is mistaken in thinking that the defender of the freedom of action can rely on the assumption that the relation is a contingent one and that, therefore, there is no contradiction between the two ways of conceiving of the event. This neo-Wittgensteinian assumption can, in fact, be applied to the relation between the understanding of any of one's own present actions and the causal explanation of the objectifiable external world. In the case in which the agent's arm-rising actually (at least, also) depends on an alien stimulation of the nerves, the agent who thought he was raising his arm, but who learned the real situation, could say: "Well, I see my arm would have risen in any case." The same response cannot be used, however, to answer the argument that *whenever* he raises his arm, an event occurs in his brain that is sufficient to cause the arm to rise. This case concerns those brain functions of the lived body that are not objectifiable, because they do not belong to the physical body's external world. In this case, the person who thinks he is acting must assume that his arm will rise as an effect of events in the brain only if it is brought to do so by his lived-bodily action, hence, by the brain functions of the lived body, however this might be possible.

It is true that, from the perspective of the physical body's external world of or prehuman nature, it is possible but not necessary that "a case of arm-rising is also a case of arm-raising."[31] From the perspective of human action, however, the opposite contingency does not hold. If, as von Wright himself assumes, "animism" is to be rejected, then it is necessary that whenever I lift my arm, I am able to do so because my arm also rises as a result of an event in the brain that is causally sufficient to make it rise, an event that, ceteris paribus, could not have occurred unless I raised my arm.[32]

My exposition of the ex post actu explanation of actions ultimately led beyond understanding good reasons to the causal efficacy of reasons or the intentions grounded on them. This exposition made it clear that, in this model of explanation, we cannot help but presuppose something close to the causality of action intentions, no matter how difficult it may be to make this compatible with von Wright's post-Wittgensteinian dualism in language games.[33]

### 3.4 The Hermeneutic Side of von Wright's Model

In continuing our analysis of the ambiguity in von Wright's model of action explanation, yet another version of his conception can be elaborated. This conception is even further from the scientistic account of explanation suggested by the "definitive" inference schema than the model of ex post actu explanation. For this reason, it accords more closely with the neo-Wittgensteinian paradigm that clearly distinguishes between the language game of the teleological-intentional understanding of action and that of the causal explanation of natural events.

Recall that in the case of ex post actu explanation, the inherent necessity (in Hegelian terms) of the answer to the question "Why did this action occur?" does not depend on the cogency of a theoretical-explanatory argument testable by means of predictions. Rather it depends on two circumstances: (1) the intelligibility of action in light of the normative cogency of the "practical inference" (under the circumstances given to him, it was (purposively) rational for him to act in this way); and (2) the fact that, if the action can, ex post actu, be shown to have been purposively rational, it necessarily has already occurred (a fact determined from a temporal perspective). In this case, the problem of verification does not involve confirming the cogency of an explanatory law-hypothesis, as in the case of natural-scientific causal explanation. Rather, it involves exclusively the empirical-hermeneutic applicability of the cogency of the "practical inference," a cogency which itself cannot be falsified. At the same time, empirical-hermeneutic verifiability presupposes that the intention (or the intention surmised by "practical inference") in light of which the action can be understood not only existed at the time of the action, but became causally effective — as always, through natural causality. This presupposition remains part of the ex post actu explanation.

This presupposition no longer obtains when purposive-rational understanding is conceived of not as an answer to the question "Why did this action occur?", but merely as an answer to the question "Why did that person do that?" or "For what reason did he do that?". We ask this question, for example, when we are not concerned with an ex post actu explanation of actions as events in an already objectified historical world, but instead are interested in understanding historical actors as virtual partners in interaction whose position one could, in principle, assume. Here, the purposive-rational understanding of action in light of the "practical inference" no longer has the function of demonstrating that the occurrence of action is somehow necessary. Instead, its function is to clarify the meaning of another's action, what the action itself is supposed to signify, by understanding the ground of the intentions. In the case of sound human action or of human action in its full sense, this meaning is, in principle, already intentionally and teleologicaly mediated and thus can be made intelligible at least in the light of a rudimentary "practical inference."

To a certain extent, von Wright confirms this view; but he ultimately revises it in favor of a more scientistic conception of "teleological explanation." First, he mentions "the mere understanding of behavior as action—for example, button pressing—without attributing it to a remoter purpose—such as making a bell ring"—and then suggests that even this kind of understanding contains a "rudimentary form of teleological explanation":

"A behaved the way he did because he intended to press the button." This can be said to have genuine explicative force when it means that A's behavior was intentional pressing of the button or an attempt to press the button, and not only a movement of some part of his body which resulted in pressure against the button.

To this extent, qua "teleological explanation," the mere understanding of a behavior as a specific action would be "the step whereby we move the description of behavior onto the teleological level, one could say." It seems to von Wright "clearer to separate this step from explanation proper, and thus to distinguish between the understanding of behavior (as action) and the teleological explanation of action (i.e., of intentionalistically understood behavior."[34]

The problem of the relation between the teleological explanation and the explicative understanding of actions becomes even clearer in the chapter entitled "Explanation in History and the Social Sciences":

An explanation in teleological terms of an act of pressing a button may result in our redescribing what the agent did as an act of sounding a bell or of calling people's attention or even of being let into a house. . . . And similarly for collective action. Something which used to be thought of as a reformatory movement in religion may with deepened insight into its causes come to appear as "essentially" a class struggle for land reform. With this reinterpretation of the facts a new impetus is given to explanation.[35]

Von Wright sees that "very much of what would normally be referred to as the "explanations" offered by historians and social scientists consists in *interpretations* of the raw material of their research."[36] He also sees that such interpretations or reinterpretations are mediated in characteristic ways by what he calls "teleological explanation." Nevertheless, because of the very interconnection of the two activities, it seems to him appropriate to separate them "in a methodological inquiry," i.e., distinguish between explicative understanding as an answer to the question "What is this?" and teleological explanation as an answer to such questions as "Why was there a revolution?" and "What were the causes of the revolution?"

This distinction, it seems to me, again obscures precisely that aspect of "teleological explanation" elucidated above, as well as suggesting a form of explanation that, once again, competes with subsumption-theoretic causal explanation. I do not deny that one can still—and, perhaps, should—distinguish between using "purposive-rational understanding" to answer the question "Why did he do that?" and answering the question "What kind of action is or was that?". What is more important, it seems, is the interconnection of these two operations as mutually supportive acts in the understanding of meaning.

Both run counter to a view of teleological explanation according to which it constitutes an answer to the question "Why did this action as an event happen?". In contradistinction to von Wright's neo-Wittgensteinian approach, the operations raise the question whether intentions are causes, even the question concerning a nomological schema for a quasi-causal explanation of motivation. For this reason, I would again argue for the terminological distinction between explicative and purposive-rational understanding, on the one hand, and quasi-causal motivational explanation, on the other. By examining von Wright's elucidation of the interrelation of the first two acts of knowledge, the ground of this distinction can be made clearer.

First, we ask: What is the foundation on which the teleological "explanation" of action, in von Wright's sense, can be employed to explicate and reinterpret actions, or what he calls "collective actions"? In other words, our question concerns the foundation on which an implicit, rudimentary "practical inference" moves the description of an action as a specific action to a teleological level. It seems to me the answer to this question must originate in the constitution of the objects of the social world, a constitution mediated principally by communication, which, therefore, diverges from the communication-free constitution of the objects of nature. The answer must refer to the circumstance that—in the case of human action, in contrast to that of natural processes—the descriptive interpretation of the object of knowledge as something determinate must be legitimated by the intentional self-understanding of the subject-object of knowledge. It does not rest on the knowing subject's interpretation alone, although that is always necessary.

This does not yet mean that every linguistic explication (i.e., in the case of social science, for example, every terminological-conceptual explication) of the meaning of human action must immediately be confirmable by the actual, linguistically articulated self-understanding of the actors. With this overblown demand, social science and history would deny any possibility of either a hermeneutic reconstruction of the meaning of human action, one that reviewed it in reflective and theoretically deepened terms, or the critique of ideology in which such a reconstruction is mediated by method.[37] (In the case of such "collective actions" as demonstrations, religious processions, revolts, and revolutions, as in the case of the rules of collective action embedded in institutions, the difference between the appropriate explicative interpretation and the purposive-rational self-understanding of participating actors is particularly clear. I do not want to suggest here that this difference can be overcome by making individual intentions conscious.) Nevertheless, an explicative interpretation of human actions rests on the methodological postulate that, in principle (that is, given sufficient schooling), the actors must be able both to participate in the language game of the social scientist and to confirm the empirical-hermeneutic accuracy of the descriptive interpretation of their actions and institutions. This they do by recognizing the meaning attributed to their actions by the description as one that is more or less well grounded in their intentions. Such a possibility exists only in the human sciences. I think it accounts for the heuristic and methodological interconnection between the answers to the questions: (1) "What kind of action is or was that?", and (2) "Why did they do that?" or "For what reason did they do that?". Thus it demonstrates the intrinsic connection between purposive-rational understanding and the explicative-descriptive understanding of actions in the sense of the hermeneutic version of what von Wright calls teleological explanation.

Because the interrelation of these two forms of understanding is unique to the human sciences, the parallel von Wright draws between the distinction of understanding and explanation in the natural sciences and the same distinction in the social sciences is unsatisfactory. It is not enough to say, with von Wright, that "the intentional or non-intentional character of their objects marks the difference between two types of understanding and of explanation."[38] This parallel implies that, in the case of "intentional objects," and thus in the case of both the social and the natural sciences, the descriptive-explicative understanding of data that answers the question "What is it?" constitutes the presupposition for answering the why-question, a question sharply distinguished from the question "What is it?" and one that requires a theoretical explanation.

It seems to me that this kind of relation exists only in social sciences that are practiced in a quasi-natural scientific way, since they presuppose a theoretical relation between subject and object and, with Hempel, view purposive-rational understanding merely as a heuristic foundation for the quasi-causal explanation of events of behavior. That purposive-rational understanding mediates a continuation and deepening of an initial, descriptive understanding of the data is not taken into account. Hence, the methodologically relevant form of understanding constituted by hermeneutics is overlooked. Such understanding does not presuppose a theoretically fixed subject-object relation as its epistemological principle, and therefore permits no sharp distinction between the what-question and the why-question. Rather, by means of methodical understanding, it serves to mediate the practically relevant process of coming to an understanding, either within everyday communication and interaction or in the transmission of the tradition in which it encounters crises (as in cases where an understanding with an alien culture must be reached for the first time or where understanding one's own culture must be reconstituted).

From the perspective of this analysis, I want to remark again on von Wright's astonishing desire to eliminate the evaluation implied in Dray's concept of "good reasons-essays" from his own model of teleological explanation. If this intention can appear to be understandable under the scientistic-theoretical version of the model, it is hardly illuminating under a purely hermeneutic version. In support of Dray's veiw, it is now clear that, in the case of human (intentional) actions, in contrast to the description of merely natural processes, the explicative interpretation of meaning cannot ensue without evaluation of the successful or intended fulfillment of normative standards.

The normative standard can be a conventional one, as, for example, in the case of the questions, "Was that a goal-kick, a move in a chess game, an expression of congratulations, or a declaration of war?". In this case, fulfillment of the norm to be evaluated is the condition of the possibility of constituting the facts of the action. The normative standard, however, can be the nonconventional standard of purposive rationality as well. This is the case in the questions, "Was that bribery, a trick, a plea for help, a putsch or an attempt at one, a purge, or the resumption of diplomatic relations?". Finally, often it may be difficult to separate conventional and purposive-rational evaluations — as, for example, in the ambiguous question, "Was that a clever move?".

It should also be noted that, at this point, neither the conventional nor the purposive-rational evaluation of actions violates Max Weber's demand for value freedom, since this is directed only against evaluation of the conventional norms or the goals of action themselves. At issue here, rather, is an immanently evaluative judgment that simply belongs to the understanding of human action.[39] As such, evaluation connected to purposive-rational understanding is also to be sharply distinguished from a substantive, "objective" evaluation of the appropriateness of an action in the sense of its normative foundations. This is so, even though the formal criterion of purposive rationality to which the attempt to understand refers is absolutely objective and thus serves to show the rationality of a hypothetical justification of the action. Is it this problem complex that leads von Wright to dispute the moment of evaluation in his model? In response, I think we must distinguish the following three contexts for a normatively determined evaluation.

1. Evaluation of the success of an action in terms immanent to its concept, whether according to conventional standards or those of purposive rationality, This kind of evaluation does not contradict the idea of an empirically descriptive understanding, but it is necessarily implied by it. Moreover, it is precisely this implication that constitutes the difference between hermeneutic and natural scientific (at least, physicalistic) empiricism.

2. Evaluation of conventional standards or of goal projections and beliefs, or of the standards of formal rationality themselves. This evaluation transcends the concept of descriptive, value-free understanding in Weber's sense; I think, however, that it represents a possibility of critical and reconstructive history and ultimately is not to be separated from the interpretive perspective of universal history. This is demonstrated by Weber's own evaluation of historical progress in terms of the process of rationalization or the sciences' approach to truth.[40]

3. Evaluation in the framework of a systematic, philosophical grounding of the validity of values (as in the work of the neo-Kantians). This context of evaluation pertains to the validity of the norms of possible evaluation on the basis of an ultimately transcendental-pragmatic metanorm, namely, that norm which necessarily is always recognized in argumentative discourse and that grounds the formation of consensus over norms.[41]

This grounding of norms, the final and systematic-philosophical grounding qua metanorm for grounding norms through the formation of consensus, should make it possible to provide a normative foundation for evaluation in the sense of paragraph 2. At the same time, we must recognize that it commits this second context of evaluation, and hence, the concrete generation of norms to material substantiation in a process of the simultaneously normative and empirical reconstruction of social history. In the present context it is essential that the hermeneutic understanding associated with the critical reconstruction of history, in the sense of paragraph 2, has the character neither of a final, transcendental-pragmatic grounding nor of a logical (deontological) grounding of norms. Finally, in the case of empirical-descriptive understanding in the sense of paragraph 1, the difference between understanding in the light of norms and understanding in the light of grounds is especially clear. This must be explicitly emphasized because of the strategy of scientistic causalists who perceive the problem of the E-V controversy in terms of the alternatives: either causal explanation or the objectively valid grounding of the maxim behind the action. That way, they completely overlook the hermeneutic inquiry that involves understanding a given action in light of the criterion of rationality that was decisive for the actor.

Here, the textual analysis of the tension is concluded with the claim that von Wright associates with the teleological model of explanation and, with it, the ambiguity—indeed, in certain contexts, self-contradiction—it implies. On the one hand, I have been concerned to indicate that aspect in the authoritative inference schema from which his critics develop a scientistic interpretation of the model, while, on the other hand, trying to show the possibility of interpreting it in terms of purposive-rational understanding. In the purely hermeneutic limit-case, this interpretation is capable of redeeming von Wright's post-Wittgensteinian arguments, according to which neither a nomological premise nor the concept of causality play a role in the cognitive application of practical inference. On the basis of this analysis, it should now be possible both to clarify the critique of von Wright's model and to assess it critically.

# 4

# The Scientistic Reinterpretation of "Intentional Explanation" by the Critics of the Neo-Wittgensteinian Approach

I would now like to discuss the positions of two critics of von Wright's model of teleological or intentional explanation, those of A. Beckermann and R. Tuomela.[1] Beckermann's massive, clearly formulated, scientistic-naturalistic critique of von Wright is part of a comprehensive dispute with both the neo-Wittgensteinian approach and the position of Dray and Mischel, which is inspired more by Collingwood. In addition, Beckermann substantiates arguments of Davidson, Churchland, and Brandt and Kim and, in his view, convincingly rehabilitates both the subsumption-theoretic model of explanation and the methodology of unified science.[2] For heuristic reasons, then, I do not want to ignore his arguments in developing my view of the third round of the E-V controversy. Tuomela is considerably more cautious; in no way can he be seen as a scientistic naturalist. He accepts the validity of von Wright's (hence, the neo-Wittgensteinian) agruments up to a certain point but nonetheless is able to rehabilitate the subsumption-theoretic model in a restricted sense. Above all, the examination of Beckermann's position is meant to indicate those presuppositions under which the problem of the E-V controversy cannot be resolved, presuppositions that von Wright continued to suggest or, at least, did not explicitly preclude. In contrast, the discussion of Tuomela's thesis should serve a positive function in helping us to begin to formulate a new "archi-tectonic" (Kant) for the theory of science. Such an architectonic is, I think, necessary to demonstrate the compatibility or complementarity of the methodological position of the hermeneutically oriented social sciences or Geisteswissenschaften with the empirical-analytic position of the quasi-natural scientific social sciences. To this extent, it will also show the possibility of resolving the crucial issue of the E-V controversy.

The purview for my highly selective discussion of these two writers emerges from my interpretation of the ambiguity in von Wright's model as elaborated in the text of *Explanation and Understanding*. To evaluate the approach of these critics, it is important to see that, ultimately, both agree with Hempel in their preconception of "explanation"; that is, they take it as more or less self-evident that any explanation—thus, even an "intentional" or "teleological explanation"—must answer the question "Why does action *a* necessarily occur?" or "Why was action *a* to be expected as an event?". Thus they ignore von Wright's account of the unique character of the "practical syllogism" as the presupposition of teleological-intentional explanation, assuming that it must comprise a theoretical-explanatory argument that involves the explanation of an event. As I have tried to show, this assumption is not at all self-evident. Nevertheless, it is legitimate to the extent that, among other questions, one can also inquire into the theoretical explanation for the occurrence of an action as an event. Not only is this actually the question in certain social sciences, but von Wright's inference schema suggests that it is his question, since ultimately the conclusion of the schema involves an explanation of why an action necessarily occurs. For this reason, and because von Wright denies the possibility of testing teleological explanations through predictions, it is understandable that both Beckermann and Tuomela question the cogency of intentional explanation and attempt to resolve the problem by modifying von Wright's schema.

In the strategy they use to resolve the demand for cogency, Beckermann and Tuomela share the following concern: they want to show that the schema of intentional explanation can be conclusive only under two premises. First, the reasons or intentions that figure in the practical inference must reoccur in an explanatory schema as causes. Second, additional premises must be included in the schema, among which a lawlike sentence *L* must be found. To this extent, both writers advocate a return to the subsumption-theoretic model, although, in contrast to Beckermann, Tuomela does not propose either a naturalistic version of the causality of action or, therefore, a causalistic version of the role of the *L* premise in intentional explanation, a version that would contradict the LC argument. Hence, although Beckermann's insistence on the causal efficacy of reasons or intentions has a naturalistic or reductionist thrust, the same insistence in Tuomela's argument points in a different direction. There, the postulated causality of intentionally understandable actions appears not to be reducible to the natural, nomological causality of behavioral events, even though this causality must be presupposed. The causality of actions, rather, appears to complement the causality of behavioral events and is therefore compatible with the analyticity of the relation between intention and action.

Given the complexity of this constellation of arguments, I shall proceed as follows. I follow the sequence of Beckermann and then Tuomela, discussing first the arguments for the causal efficacy of intentions and then the arguments for the necessity and possibility of a lawlike premise in the schema of intentional explanation. My object is to consider both the extent to which Tuomela confirms and specifies Beckermann's critical theses, as well as the extent to which he limits or corrects them. I also wish to contrast Beckermann's scientistic position with a position that is its polar opposite, namely, Rex Martin's historically and hermeneutically oriented critique of von Wright's model of intentional-teleological explanation.

## 4.1 Beckermann's Insistence on the Causal Efficacy of Reasons and Intentions

The preceding interpretation of von Wright makes it clear that Beckermann's account of the structure of intentional explanation begins from premises that a hermeneutic account in no way must or should accept. For example, Beckermann assumes that of the three concepts mental explanation, intentional explanation, and explanation in terms of reasons, "the concept of mental explanation must be considered the most comprehensive" since it is involved in explaining "spiritual (*geistige*) states" and "intentions, plans, goals, wishes, etc."[3] Someone familiar with philosophical strategies can anticipate in this the possibility of a certain hypostatization of intentions as entities that can become the theme of psychology, perhaps as events or dispositions that can be understood as causes. This anticipation is confirmed to the extent that Beckermann understands intentions in the extremely wide sense of "wishes," i.e., "having the desire to," "feeling oneself obliged to," "being convinced that it is morally desirable that," etc. Here, he echoes Davidson's "pro attitudes," under which Davidson includes "desires, wantings, urges, promptings, and a great variety of moral views, aesthetic principles, economic prejudices, social conventions, and public and private goals."[4]

The objection that can be raised to this starting point is that it overlooks a decisive difference between intentions (and volitions, in the sense of decisions of the will) and "pro attitudes" or intellectual states (a difference both von Wright and Tuomela always recognize). No matter how difficult it may be in practice, we can always distance ourselves from any "pro attitude" through a decision of the will, for example, through a decision grounded in ethical responsibility. Hence, we can distance ourselves from the action to be expected on the basis of the pro attitude. Adoption of such a distantiation is at least meaningful even if it is denied by naturalists. This means we must reckon with the possibility that the prediction of an action on the basis of someone's pro attitude can miscarry. Indeed, we must reckon with the possibility of a "good reasons-essay" that "explains" (I would say, "understands") the failure of the prediction by referring to the distantiation from the pro attitude effected by responsible free choice. In this case, we can always clarify failure of the prediction through the supposition that "perhaps the actor did not corroborate his pro attitude in the decision of his will, but rather rejected it." In principle, however, it makes no sense to speak as though someone could have distanced himself from the *intentions* that had to be presupposed for his action. That is, one can, of course, change one's intentions over time; moreover, following Spinoza and Freud, we have good reasons for supposing that the person who changes his intention must somehow be in the position to change his inherent disposition corresponding to the intention, and that this change rests on a transformation of affective wishes or on the sublimation of the libido. But the intention that must be presupposed in an "intentional explanation," in von Wright's sense, cannot be changed, *per suppositionem*.

Thus, if one wants to do justice to the LC argument, one cannot simply subsume "intentional explanation" under "mental explanations," in Beckermann's sense. In the relevant version, this argument does not refer to intellectual states or pro attitudes but, rather, only to intentions. In principle, pro attitudes can be seen as entities (natural events or temporally lasting, inherent dispositions) that temporally precede the action and are contingent in Hume's sense of causal explanation. That means they can be conceived of as antecedent conditions in the sense of the subsumption-theoretic model of explanation. In understanding actions, however, intentions can and must be considered inseparable, in principle, from the intended, identifiable action. If the action is understood in purposive-rational terms in light of a "practical syllogism," then the imputed reasons (goal intentions and beliefs about means) are not conceived of as antecedent conditions of the decision to act but, rather, as premises in the sense of a normatively correct, hence rationally necessary, intention transfer.

In this rejection of Beckermann's starting point it is easy to forget that he begins with the assumption that intentional-teleological explanation is meant to give a theoretical-explanatory answer to the question "Why does or did action $a$ occur?". This question, which views the action as an event, cannot be dismissed by pointing to the LC argument, since, obviously, if an action can be objectively identified in space and time, it must be viewed as an event, the occurrence of which motivates the question of why. If the LC argument is correctly understood, however, we do not even have to reject analysis of the action as an event. This analysis does not mean that the action interpreted in light of an intention is always—or, in relation to any conceivable context—identical to a specific event of muscle-moving, as Beckermann seems to suppose.[5] Identifying an action as an event merely requires that the action qua lived-bodily movement necessarily correspond to *some* muscular movement, since that alone allows its identification in space and time. Von Wright himself suggests this point in claiming that an action has a result that is a natural event and therefore necessarily possesses antecedents and consequences in the external world.[6] Indeed, only under this premise is it conceivable, as von Wright correctly assumes, that the relation of causal necessity between natural events can and must be seen as an implication of the relation of bringing something about and doing something, that is, as an implication of action qua "interference with the course of nature."[7]

If one now asks why a singular action occurred as an event in the sense elucidated above, the answer cannot consist in simply pointing to the LC argument and the normatively conclusive intention transfer between volitional-cognitive reasons and the decision to act, a transfer which, a priori, can be seen as necessary. Even if the answer is mediated by a purposive-rational understanding of the action as a generic action in light of a "practical inference," with regard to an existing action, the answer must also be able to presuppose the causal efficacy of the reasons or transferred intentions. Again, von Wright implies this. As we saw in the example of the assassin, the fictional premise that "nothing happens" is comprehensible only under two assumptions: (1) a conceptual distinction is assumed between the transfer of intentions that are generally intelligible in light of the "practical inference" (i.e., intentions to be postulated as rational in a normative sense) and the real efficacy of this transfer in the case of a specific event; and (2) although difficult to understand, the presupposition that, in a case where no conceivable external or internal obstruction neutralizes the efficacy of the premises, this conceptual difference could actually result in the nonrealization of the action intention or the resolution.[8]

Thus I can agree with Beckermann that an intentional explanation must presuppose the efficacy of the intentions. I do not think, however, that this means the causal efficacy of the understood intention (which must be presupposed in every case of empirically correct generic interpretation) can be reduced to the causality of the corresponding natural event (i.e., the activity of nerves and muscles). I shall try to make this clearer by referring to one of Beckermann's examples.

Beckermann correctly emphasizes that the intentional-teleological explanation, "Peter beckoned with his finger in order to signal Maria to come to him," does not serve as an explanation of the action that is present as an event simply because one can assume correctly that Peter had good reason and therefore the intention to do what he did. Peter could also suffer from a nervous twitch in his right hand and not have beckoned at all, but simply moved his hand nervously. If that were the case, then, although one had correctly grasped Peter's intention, this intention would not have been causally effective in the event, and thus the explanation would be false.

This example seems to demonstrate that, where intentional explanation is used to explain motives, it must presuppose more than the presence of good reasons, in other words, the purposive-rational intelligibility of the action in terms of a "practical inference." In addition, it must presuppose and prove the efficacy of these reasons, as is required in court, for example. Nevertheless, in no way is it demonstrated that the causal efficacy of the intention is identical to the causal efficacy of the nerves or muscle activity corresponding to the intention. Therefore, neither is it identical to a causal determinism. This point can be clarified by modifying the premises of the example.

Assume that Peter had, in fact, long passionately desired to make Maria unfaithful to his rival. At a party he played with this idea and thought that he could beckon her over; but, whether out of fear of a fight or because of good taste, he dismissed the idea. Nonetheless, because of his desire to win Maria and his nervous constitution in general, he had developed a nervous twitch in his hand that always appeared whenever he saw Maria with his rival. If it appeared in this instance, then the "explanation" would be false even though intention was correctly inferred and causally effective on the corresponding activity of a nerve or muscle. It would now be false as an intentional, purposive-rational understanding of the actual behavior.

It is easy to see the identity between this case and the example we examined above, of the nephew who is supposed to have murdered his uncle in order to inherit his fortune. Such an explanation can be false, for two opposite reasons—the intention to commit murder did not become causally effective (by chance, the nephew quarreled with his uncle and killed him); or the intention to commit murder became causally effective in such a way that it produced a disposition to irrationality and violence. (Because of an irritability produced by the intention to commit murder, the nephew fought with a stranger without knowing it was his uncle, and killed him.)

Two points follow from this example for the case in which a valid intentional explanation is to function as a causal explanation in terms of motives, that is, where it is to explain the occurrence of an action as an event, as Beckermann supposes. First, it is not enough to give a correct account of the good reasons in terms of which a possible understanding of the action can be achieved. Second, it is not sufficient to assume correctly that the intention posited as rational was causally effective in the sense that it brought about the explanandum qua behavioral event through corresponding activity of nerves and muscles. Rather, we must assume that the correctly posited intention, as such, that is, the intention presupposed in a purposive-rational understanding of the action, itself became causally effective with regard to the behavioral event corresponding to the action. This means, however, that even if we are concerned to answer the question "Why did this action qua event occur?", the validity of an intentional explanation depends on the causal efficacy of the intention, in the sense that it intentionally brings something about (von Wright) and not simply in the sense that it agrees with the causal, nomological character of the activity of nerves and muscles. In the scientific objectification of action intentions, we cannot avoid talking about the causal efficacy of an intention and of the good reasons mediated by it. What I have said here shows, however, that, in addition to the natural, lawlike causality of the activity of nerves and muscles, we must presuppose a "causality of freedom," in Kant's sense.

This analysis of the causality of action or intention agrees with my interpretation of von Wright; it is hardly compatible with Beckermann's position, though it may well accord with Tuomela's. Before attempting to confirm this suspicion, I want to discuss Beckermann's views further, to try to answer the question whether an intentional explanation in von Wright's sense can recur to causally effective reasons or intentions (Beckermann's "central explanatory facts"[9]) even when it functions as an answer not to the question "Why did the existing action occur?" but to the question "Why, i.e., for what reasons making the action rationally intelligible, did x do what he did?".

## 4.2 Beckermann's Scientistic Fallacy

Beckermann himself seems to want to pose this question in examining Dray's and Mischel's explication of the "good reasons-argument." He states that according to these writers, "the historian's question "Why did A do x" is less like the natural scientist's question "Why did event E occur?" than the question "Why did you do that?".[10] Beckermann admits that because the latter question is formulated in the second person, it is in fact a why-question that demands justification. Then he commits what I want to call the "scientistic fallacy" characteristic of representatives of a unified methodology, a fallacy which, I had to surmise, is one of the reasons for the ambiguity of von Wright's model. Because the question "Why did A do x?" is formulated not in the first or second person but in the third, Beckermann concludes that the why-question demanding justification must turn into a question demanding explanation for the existence or occurrence of the action as a spatiotemporal event. This explanation is the analogue of the natural scientific question about causes, and it must be answered not by referring to good reasons but by referring to the causally effective "possession of good reasons."[11]

In the following pages I shall demonstrate that the basis for Beckermann's conclusion is a deeply rooted and highly characteristic premise of contemporary analytic philosophy.[12] Beckermann assumes that with regard to both actions and beliefs ultimately there are only two methodologically relevant types of why-question and answer: (1) that pertaining to the explanation of events, and (2) that pertaining to the objectively valid grounds or justifications for a law or the truth of something. As direct discourse, the latter type of question would be directed toward another in dialogue (in the second person) or toward oneself in monologue (in the first person). In contrast, the former type of question would comprise questions (in the third person) about the occurrence of others' actions and beliefs as events in the objectifiable world discussed by us (I, you, or they who, as speaking subjects, form the "limit of the world"). In other words, one would have to distinguish between only two kinds of question: (1) those belonging to a normative logic of science and ethics (or deontological logic?), that refer to what is valid; and (2) those concerning empirical natural science, which refer to what "is the case."

This conception of possible alternatives follows the *Tractatus Logico-Philosophicus*, overlooking the possibility of conceiving of the other or others one discusses in the third person (singular or plural) as virtual partners in communication or interaction. In other words, it ignores the possibility of viewing human beings as contemporaries or subjects of history whose actions and beliefs one attempts to understand by virtue of the reciprocity between self-reflection and the anticipation of alien intentions and cognitive presuppositions. For the scientistic approach, the move from formulation of the why-question in the first and second person (i.e., the formulation demanding grounds or justifications) to the question as posed in the third person (the reasons for the actions and beliefs of others) is equated with the transition to the observer's perspective. Thus it is transformed into a why-question that demands explanation of an event and conforms to the theoretical subject-object relation of natural science. To this extent the hermeneutic distantiation from others, insofar as they are the alien subjects of action intentions and beliefs, is confused with the theoretical distantiation in terms of which they appear as the mere object of one's own action intentions and beliefs.

Another drawback of this confusion is that it overlooks the possibility of a hermeneutic self-distantiation in answering the justification question in the first or second person. Beckermann seems to assume that the answer to the question "Why did you do *x*?" or "Why did I do *x*?" is immediately identical with the answer to the question "Why should one act in this way in a situation of type C?".[13] In a conversation or monologue, however, it is possible that the answer will not be "because I was in a situation of type C and in a situation of type C one ought to do *x*," but, rather, "because I believed that I was in a situation of type C and thought it was best in such situations to do *x*." In other words, it is possible that the answer is already related to one's own intentions and beliefs, intentions and beliefs that can be made a theme for reflection and even placed in question. For this reason, the transition to the desire to understand someone in the sense of the question "Why, i.e., for what reasons plausible to him, did he act in that way?" can always be grasped as the emergence of the hermeneutic inquiry out of the reflective perspective of dialogue.[14]

Hence, the indirect methodological advantage of discussing the good reasons-argument in terms of the alternative between explanation of events and justification or grounding is that, *via negationis et eminentiae*, it clearly illuminates the hermeneutic inquiry that is overlooked. Such an inquiry involves coming to an understanding between virtual co-subjects of possible argumentation, and it must, so to speak, take its place between the two poles of purely objectivistic argumentation. It must presuppose that, although the actions and beliefs of other discussion partners are somewhat estranged by being formulated in the third person, they remain intelligible in two ways—on the one hand, in light of universally valid, intersubjective criteria of rationality, and, on the other, under the hypothetical premise of particular, subjective volitional and cognitive presuppositions that are not universally valid but can be attributed to others on the basis of one's own subjectivity. This means that, in a way, these actions and beliefs are open to participation and critical evaluation in a hermeneutically expanded communication community. It thus becomes clear that a "good reasons-essay" involves a methodical, hermeneutic contribution to intersubjective understanding. Hence, in contrast to both the explanation of an event and deductive or inductive grounding or justification, it cannot be abstracted from the pragmatic dimension of knowing subjects nor made the theme of a purely logico-semantic explication. This circumstance may be the reason that for decades it has been almost hopeless to validate the specifically hermeneutic interest in knowledge in the terms of the framework of the modern logic of science or to consider this interest in epistemological rather than merely empirical-psychological terms. (This point is still a precarious one in analytic philosophy.[15])

As Beckermann points out, Dray and Mischel, both of whom are indebted to Collingwood and hence to a preanalytic tradition, have long emphasized that intentional explanations can be seen as justifications only in a relative sense.[16] They show only that the action to be explained would have been rational "if the situation were as the actor imagined it to be" or that this action was the thing to do "from the standpoint of the actor." This is a clear enough statement of the fact that, or the way that, the generally valid criteria of rationality that are presupposed for possible justification are to be introduced into the specific hermeneutic context in which one hypothetically puts oneself in the other's position. (The criteria of rationality relevant to a good reasons-essay, first, involve only the minimal criteria of formal rationality.) Beckermann believes he can show that the position of Dray and Mischel is "cogently refuted" by the fact that

there are cases in which we accept statements about an actor's intentions and beliefs as intentional explanations even though the reasons that the actor had for performing the action are not good reasons and, similarly, there are also cases in which the actor's reasons were in fact good reasons but we do not accept the fact that he had these reasons as an explanation.[17]

As an example of the first thesis, Beckermann uses the following: "Hans wears an amulet because he does not want to get ill, and believes that his amulet will keep illnesses away from him." Beckermann thinks the obvious "irrationality" of this behavior precludes all discussion of understanding in terms of "good reasons"; nevertheless, he claims that we can speak of a correct causal explanation of the event that refers to the "possession" of specific, causally effective if irrational reasons, hence, to certain "explanatory facts."[18] The positions of both Dray and Weber throw light on this argument by making it absolutely clear that, precisely in this case, the attempt is usually that of using generally valid criteria of rationality, as they are represented by the formal schema of purposive rationality or of the "practical inference," to clarify a behavior that is alien to a rationally enlightened contemporary perspective. That this is exactly the minimal hermeneutic point of the good reasons-essay is made clear in an example used by the anthropologist Kroeber and cited by Rex Martin in his critical account of von Wright's *Explanation and Understanding*.[19]

The example involves a primitive man who has accidently inflicted a knife wound on his own leg and now attempts to heal the wound by carefully cleaning the knife. In von Wright's view, everything depends on establishing the premises of a "practical inference" in light of which one can explain the "savage's" strange behavior in "intentional-teleological" terms.[20] I believe this is correct to the extent that a certain victory is already gained by purposive-rational understanding (and, hence, by a good reasons-essay) if we can say: "The man wanted to heal his wound, and we can show that he believed that this was the way to do it." The triumph of understanding is that the anthropologist can say to his enlightened contemporaries or peers: "See, he is a thinking person just like you and me; he did not act completely irrationally but in a purposive-rational way. If you could share his beliefs, you would rationally have to act in exactly the same way in the same circumstances."

Of course, the enlightened contemporary would not be completely satisfied by this demonstration if he really wanted to understand the "savage." Martin's attempt is to demonstrate this point and to criticize von Wright from a historical-hermeneutic perspective. He doubts that establishing the second premise of the explanation schema (the reference to what the "savage" actually believed) "really matters all that much in these cases," since, in general, we find an action sufficiently intelligible if "we can say that the doing of A is the sort of thing done when someone intends E."[21] In contrast, where this is not the case, as in the present example, neither establishing the premise about what the agent believes nor the possibility of constructing a "practical inference" will be enough to guarantee an adequate understanding. Such understanding, rather, will require additional information (by telling a story, for example) which can "fill in on" the savage's belief about the means-end relationship expressed in von Wright's inference schema. This "filling in" is not supposed to be equated with explanation of the belief that was unintelligible under the first explanation; according to Martin, it is, rather, already presupposed in the first explanation in order to make plausible the premise about the agent's belief. What is meant should become clear in Kroeber's analysis of the situation:

The savage and the peasant . . . have observed certain indisputable facts. They know that cleanness aids, dirt on the whole impedes recovery. They know the knife as the cause, the wound as the effect; and they grasp, too, the correct principle that treatment of the cause is in general more likely to be effective than treatment of the symptom. . . . They fall back on agencies more familiar to themselves, and use, as best they may, the process of magic intertwined with that of medicine.[22]

This discussion allows me to dispute Beckermann's scientistic reduction of "intentional explanation" and to clarify its possible position within the wider methodological context of hermeneutic procedures of knowledge. I think Martin misapprehends the specific achievement of purposive-rational understanding when he contrasts the reference to the premises of a "practical inference" to the everyday intelligibility of a particular way of acting in view of specific goal intentions. For his part, Dilthey viewed the latter intelligibility as merely a "pragmatic understanding" in the everyday framework of a "common sphere" (such as the workplace) and convincingly distinguished it from the skilled "hermeneutic understanding" that becomes necessary wherever pragmatic understanding encounters difficulties (thus, in the confrontation with alien forms of life or in the case of a crisis in the understanding of one's own religious, legal, or literary tradition).[23] Particularly for modern human beings, it appears that purposive-rational understanding of strange actions achieved by establishing the premises of a "practical inference," in von Wright's sense, is indispensable as a means of access to historical-hermeneutic understanding.

Nevertheless, it is indisputable that if goal intentions and beliefs about means are completely incomprehensible, the hermeneutic interest in knowledge cannot rest content with showing a mode of action to be purposive-rational in formal terms. Indeed, I think one can claim that it is precisely purposive-rational understanding that can and must find a clear way to raise the question of the substantive comprehensibility of assumed goals and beliefs. At this point, Martin's demand that the practical inference be narratively "filled in" in the context of a story seems to become relevant. Von Wright does not fully grasp the specific hermeneutic thrust of this demand in supposing it to amount to either a verification procedure for establishing the premises of the "practical inference" or the beginning of a new "belief-explanation."[24] Here again, the ambiguity or, in this case, the scientistic-hermeneutic equivocation we have explored in von Wright's approach comes into play.

Von Wright's view that the issue concerns only verification of the premises of the "practical inference" or a new "teleological explanation" becomes understandable in view of his assumption that the "practical inference" serves to explain an action as an event. In contrast, I have pointed out that the "practical syllogism" can possess only a normative cogency; moreover, if it is to be placed in the service of hermeneutic understanding, as Martin supposes, then, I think, it makes sense to distinguish between establishing the cogency of an inference schema by verifying its premises and substantively filling in the inference schema to achieve a better understanding. It is true that this "filling in" cannot improve the formal cogency; it can, however, demonstrate the plausibility of the substantive connection between the elements of the inference and, above all, show the plausibility of the connection between the primary goal intention and the action. In this way the action does not follow from the premises in a formal (whether practical-normative or theoretical-explanatory) sense alone; the connection, rather, also appears plausible in a substantive sense, irrespective of the rationality of the inference schema. Now, one might object that this kind of plausibility can be achieved only through another teleological explanation of the volitional-cognitive presuppositions of the first explanation in light of this "rational syllogism." Such an objection, however, derives solely from an interest in formal logic; it does not consider the hermeneutic achievement of the historian or cultural anthropologist who, without engaging in a logical regress from the "explanation" to its premises, makes deeper understanding possible by embedding purposive-rational understanding within a narrative. At this point, it seems to me, we must reconsider the hermeneutic interconnection between the purposive-rational understanding of actions and the explicative description of their meaning.

I do not want to suggest that a deepening of explicative-substantive understanding can be completely independent of the attempt to justify the volitional-cognitive presuppositions of actions understood in purposive-rational terms. Indeed, it is not completely independent of the attempt at a critical reconstruction and evaluation of the ultimate goals and normative maxims of individual people or cultures in terms of a universal ethics, or of its deepest convictions in terms of a philosophical-scientific world orientation that is itself mediated by efforts to understand.[25] All understanding of action—from the good reasons-essay based on the minimal claim of formal, purposive rationality to the good reasons-essay that makes substantive claims—seems ultimately to stand under the same regulative principle calling for hypothetical justification in light of common normative standards of the human communication community. The hermeneutic interest in knowledge is an interest in the possibility of achieving mutual understanding. It cannot be satisfied by definitively relativizing "good" reasons with respect to differences in forms of life as ultimate normative standards; ultimately it can be satisfied only by relating differences in reasons to differences in situations.[26]

We turn now to Beckermann's second argument against Dray's conception of good reasons-essays: namely, that often we do not count as an explanation the fact that someone had good reasons for his action. I have already admitted that in the case of explaining the occurrence of an action as an event, we must insist on a proof of the causal efficacy of the reasons as motivating reasons. Now I want to add that if one is interested in the kind of explanation of actions as events that is prognostically relevant (an interest characteristic of the empirical-analytic social sciences and that differs from von Wright's interest in historical ex post actu "explanation"), then, the fact that the causally effective reasons are good ones (and not more or less bad) is irrelevant to judging the validity of the explanation. This fact now retains only a heuristic significance within the "context of discovery"; nevertheless, even in this case, we must establish that the imputed reasons or reasoned intentions did not lead to the action simply because of their causal efficacy, but that they did so because the agent acted according to the sense of the imputed motives.

This requirement must also be imposed on an intentional explanation of events; it thereby distinguishes the explanation, as a hermeneutically mediated explanation, from causal explanation in the natural sciences. The requirement, however, illuminates as well the extent to which a good reasons-essay is concerned not with the causal efficacy of good or bad reasons for acting but, rather, with the hermeneutically mediated distinction between good and bad reasons.[27] Because of this concern, it focuses on generic actions or modes of action by attempting to achieve a historical understanding of single actions in light of a normative standard. Even in this case, we must take it to be self-evident that the hypothetical reasons or intentions we impute to agents did become causally effective. Nonetheless, the achievement of knowledge is characterized not by proof of this causal efficacy but by the empirically correct understanding of the reasons as good or bad (or more or less good) ones.

This analysis signals a decisive methodological distinction, which is not primarily dependent on the onto-semantic character of the entities (intentions, actions) but, rather, is grounded in the kind of inquiry and in the corresponding disclosure of the cognitive theme. I can clarify my point in the following reflection. If we are interested in a prognostically relevant motivational explanation of actions as events, then we will not only insist on proof of the causal efficacy of the imputed intentions, we will assume the importance of the fact that, in the individual case, the action intentions (to which one can attribute merely a "causality of freedom") correspond to natural events or to the inherent dispositions of the organism. It will also be important that these natural events or dispositions are subsumed under nomological, psychophysical connections or at least under the quasi-nomological regularities of the social quasi-nature of human beings. These nomological or quasi-nomological regularities do not determine well-grounded intentions as such but, rather, the corresponding natural events or dispositions to which an explanatory psychology or social science as a generalized science of behavior can refer in determining its objects. Put briefly, these sciences are primarily interested in the reified motivational structure of human quasi-nature. Conversely, the Geisteswissenschaften resort to an external explanation only with regard to that which ultimately cannot be understood in terms of good reasons. It is only in these cases that they refer to biological nature or to the historically sedimented quasi-nature of human beings.

In the following the distinctions I have elaborated in this section will permit an evaluation of Tuomela's position with regard to the causality of action intentions. In conjunction with this, they will also permit a critical assessment of Beckermann and Tuomela's attempt to reinterpret the schema of intentional explanation in subsumption-theoretic terms.

## 4.3 Tuomela on the Logical Connection Argument and the Causality of Actions and Intentions

Tuomela also criticizes von Wright's model of intentional explanation for the reason we cannot help supporting: for not taking into account that the agent's intention produces—and, to this extent, causes—the action to be explained. The principal thrust of his critique seems to be to question the New Dualism that lies at the base of von Wright's position. Tuomela postulates explicitly that the causal efficacy of the intention can "cross boundaries of conceptual frameworks," since the effective intention and the action to be explained involve psychological characteristics of singular events, whereas the descriptions that a causal theory presupposes to explain the causal connection are "likely to be physical." That is, they must "come from future neuro-physiological science."[28]

In evaluating this claim within the present framework, it seems to me that the causality Tuomela posits is of decisive importance. It is true that this causality cannot easily be reconciled with the neo-Wittgensteinian differentiation of language games. Nevertheless, it does not cast doubt on the neo-Wittgensteinians' LC argument, since the descriptions that are presupposed in a causal nomological theory do not refer to the intention (itself also effective) or the action that forms the explanandum of intentional explanation. Tuomela explicitly confirms that he does not want to say that "generic actions are caused or causally explainable" or that on the basis of causal explanation one somehow could predict unknown future instances of such generic actions. "For conceptual reasons, there cannot be causal or other deterministic laws on the basis of which such predictions could be made."[29] Here, if I understand Tuomela correctly, he is substantiating the distinction, in principle, between the contingent relations of natural events (in Hume's sense) and the relation between intentions and action explananda. He does so by distinguishing: (1) the singular events that correspond to the intention and the action to be explained in the individual case; (2) their possible generic description within the framework of a causal nomological theory; and (3) the possible explicative interpretation of their meaning in the sense of generic intentions and actions. Tuomela seems to confirm this insofar as he agrees with von Wright's version of the LC argument.[30]

If this interpretation is correct, the relation of causal efficacy that Tuomela postulates between the objectified intention, and the action it brings about, refer to the corresponding, singular events in each case, insofar as they are assumed to exist—that is, insofar as they are independent of both their comprehension as generically describable objects of causal nomological explanation and their generic explication as understandable elements of the "practical inference." Hence, in a "third" language game, so to speak, talk of an "intentional causality" could at least be reconciled with the neo-Wittgensteinian distinction between understanding action and explanation in terms of natural laws of the natural event corresponding to the action. In addition, Tuomela seems to confirm this inference insofar as he emphasizes that the observable parts of the existing instances or exemplifications of a specific kind of generic action are caused by "effective intentions," namely, "tryings" to bring about a specific action.[31] But how, under these premises, are we supposed philosophically to conceive of the type of causality in action and intention to be postulated?

As far as I can see, Tuomela's answer to this question lies in the statement:

Trying to do something is an important form of self-activity. . . . I agree with Chisholm . . . in that, e.g., in raising one's arm one makes cerebral events happen in his head and that these cerebral events are causes of bodily behavior. Thus our notion of trying involves, but is not identical with, making brain events happen. The general underlying idea in our account of agency is that an agent is a coherent and unified psycho-biological being capable of directed self-activity and self-control. In this general sense an agent can be said to have causal power.

If, for the moment, one ignores Tuomela's use of the term *causal power*, which he shares with Chisholm and applies to actions, intentions, and actors, then this explication of self-activity seems to contain no element that conflicts with the distinction between the language game of caused natural events and that of reasoned actions. Tuomela carefully distinguishes what von Wright calls "Humean causality," the causality that presupposes the contingency of the observed relation between natural events, from the causality of action or intention that the former already presupposes in the case of "causing." That way, he permits the latter to be identified with a "non-Humean causality," the possibility of which von Wright sometimes concedes. Speaking of the "unified psycho-biological being" of the agent, however, seems to come close to the elucidation I have already given of the special relation (of identity) of the actor to his body qua lived body. As I have indicated, this relation differs in a phenomenologically significant way from the relation to alien bodies and to one's own physical body in the case where bodily movements are externally (physically or biopathologically) provoked. Nevertheless, as noted, Tuomela distinguishes singular events, which are presumed to exist and which are caused by action intentions, from both generic natural events that can be explained in causal nomological terms and generic actions that can be interpreted in the light of an understanding of intentional meaning. To this extent, I think, Tuomela reconstructs precisely the problem Kant answered with the concept of a "causality of freedom." Tuomela seems to confirm this in establishing that singular actions are not determined by causal or other (statistical) laws, though they can be, and normally are, determined by the actor's "intendings" in such a way that these "intendings themselves need not, and at least cannot always, be predetermined by other further determinations (as long as man can be regarded as an agent)."[32]

Tuomela's answer, of course, differs from Kant's, insofar as it argues that action intentions or decisions of the will which themselves are not determined are, nonetheless, capable of causing changes in the world of experience that stands under natural laws. Again, this difference reflects Tuomela's fundamental belief in the necessity of crossing boundaries of conceptual frameworks and, in particular, those of the post-Wittgensteinian New Dualism, in which the sense of the Kantian dualism of the "two worlds" of "noumena" and "phenomena" is retained.

In this connection it seems interesting to recall Nicolai Hartmann's "real-ontological" extension of the Kantian account of the "causality of freedom." This extension was motivated primarily by Hartmann's concern with the ethically and ontologically relevant problem of human responsibility for the result of action. He begins by claiming that indeterminism is a false solution to the problem of the freedom of the will, since the issue is precisely one of illuminating the teleologically oriented final determination of the real world by the human "causality of freedom." Hartmann thinks it conceivable, insofar as possible, that causal chains of natural events are never determined teleologically, and therefore remain open to a "teleological reformation" by the final determination of human beings. To the extent that these human beings acquire a knowledge of causal laws, they can choose chains of events as a means of realizing their goals.

This conception, which "sublates" (aufhebt) the Kantian dualism of noumena and phenomena into a real-ontological theory of "levels," seems, prima facie, to effect an elegant mediation of the causal nomological character of nature with the freedom of action qua final teleological determination. It does not, however, seem really to resolve the problem Kant left unresolved, for which the theory was proposed. Hartmann's "final determination" involves a final determination of ontological levels of the real world; the problem, then, is how it can influence actual (as opposed to possible) chains in nature and do so in such a way that changes in the real world can be attributed to a "causality of freedom," not, of course, as regards their natural law-likeness but as regards their causal determination. It is much more plausible to resolve this problem under von Wright's premises, according to which the conception of a "universal causal determinism" appears as an illegitimate totalization of that causal determinism of nature which can itself be conceived of only under the presupposition of experimental action. From this fascinating perspective, the assumption of a certain "indeterminism" in nature appears indispensable for resolving the problem of the freedom of action; for, resolving this problem is itself the presupposition for resolving the problem neither Hume nor the neo-Humeans could resolve—the problem of the pragmatic causal necessity of experimentally manipulatable relations between changes in system states. (In this context, "nature" need not refer to the object of proto-physical or macro-physical manipulation in experiments, even if it can be the object of "nonclassical" theories that must be tested experimentally.) Such a solution is not incompatible with the form of the causality of actions, actors, or intentions that Tuomela postulates.

This concludes my analysis of the fundamental possibility—indeed, necessity—of presupposing the causal efficacy of intentions in intentional explanations that explain actions as events and thus necessarily include the "bringing about" of natural events. I now turn to the question of whether—and, if so, to what extent—it is possible or necessary to reinterpret von Wright's proposed schema of intentional-teleological explanation (which, as we saw, seems to involve explanation of an event, and hence, differs from the pure schema of the "practical inference") in terms of a subsumption-theoretic schema. Again, I shall begin by discussing Beckermann's suggestions and arguments against the neo-Wittgensteinians.

### 4.4 Critique of Beckermann

By refuting the LC argument, Beckermann believes he can show that an intentional explanation must be grasped as a causal one, insofar as it subsumes the explanandum under a universal law. He bases this claim primarily on an argument used by Churchland.[33] In evaluating this argument, I think it is advisable to remember that Beckermann is not interested in intentional explanation, insofar as it is a systematization of purposive-rational understanding, but only insofar as it gives an answer (at best, mediated by purposive-rational understanding) to the question why a certain event occurred or had to occur. If an "intentional explanation" is meant to assume this kind of function, then apparently it must be able to take the form of a subsumption-theoretic, causal explanation, since, as we have seen, the explanation schema von Wright proposes (not to mention the purely normative schema of his "practical inference) is not conclusive as a theoretical-explanatory argument. That is, it cannot be tested (or falsified) by predictions. From this consideration it naturally does not follow that there actually are intentional, causal explanations that can be grounded in universal laws and falsified (that is, tested without the use of ad hoc clauses). Indeed, the critical thrust of the LC argument is directed precisely against this possibility. Thus it is crucial to see whether Beckermann can find an example that vitiates it.

In Beckermann's view, the following explanans schema represents just such an example. The antecedent conditions are:

($A_1$) H does not want his telephone to be disconnected.
($A_2$) H knows that his telephone will not be disconnected if he pays his telephone bill.
($A_3$) H knows that there is no other way to prevent his telephone from being disconnected.
($A_4$) There is nothing that H wants more than the goal specified in ($A_1$).
($A_5$) H is able to pay his telephone bill.

These conditions are combined in the following law:

($L_1$) Whenever ($A_1$) ($A_2$) ($A_3$) ($A_4$) and ($A_5$) are fulfilled, H pays his telephone bill.[34]

Using this explanans schema, Beckermann convincingly argues that it is "not imaginable" that under these premises H would not pay his telephone bill. If he did not pay it, one could assume that one of the five antecedent conditions was not fulfilled.[35] Beckermann illuminatingly adds that it is not possible to assume as a counterargument that someone who wants to demonstrate the irrational freedom of his will would not pay his bill, for, in this case, condition $(A_4)$ clearly is not fulfilled.

At this point at the latest, however, a defender of the LC argument could exclaim: "To whom are you saying all this? Doesn't your appeal to the 'unimaginability' of falsifying the so-called law indicate that a normal empirical law is not involved here? Isn't it, rather, a principle that can be comprehended in conceptual-analytic terms and that involves the correct transfer of intentions in a 'practical inference'? In short, isn't it a normative principle of rationality that is masked as a law?" Beckermann himself recognizes that the "law" $(L_1)$ is "not only factually true" but also has "that 'conceptual character' that the proponents of the Logical Connection argument claim." Nevertheless, with Churchland, he believes "a deeply anchored theoretical-nomological principle is involved." In this connection, he cites the following passage from Churchland:

It is difficult, perhaps impossible to deny $L_1$ without undermining the conceptual machinery which makes such understanding possible, or better constitutes it, but none of this entails that $L_1$ is "analytic" in any sense inconsistent with its being nomological in character. One could not deny the principle of mass-energy conservation without threatening similar havoc in the conceptual framework of modern physical theory, and one would encounter similar difficulties in trying to describe a non-controversial case which would falsify that principle. If there are any relevant differences between these two cases, they are differences only in degree.[36]

Beckermann ultimately bases this answer on an appeal to Chihara and Fodor's "Operationalism and Ordinary Language" and to Brandt and Kim's "Wants as Explanations of Actions".[37] According to Beckermann, intentions and beliefs are "mental states," and as such, "theoretical entities" of such a kind that any explication of them that refers to the actions they imply (as is presupposed in the LC argument) already involves an empirical theory that can be revised in the progress of science.[38] Hume's reference to the contingency of the causal connection between observable events, therefore, is said to be irrelevant to the connection of intentions, beliefs, and actions in an intentional explanation; for, even if it still is expressed in ordinary language, the latter connection always already implies a causal theory that can use psychological terms.[39]

This modern form of scientism and "theoreticism" thus absolutizes the notion of "theoretical concepts," which had its original paradigm in concepts of modern physics that could not be perceived, for example, "gravitation potential" and "electron." Its fatal aporia seems to lie in the disavowal of its own presuppositions. If it is no longer possible to distinguish between "analytic" and "synthetic," between "criteria" and "symptoms" or between the normative conditions of experience and falsifiable empirical hyptheses, then precisely that concept of a revisable empirical theory in whose name this leveling is undertaken loses its meaning; theories, rather are immunized against possible falsification. This point becomes clear if we focus on the conceptual system in terms of which scientists both understand their intentions, beliefs, and actions and standardize them as the conditions of inter-subjectively valid science. Now, suppose that this conceptual system can, in principle, be completely understood as the result of an empirical theory, so that the objects of epistemology are simply competing theories. Ultimately the instrument for—or premise of—every possible critical evaluation of theories would be destroyed, and the question concerning what are to be classified as competing "theories" in the first place becomes a problem.

The fate of the Popperians' "principle of proliferation" offers an illuminating example of the logic of absolutizing the concept of empirical theory. In a similar way, Feyerabend applies it to the theory of science, and Albert to different moral theories. Both fail to reflect sufficiently on the necessity of scientific or ethical standards for (or the normative conditions of the possibility of) critically comparing scientific theories or ethical systems. Feyerabend draws the ultimate consequence of scientism or "theoreticism" when he refers to scientific theories, theories of science, different kinds of ethics, metaphysical systems, religions, myths, fairy-tales, even astrology and theories of exorcism, and any-thing else that might possess a truth claim. In his view, these theories should be presented to the evaluation of children in a nonprejudicial way, that is, without pointing to any standards for or premises of critical comparison.[40]

One might object that the consequences to which I have referred can be avoided, since the conceptual system in which we understand the normative conditions of the possibility of empirical science can be seen as prescientific, that is, as provisionally justified. In other words, without prejudice to its function as a premise, the conceptual system can subsequently be explicated as an implicit theoretical conceptual system and revised by empirical theories. One proceeds in the same way with the conceptual system that is thereby provisionally presupposed, and so on, ad infinitum.[41] The answer to this objection is: An empirical science such as psychology would doubtless proceed in this way with regard to wishes, volitions, intentions, beliefs, and the actions corresponding to them; nothing prevents it from doing so. Philosophy, however, can and must establish a constant complementarity between the progress of empirical science, a progress that depends on the revisability of both theories and theoretical concepts and the normative conditions of the conceivability and controllability of anything like empirical theory, falsifiability, revisability, etc. These conditions can be understood a priori and are presupposed by the progress of science.[42] To return to the problem of intentional explanation, in principle, one cannot dispute the possibility of distinguishing between falsifiable theories and normative principles that are immune to falsification; the unrestricted use of the concept of "revisable empirical theory" in referring to conceptual and analytic relations does not take it seriously.[43]

At this point, Beckermann might perhaps object that talk of immunizing theories against falsification overinterprets, and thus distorts, his reservations about sharply distinguishing between conceptual-analytic distinctions and causal relations that can be grounded in empirical theory. In his view, intentional explanations interpreted in causal-theoretical terms are not absolutely immune to falsification; rather, "quasi-analytic" hypotheses about the laws to which they recur are no different, in principle, from normal empirical hypotheses about laws. Even these are not clearly falsifiable by "test propositions" in the naive sense of falsification. These "test propositions" cannot be derived from the hypotheses alone; rather, they refer to them and to an entire series of additional assumptions (for example, about testing instruments and procedures) which themselves include theoretical hypotheses.[44] Hence, from the falsification of "test propositions" it follows only "that there must be a mistake somewhere in the system of assumptions in use."[45] In principle, according to Beckermann, testing "quasi-analytic" hypotheses about laws in the case of "intentional explanations" can be conceived of in the same way.

If this is supposed to be the meaning of Beckermann's statement that $L_1$ in the schema of the "intentional explanation" of paying the telephone bill could be a "normal empirical causal law," then he seems to underestimate the seriousness of the situation in the case of the example.[46] This can be seen if we complete both it and Churchland's inference schema, which it uses. Actually, the schema of the explanans reproduced above is not sufficient to deduce that H payed his telephone bill. At least two further antecedent conditions are missing:

($A_6$) H is not prevented from paying his telephone bill.
($A_7$) H is capable of acting in a purposive-rational way.

We acquire the first of these additional conditions ($A_6$) by means of a trivial consideration—i.e., as in von Wright's inference schema—by including in the explanans the reservation "unless H is prevented" in the sense of a condition of normalcy. As Tuomela points out, one must take this step as soon as the schema of an intentional explanation is no longer viewed as the schema of a purposive-rational understanding in light of a "practical inference," but, rather, with Beckermann, as a causal, nomological explanation of an event. The premise "($A_5$) H is able to pay his telephone bill" usually is understood already to contain ($A_6$). More important is another condition of normalcy, to which Tuomela refers as well and which is also required when the schema of the "practical inference" is reinterpreted in terms of the explanation of an event. Here, I refer to the formal criterion of purposive rationality to which we refer as the minimal criterion of rationality in a good reasons-essay that makes use of the "practical inference." In the case of the causal-theoretic reinterpretation of understanding in terms of an intentional explanation of events, this normative criterion must be made explicit as an antecedent condition ($A_7$); whereas, in the case of understanding, the norm of rationality is presupposed as part of the constitution of the categorial meaning of the required cognitive achievement, in the reinterpreted case, its fulfillment must be seen as a contingent, causally effective condition and brought under control.

Given these two additions to the explanans, it is now, in fact, unimaginable that H would not pay his telephone bill. At the same time, however, it becomes clear that, in this case, the assumed laws are actually immune to falsification and that this immunity can be established a priori; hence, these laws differ from lawlike explanations that are difficult to falsify, the kind of explanations on which Beckermann perhaps focuses. At least the rationality condition cannot be established ex ante as the premise of specific predictions; that is, it is not reducible to those features of behavioral dispositions that can be identified empirically. Therefore, fundmentally it is always possible to reject a falsification of the intentional explanation of events by showing that the rationality condition was not fulfilled (in the case of complex inference schemata, this demonstration can, in a practical sense, be highly plausible).

In spite of all these arguments in favor of the LC argument, I think that Beckermann and Churchland's account of intentional explanation as a "quasi-analytic" (and, simultaneously, causal nomological explanation) contains a kernel of truth. I have criticized the "theoretical" grounding of this account; but completely independent of this grounding—indeed, precisely under the premises of a hermeneutic version of the force of the LC argument—we can see the following: The presumption of the advocates of the LC argument is that by recurring to the "quasi-analytic law ($L_1$), Beckermann's or Churchland's intentional explanation amounts to nomologically disguising a normative principle of rationality. This claim is not completely pertinent, because the successful explanation of an action as an event makes a different use of the normative principle of rationality than does purposive-rational understanding. In other words, Beckermann's example of an intentional explanation—let us say, the "event fact" that H pays his telephone bill—is not identical to a successful ex post actu "explanation" in von Wright's sense. That is, it is not the same as the empirically and hermeneutically correct understanding in which an action that is already necessarily present to the ex post perspective is seen in light of a "practical syllogism." Beckermann has done what von Wright calls dogmatic for conceptual reasons in his example of the assassin, though he admits that it "may be reasonable." In von Wright's words, he has presupposed "the validity of the practical syllogism as a standard for interpreting the situation"—which, I think, means that he has used the normative principle of rationality associated with purposive-rational understanding as an unfalsifiable yet empirically valid law. Such a procedure, however, is indisputably possible and, in a certain sense, rational. How can it be understood?

It is interesting that, to a certain extent, we can sublate the conceptual difference between normative principles and laws in an intentional explanation (i.e., one mediated by purposive-rational understanding) of an action as an event. This we accomplish by hypothetically presupposing that human beings behave rationally in the premises of the explanation. That is, we presuppose that they follow a normative principle of rationality as though, by their action, it were to be made an empirically valid universal law. Obviously this formulation alludes to one of Kant's versions of the "categorical imperative"; it is meant to indicate that, by assuming they are followed, we can make nomological and explanatory use not only of the minimal criteria of purposive rationality but of other normative principles that are set over mere purposive rationality. Insofar as we admit a corresponding premise of rationality into the explanans, it is true that we immunize the quasi-law against possible falsification and thereby provide a kind of justification for discussion of disguising a normative principle as a law. An explanation of this sort, however, remains meaningful insofar as one can understand it as a (more or less counterfactual) anticipation of an "ideal law" that human beings ought to realize or put into effect.

Although the quasi-law is immune to falsification, since it is a normative principle in disguise, the causal explanation that uses this normative principle as a law is not absolutely immune to falsification. It can prove empirically true; this may often be the case in simple explanations of action events mediated by purposive-rational understanding.[47] In these cases the explanation has successfully anticipated the empirical-nomological validity of a normative principle of rationality. Nevertheless, it can be falsified indirectly if we find ourselves required to deny that the rationality premise has been fulfilled. In this case, the intentional, causal explanation is exposed as a counterfactual anticipation of an "ideal law." At the same time, we are presented with the task of giving an empirical explanation for the divergence of the actual action from the rational norm which is not falsified as such. More precisely, we must both clarify this divergence by uncovering reasons and explain it causally as a predictable event.

At this point I want to make the following supposition. We have seen that human actions involve unfalsifiable normative principles that can also be considered ideal laws. Further, realization of these laws can be successfully or unsuccessfully anticipated in such a way that the question arises why the rational norm was not followed or why the ideal law was not realized. This circumstance may be the foundation for the fact that, in the realm of culture as opposed to nature—i.e., in the world still to be realized by human beings—it is not only hopeless but absolutely meaningless to search for universal and contingent laws, in Hume's sense. From the Stoics to Kant, Schelling, Hegel, and Peirce, the possibility of ultimate identification of the categorial structures of universal laws and universal principles of rationality has been recognized. It is precisely this identification that Churchland and Beckermann implicitly use and that speaks against scientistic reductionism. This means that a law-governed rationalization of the universe can be conceived, if at all, only as the possibility *assigned* to human beings of forming "habits of action" (Peirce).[48]

The scientific correlate of this practical task of realizing norms as ideal laws seems to be one of reconstructing human history as the history of divergences from ideal norms. Such a reconstruction must be a critical-hermeneutic one, that is, one that is appropriate both normatively and empirically. At the same time, it includes the task of a causal explanation of the occurrence of the events of human history, an explanation that can be either hermeneutically mediated or, in the case of that which can no longer be understood, naturalistically and nomologically mediated. In attempting such a historical reconstruction, we first encounter the sociocultural norms or systems of rules that are interesting from a social scientific or historical perspective and that include the contingent institutions or conventions of religion, custom, law, art, economy, style, sport, and so forth. On the one hand, as rules that are more or less consistently followed, these offer the intelligible reasons for human actions and thus, in principle, can be legitimated or criticized. On the other hand, as regularities—for example, dispositions to behavior—they supply quasi-laws that permit at least statistically relevant, quasi-causal explanations of historically and culturally determined behavior. There are cases in which even an understanding or quasi-causal explanation of action in light of such a system of rules (which, as culturally determined regularities, represent a human quasi-nature) is no longer possible, as in the case of behavior that is clearly pathological. There are also instances in which this understanding or quasi-causal explanation is unsatisfactory because of universal invariances in behavior. Here, we can look at the residual instinctual gestures that are the theme of ethology or at anthropologically universal structures that are also contingent, such as the conditions of linguistic competence as delineated by Chomsky and Lenneberg. Only in these cases, however, will we recur to purely universal laws of human nature, even though any complete explanation of an event of human action naturally presupposes these laws as a *conditiones sine quibus non.*

We now turn to Tuomela's subsumption-theoretic reinterpretation of teleological-intentional action.

## 4.5 Tuomela's Revision of von Wright's Schema of Teleological or Intentional Explanation

Tuomela proposes the following "amended version" of von Wright's schema of the "practical inference" as a way of allowing its logical cogency as a "theoretical explanation":

($P_1$) From now on, A intends to bring about $p$ at time $t$.
($P_2$) From now on, A considers that unless he does $a$ no later than at time $t'$, he cannot bring about $p$ at time $t$.
($P_3$) "Normal conditions" obtain between now and $t'$.
(L) For any agent A, action $a$, and time $t$, if A from now on intends to realize $p$ at $t$, and considers the doing of $a$ not later than $t'$ necessary for this, and if "normal conditions" obtain between now and $t'$, then A will do $a$ no later than when he thinks time $t'$ has arrived.
(C) No later than he thinks time $t'$ has arrived, A does $a$.[49]

Given what has been said about the possibility of inserting the "practical inference" in an explanation of an event that can be tested prognostically, the meaning of this alteration of von Wright's schema is self-explanatory:

According to Tuomela, the additional premise ($P_3$) contains the "unless he is prevented" clause that von Wright placed in the conclusion. I hypothesized that he did so because it has nothing to do with either the understandable decision (or intention transfer) that A makes on the basis of the "practical inference" or the insistence on that decision. Hence, von Wright denies that the clause belongs in the explanans of an "intentional explanation." In a prognostically testable explanation of an event, however, the clause is causally relevant, and naturally it belongs in the explanans. Accordingly, Tuomela also changes the conclusion, replacing "sets himself" with "does."

Tuomela argues that, in addition to this not-prevented clause, ($P_3$) also contains certain ceteris paribus conditions not made explicit by von Wright in his schema:

(1) A then had no other goal $p'$ which he preferred to $p$; and (2) there was no other action $a'$, also necessary for $p$, such that A preferred $a'$ (or rather $a'$, together with its various consequences) to $a$ (with its consequences).[50]

According to Tuomela, these conditions indicate that von Wright's schema of the "practical inference" already represents an abstract simplification of the complexity of human decision-making situations insofar as agents normally pursue many goals and believe they know many competing ways or means of reaching them.[51] Finally, among ceteris paribus conditions, Tuomela mentions a special assumption regarding the rationality of the agent, "so that, e.g., his present emotional state or his having an Oedipal complex or his miscalculations should not disturb his deliberation."[52] I have already pointed out that this crucial innovation says that the principle of rationality implied in the "practical inference" is now to be used in a theoretical and explanatory manner, as opposed to a hermeneutic one; the normative standard of understanding becomes a quasi-dispositional causal factor.

In his reply to Tuomela, von Wright remarks that his amendment makes sense only if the first and second premises are also changed, so that "one could allow for a time-interval between the intention and cognitive attitude, on the one hand, and the execution of the action, on the other hand," and thereby allow room for the intervention of "factors of an 'irrational' character."[53] Apparently von Wright precludes such a possibility from the beginning by means of the formula "from now on," that is, by supposing that the conditions of the "practical inference" remain true. Here, I want to return to the objection made above. Either von Wright's version of the LC argument makes the "from now on" formula superfluous—indeed, meaningless, since, in principle, it is not possible to verify the duration of unchanged beliefs or intentions independently of the action itself (to this extent, it is evident that von Wright's schema is not that of a prognostically testable explanation of events; hence, within his account, a special premise regarding the agent's rationality makes no sense); or, if the beliefs and intentions are to form the volitional-cognitive complex of an intentional explanation of events, in a certain sense it is possible to identify them independently of the action to be expected. In this case, the rationality condition seems necessary and meaningful even if one presupposes the "from now on" clause; for, to the extent that an independent identification of goal intentions and beliefs about means is at all possible, establishing the duration of these conditions no longer can guarantee the inference in the sense of the rationality of the "practical syllogism." Goal intentions, beliefs about means, and the rationality of the agent must now be seen as quasi-dispositions of the agent, and they must be established independently of each other and of the action to be expected. In fact, we have good reason to suppose that the causal efficacy of intentions, beliefs, and rationality (if it can already be assumed, as, I think, we cannot doubt) must be mediated by inherent dispositions.

In my view, this last reflection also indicates how, regardless of the LC argument, one must conceive of the possibility of an independent identification of goal intentions and beliefs about means such that they function as antecedent conditions in a quasi-causal explanation of actions as events.

I have already suggested that von Wright's way of substantiating the LC argument is not completely satisfactory for the empirical scientist, and I can now explain this more precisely. Nevertheless, we must first consider Tuomela's analysis of the law $(L_1)$ that forms the basis of the transformation of von Wright's schema into a subsumption-theoretic explanation.

Tuomela sees at once that the "law" $(L_1)$ is not contingent and that the intentional explanation to be subsumed under it represents a covering-law explanation only "in a Pickwickian sense."[54] He continues with the interesting interpretation that his "amended version" of the "practical syllogism" therefore deals only with an "idealized agent." Moreover, the "idealized reconstruction" of the internal relations within our "commonsense conceptual system" implied here can be compared with Chomsky's distinction between the linguistic competence of the ideal speaker-hearer and actual performance. In light of this distinction, Tuomela comes closer to transforming the schema of intentional-teleological explanation into an empirical, relevant, "covering law" explanation of human action.

He admits that the study of "competence" aids the understanding of action insofar as we can understand "an agent's actual deliberation" as the instantiation of the "conceptual structure defined by our above schema of the practical syllogism."[55] (Tuomela seems to mean his "amended version." Nevertheless, I would emphasize that the subsumption-theoretic transformation of the schema is neither necessary nor relevant to understanding in light of the practical syllogism.) By citing the reason imputed to the action, such an understanding already places it "in a larger culture-dependent setting of goals, values, norms and other standards together with some accompanying beliefs and opinions".[56]

In the spirit of Tuomela, I would add that the culturally dependent standards and conventional rules of behavior are also already to be considered intelligible reasons for following or diverging from the principles of purposive rationality. One need only think of Max Weber's concrete analyses of the way Catholic and Protestant ethics impede or accelerate the modern "rationalization" of strategic economic action. On the sociohistoric level, but still in the sense of hermeneutic understanding, the theme of these analyses is the habitualization of "performance," as opposed to ideal "competence." Nevertheless, for Tuomela, understanding in terms of ideal competences is insufficient as an explanatory theory of "performance," i.e., the "actual behavior and dispositions to behave of blood-and-flesh agents." If I understand him correctly, Tuomela wants to transform the "noncontingent" "quasi-law" (L) into an empirical and explanatorily relevant law (L') by replacing the condition of rationality (which cannot be operationalized through any "finite list" of empirically identifiable dispositions) with a specific list of assumptions about empirical dispositions. This list comprises assumptions about a person's "know-how," general abilities, personality traits, skills, and emotions, as well as assumptions about the relation between the psychological features of a person's system of knowledge, for example, and the natural and social world.[57] Tuomela also assumes that every person has internalized a particular society's system of norms.[58] Hence, at least according to his conception, the specific list of an agent's dispositions in (L') can be supplemented with dispositions not specific to personality in any psychologically relevant sense; rather, they are role-specific in a sociologically relevant sense.

Within the context of our investigation, a crucial question now arises with regard to this final transformation of von Wright's inference schema: whether or to what extent the schema shows that teleological-intentional explanation is not only a special form of causal explanation but also a covering-law explanation in Hempel's sense when it serves as a theoretical-conclusive explanation, i.e., wherever it serves as a prognostically testable answer to the question why an action occurs. On the one hand, Tuomela denies that the empirically and explanatorily relevant law (L') is "a generalization with a high degree of lawlikeness."[59] Apparently there are two reasons for this denial: *First*, the generalization refers to a relation between actions and "wants, desires, duties and other related conative attitudes." The relation can therefore be understood as internal or "quasi-analytic." *Second*, Tuomela fundamentally assumes that wants and other quasi-natural dispositions can be over-ruled by the free choice constitutive of intentions. He emphasizes, however, that "any (for the scientist) 'concretely usable' version (L')" is a synthetic generalization insofar as "the question of what specific (teleological) conceptual frame a given society has internalized is not merely an a priori or a merely conceptual problem."[60]

In view of the question posed, Tuomela's position is ambiguous, and thus is unsatisfactory at a crucial point. It is not clear how he understands the step from the "noncontingent" (L) to the "contingent" (L') that depends on replacing the condition of rationality with dis-positions that can be established empirically. That is, it is not clear whether this is to be seen as at least an approximation of a covering-law explanation according to the model of natural science. It seems to me that the ground of this ambiguity is that the talk of "synthetic" or "contingent" generalizations or laws is itself ambiguous.

On the one hand, normative principles conceived of as laws and natural laws in the sense of empirically falsifiable hypotheses differ in that the former must be understandable in conceptual-analytic terms, whereas the latter must be assumed synthetic, hence, epistemologically contingent. On the other hand, both real natural laws and principles of rationality used as laws are assumed to be universally valid. (The possibility I presupposed above of an anticipatory identification of the structure of rational norms and laws consists in just this aspect of universal validity.) Now, however, the contingency of empirically es-tablished rules rests on the independence of sociocultural forms of life. Hence, even if they are generalized by (L') as a contingent gen-eralization, this contingency is in no way analogous to the contingency of natural laws; for, in the social or cultural sciences, even regularities that are relevant to empirical causal explanations because they are falsifiable can be understood to be unnecessary. They are not definitive regulations; thus, in principle, they can be legitimated or criticized. In the sphere of action, the only rule-dependent regularities that no longer seem relativizable as socioculturally determined regularities are those that can no longer be conceived as contingent or falsifiable. These are the normative principles of rationality.

From the viewpoint of "methodological unity," one could object that it is also impossible in the natural sciences to know whether a law is universally valid or whether it is simply a regionally valid reg-ularity based on a law yet to be discovered. The response to this is,

I think, as follows: In natural science, if one reckons with the possibility of relativizing laws in the above sense, then one reckons with the derivability, in principle, of all regularities from boundary conditions and universally valid laws, in the formulation of which no proper names or distinguishing marks need appear. This is not the case with regard to regularities that are socioculturally conditioned and that can be presupposed in hermeneutically mediated, causal explanations. Before these can be conceived of scientifically as regularities, they are already understood as culturally relevant rules, not laws which, possibly, are universal. Hence, they can be formulated only by recourse to proper names and specific distinguishing marks. This holds, for example, for the hermeneutically mediated causal explanation of the maxims of behavior for Japanese samurai or for those of a Jesuit missionary of the seventeenth century, of a Calvinist silk merchant from Lyon before the lifting of the tolerance edict, or the rules a German or English judge or prosecutor must follow in performing his professional duties.

Moreover—and this seems to me the strongest counterargument—we cannot overlook the problem of how the rule-dependent regularities of human cultural life are to be derived from contingent universal laws and the boundary conditions assigned by these laws. On the one hand, such regularities can be considered universally valid if the boundary conditions of the action can be explicated without using proper names or distinguishing marks. In this case, they can be grounded only in universal but noncontingent principles of rationality, of which they are the situational application. On the other hand, such regularities must be considered contingent where they cannot be grounded in rational principles, even if all special conditions of the situation are taken into account. In this case, they are always already understood as deviations from the universally valid principles of rationality that can be presupposed as the ideal laws of human action. These deviations can themselves be understood in one of two ways: It may still be possible to see them as applications of rational norms in the context of violations of other norms as, for example, in the case of an error resulting from misapplied rules of inference or in the case of a strategy of self-deception or the deception of others. Or one can assume that wherever human action violates rational principles in the widest sense—whether in the logical-cognitive or the ethical sphere—purely contingent laws of human "first" nature have enforced themselves by means of the contingent regularities of the socially and historically sedimented quasi-nature. This would be the case in individual or collective regression.

Let us assume that the human determination Kant thought could be accomplished only in the history of the species consists in realizing the principles of rationality as ideal laws of human "second nature." Then we cannot but consider the scientistic ideal, the notion of universal contingent laws of a possible causal explanation of human action, as a way of supporting total regression on the part of human beings. Suppose, also, that scientism's mental reservation is that, nonetheless, a progressive rational science of causal explanation should still be possible as a human project in the sense of realizing human "second nature." Then one can see the notion of the pure, causal lawlikeness of social scientific explanations only as a paradox.

I doubt that anything essential changes if the idea of causal lawlikeness is liberalized in terms of probabilistic lawlikeness. Scientism is still paradoxical. Even if probabilistic laws of human behavior were compatible with freedom of choice in the individual case, as universal contingent laws, they still would not be compatible with the thought of either real behavioral innovations, in the sense of progressive science, or the progressive cultural human history that this presupposes.[61] Hence, it cannot be the case that the reasoned intentions—in the light of which we can understand human action—represent only the limit case of dispositions that allow explanation of human actions in terms of probabilistic laws.[62]

A heuristic view of empirical social science is, of course, not only conceivable but obvious. According to this view, empirical social science is not primarily interested in understanding good or bad reasons for human action, nor in an empirically and normatively appropriate reconstruction of human history in light of the possible realization of normative principles of rationality. Rather, it is primarily or exclusively interested in which good or bad reasons or intentions are causally effective dispositions—that is, in which ones determine the actual average behavior of human beings in specific societies or at specific social levels in a prognostically relevant form. To this extent we can, in fact, treat intentions as limit cases of dispositions within the framework of subsumption-theoretic, causal, or probabilistic explanations. From the standpoint of the logic of science, this position cannot be contested, since (a) it leads to results that are empirically true and (b) within the logic of science, the cognitive interests presupposed in the inquiry count as prescientific and contingent from an empirical-pragmatic point of view. In light of our philosophical reflections, however, one cannot help noticing that those social scientists who view reasoned and understandable intentions as merely the limit case of dispositions are interested in the "reification" of human action in terms of the human quasi-nature that is historically sedimented at any given tine.[63] This fact cannot be considered using the logic of science; hence, just as I objected to an explication of explanation and understanding that abstracts from the pragmatic dimension of acts of synthetic knowledge, so I question the epistemological relevance of an abstract logic of science of this kind.

With this objection I come to the final section of my investigation. In it, I attempt to explicate the result of the third round of the E-V controversy, and to do so in light of expanding the epistemological foundations of the theory of science.

# III

## Results of the
## Critical Reconstruction of
## the Third Round of
## the Explanation-Understanding
## Controversy

# Introduction to Part III

At this point let us attempt to answer the questions with which we began our investigation of the third round of the E-V controversy. We start with the second question, concerning the upshot of this third round as it was fought by von Wright and the defenders of the subsumption-theoretic model of causal explanation.

In a certain formalistic sense—one, however, that the defenders of the modern logic of science consider constitutive of the "context of justification"—we can say that the schema of subsumption-theoretic causal explanation associated with Hempel's model of a unified methodology has victoriously achieved a monopoly. If one wants an "explanation," in Hempel's sense—that is, an answer to the question why an event occurs or does not occur—the answer must produce the subsumption-theoretic form of a causal explanation. This necessity applies as well to the case of *action* events wherever explanations of them are possible. In this sense, the jurisdiction of Hempel's D-N model has been confirmed by recent writers concerned to explain human behavior in light of the normative systems of rules in the sense Dilthey and Hegel have called "objective spirit." As I think our discussion has shown, even von Wright's model of "intentional" or "teleological" explanation is not justified if it attempts to compete with Hempel's model in answering the why-question he presupposes with regard to actions.

Nevertheless, we should recall everything we have said about the ambiguity in von Wright's model and about the scientific restriction on the meaning of the preconception of "explanation." It would be absolutely wrong to conclude from the formalistic monopolization by the subsumption-theoretic model of explaining events that the neo-Wittgensteinian approach is proven false, or indeed, that the Geisteswissenschaften's claim to methodological autonomy is contradicted by the conception of methodological unity. Rather, what is suggested, it seems to me, is that we should question the epistemological presuppositions under which the third round of the E-V controversy was conducted. This applies especially to the scientistic side, but, to a great extent, to the neo-Wittgensteinian side as well; for our critical reconstruction of this most recent debate has made evident that we cannot give a clear, positive answer even to our initial question whether the neo-Wittgensteinian approach adequately reflects the motives and interests of the hermeneutic philosophy of the Geisteswissenschaften.

The neo-Wittgensteinian strategy that von Wright pursued (or, more exactly, the strategy he pursued in the third chapter of *Explanation and Understanding*) at least could not radically question the premises of the subsumption-theoretic model of causal explanation. Therefore, the strategy could not make it clear that the methodological claim of the hermeneutic tradition does not amount to a competing model for explaining events but, rather, defends the method of *Verstehen* as the answer to a different question, one possible only in the Geisteswissenschaften. Thus, we cannot avoid the conclusion that the discussion of "alternative models of explanation" is similar to the earlier discussion between Hempel and Dray, in that it reflects a frustrating and unselfconscious confrontation between fundamentally different preconceptions of explanation. More to the point, we lack a definitive resolution of the issues disputed in the E-V controversy, for two reasons. On the one hand, there has been insufficient recognition of the partial accuracy of the Hempelian monopolization of the subsumption-theoretic model of explaining events in general. On the other hand, the source of the illegitimacy of Hempel's claim (which already amounted to a *petitio principii* in the discussion with Dray) has not been clarified sufficiently. This source lies in the fact that, in the final analysis, the claim of methodological unity ignores that cognitive interest in hermeneutic understanding that is possible and necessary only in the human sciences.

In spite of these reservations, I believe that von Wright's neo-Wittgensteinian approach (and especially the pragmatic foundation he develops in the second chapter of *Explanation and Understanding*) can contribute to genuine resolution of the central problem of the E-V controversy. For this resolution it is necessary to cast doubt on the highly abstract, logico-semantic method of explicating "scientific systematizations" that is characteristic of the prevailing logic of science.

# 1
## Resolution of the Controversy: Forms of Inquiry and Cognitive Interests

### 1.1 The Inadequacy of the Logico-semantic Explication of Synthetic Acts of Knowledge

I want to formulate the principal objection to the formalistic over-evaluation of the monopoly of the subsumption-theoretic form of explaining events and to its failure to acknowledge the actual interest of hermeneutics. As we have seen, the logico-semantic method of explicating "scientific systematizations" focuses on these in abstraction from "merely pragmatic," contextual presuppositions such as the kind of inquiry and cognitive interest of the subject of knowledge. This strategy does not give epistemological reflection the room to explicate synthetic acts of the knowledge, such as explanation and understanding, as answers to kinds of inquiry that may differ from one another. In neither the case of the causal explanation that supplies the paradigm for a unified methodology nor in the methodical, disciplined under-standing intended in hermeneutics does this strategy provide an ex-plication of the categorial preconception of hypothesis-construction. This preconception, however, represents the condition of the possibility of both causal analytic and hermeneutically relevant acts of knowledge; it does so, on the one hand, in the sense of the experimentally verifiable nomological and causal necessity of state alterations within sufficiently closed systems and, on the other hand, in the sense, for example, of the understandable reasons (intentions and beliefs) of virtual co-subjects that can be adapted to the schema of a "practical inference."

With regard to causal explanation, the significance of this objection to the logico-semantic method of explication becomes clear if one recalls that the D-N model is in no way sufficient to distinguish a real causal explanation, one relevant to natural science, from a mere "grounding" of our expectation of an event on the basis of either general symptoms or even expert information. To that extent the fact that one can also give the logical form of D-N explanation to the explanation of actions on the basis of norms of behavior typical in certain situations—i.e., on the basis of culturally specific and institutionalized systems of norms and beliefs—can say nothing from a methodological standpoint and can therefore be misleading. An explication of the presumed synthetic act of knowledge (produced to answer a specific question) can show that the condition of its possibility does not lie in the categorial preconception of the causal nomological necessity of a connection between events but rather in the preconception of hermeneutic understanding that refers to intelligible reasons.

For example, suppose we want to "explain" Cleopatra's suicide by snake bite. We assume she wanted to die in order to avoid being taken prisoner by Octavius and to evade the disgrace of being presented in the Romans' triumphal parade. We first make her choice of method comprehensible by referring to the Egyptians' religious tradition; then we construct a causal explanation of the event that uses both her intention to die and become immortal and her religious beliefs as a volitional-cognitive causal complex. In addition, this causal explanation presupposes a lawlike premise according to which all Egyptian queens wanting desperately to die and at the same time become immortal choose death by snake bite. It is now clear that in this case, as well as countless similar cases of "historical explanations," only two procedures are methodologically relevant to the historian (1) hermeneutic mediation of the person's possible motives achieved by interpreting the available source material on the political situation and the cultural tradition; and (2) verification of the hermeneutic accuracy of the explanatory interpretation of the act of suicide. Testing psychological theories about the motivation behind the suicide by observing similar cases is not included. From the standpoint of the theory of science, the obvious explication of this kind of explanation is that it is not a prognostically relevant, subsumption-theoretic explanation of an event, but, rather, an ex post actu understanding in light of a "practical syllogism" that is possible only from the historian's perspective. Therefore it has the character of a quasi-causal explanation of an event only because, from an ex post perspective, action whose meaning has been correctly understood must also actually have occurred. Indeed, as I have tried to show, this is precisely the point of von Wright's model of explanation (even though it is not corroborated by the form of the conclusion to the inference schema that uses the present tense).

Given an ex post actu understanding of the meaning of the historical action, it may be possible to construct a case of subsumption-theoretic causal explanation by distilling a lawlike premise from the historical background of the motives involved. In most cases, however, this construction reflects a procedure of methodologically parasitic hypostatization that, frankly, is comical. The historian may contribute much to a better understanding of actions on the basis of methodical hermeneutic procedures applied to reasons, goals, beliefs, and norms or maxims; the logician of science, however, simply uses them to compose the volitional-cognitive, causal complexes and regionally restricted quasi-laws, on the basis of which he constructs the subsumption-theoretic causal explanations of unified science and tests them in empirical observation. In this process he must always silently assume that even in the critical analysis of sources one can equate the historian's *communicatively mediated* empiricism with empirical observation in general, an assumption I believe is either false or inconsequential. This small study indicates the fatal significance of the presumption to which representatives of methodological unity subscribe: that *Verstehen* is not a cognitive achievement associated with a method but, rather, a psychological-heuristic presupposition for discovering explanatory hypotheses. As we have seen, this presumption reduces understanding to the element of "empathy" that actually belongs to the hermeneutic, cognitive achievement as the specific moment of sensuousness.

To be sure, we can cite counterexamples to the cases of ex post actu explanation already recounted. In these cases an explication which shows that the act of knowledge is a subsumption-theoretic causal explanation cannot be dismissed as an additional, parasitic construction, even though the explanation of the event of action is mediated by an intentional-explanatory, purposive-rational understanding. This is the case, for example, when it is possible successfully to anticipate the validity of normative principles of rationality, and hence, to use them as laws for prognostically relevant, causal explanations of human behavior. This could well be possible in modern industrial society with regard to the domain of economic and technical action, in which purposive rationality is assumed; but it may also be possible in the normally functioning systems or spheres of nonstrategic human interaction with regard to certain universal norms of moral reciprocity one necessarily acknowledges if one is ready to enter into communicative processes of coming to an understanding. Ultimately we can reduce the general structure of such subsumption-theoretic causal explanations and predictions to the commonsense truth that, if we can understand the rationality of the way in which our fellow human beings behave, we can rely on their behaving in this way.

Such conversion of understanding into the explanation and prediction of events is also possible because of the contingent, institutionalized, or habitualized rules and conventions of forms of social life, rules, and conventions that form the historically sedimented quasi-nature of human beings at a cross section of time and within delimited regions. The conversion not only is possible with regard to behavioral norms compatible with the normative principles of rationality, insofar as they represent the substantive specification of such principles in specific situations, it is possible as well with regard to behavioral norms that contradict norms rational in the widest sense, which block the latter's realization. At this point it is no longer possible to dispute the methodological uniqueness of the subsumption-theoretic causal explanations that occur in the social sciences. This uniqueness consists in the fact that the possibility of understanding the actions of virtual co-subjects in light of good reasons now possesses, at most, only a heuristic character. For prognostically relevant explanations, only one aspect of the (good or bad) reasons counts, and that is their causal efficacy in the quasi-nomological context of institutionalized or habitualized rules of behavior. Empirical research in such possibilities of explaining human behavior ultimately must refer to the present, since the test of validity is mediated through prognosis. Hence, ethnological, anthropological, and historical investigation of motives and culturally relative rules of behavior can be viewed as collecting examples and counterexamples to confirm psychological and sociopsychological theories about motivation.

From a certain perspective, given the standard point of view, forms of behavior in archaically structured primitive cultures offer especially propitious material for testing the theoretical-explanatory theories of the empirical social and behavioral sciences. The communicative relation between these cultures and the scientific civilization of the researchers that study them is relatively one-sided; hence, over an extended period of time, something like a quasi-natural, scientific, subject-object relation often is produced, which makes it possible to verify particular predictions, using controlled and reproducible tests. Here, however, the basic condition of experimental, causal analysis is the existence of a sufficiently closed object-system, and in modern industrial society that is difficult to achieve because of the distorting effects of self-fulfilling and -denying prophecies: the subject-object of the modern behavioral sciences suffers an inconvenient reaction to conversion of communicatively mediated understanding of motives into prognostically relevant, theoretically oriented causal explanations. To a certain extent these reactions provide a corrective counter-movement to scientistic reification and historical abstraction.

Now, however, how can we understand or adequately ground these facts from the standpoint of the theory of science? On the one hand, in the case of the human sciences and only in that case, an ostensibly causal explanation styled along subsumption-theoretic lines can obscure the methodologically relevant cognitive act of purposive-rational understanding; whereas, on the other, it is possible to perform a methodologically relevant, subsumption-theoretic conversion of purposive-rational understanding into a merely heuristically relevant act, preparatory to a quasi-natural scientific causal explanation. Thus, from a methodological standpoint, the question is: How is it possible for the human and social sciences to include hermeneutic as well as quasi-nomological and causal-analytic research orientations?

## 1.2 Expansion of the Epistemological Foundations of the Theory of Science in the Direction of a Transcendental Pragmatics

It seems to me that, to answer the question just posed, it is essential to reflect on a situation which neither the logico-semantic method of explication nor the neo-Wittgensteinian onto-semantic conception of the dualism in language games even acknowledges, much less clarifies. Neither school sees that the human sciences differ from the natural sciences (or, at least, from physics) precisely insofar as they offer a methodologically different starting point for efforts to gain knowledge.

Strictly taken, the logico-semantic way of explicating the neopositivist logic of sciences (i.e., the explication that abstracts from the pragmatic dimension of acts of knowledge) can focus only on the deductive (or inductive-probabilistic) relation between explanans and explanandum, which it sees as the *conditio sine qua non* of an adequate explication of "scientific systematizations." It therefore overlooks the conditions of the relevance of all synthetic acts of knowledge. It overlooks the condition of the relevance of causal explanation itself insofar as it is unable to elucidate the difference between (1) a scientifically innovative explanation and a prediction that represents only the deductive application of this explanation; (2) real universal laws and pseudonomological general propositions; or (3) real, universal laws in general, and causal laws. Nevertheless, in spite of abstracting from the pragmatic dimension, in absolutizing its intention with regard to methodological unity—that is, in absolutizing its intention to make either strong or weak causal explanations paradigmatic—it silently absolutizes one possible interest that human beings take in knowledge. The interest in natural sciences or physics seems to be given a monopoly as the only possible scientific form of inquiry. To this extent, even in its late phase of formalistic asceticism, neopositivism perpetuates a scientific prejudice that blocks the progress of enlightenment in the theory of science.

For its part, the neo-Wittgensteinian onto-semantic conception believes that it can ground a clear differentiation of mutually exclusive conceptual frameworks on the basis of the logical analysis of language games. This differentiation is both ontological and a feature of the theory of science. It distinguishes between the nomological, causal explanation of (natural) events, on the one hand, and the intentional-teleological explanation of actions, on the other, and it may be supplemented by an equivalent distinction between laws and rules or norms. Under favorable contextual presuppositions, such a differentiation may be able to explicate the ideal-typical distinction between causal explanation and the hermeneutic understanding of action in an appropriate way; but it thereby remains fundamentally exposed to the temptation to confuse hermeneutic understanding with an explanatory act of a peculiar kind, one that arises from the theoretical subject-object relation of "science" in the same way that causal explanation does. Accordingly, it fails to see that hermeneutic understanding is to be comprehended in the context of practically relevant communication, and lapses into the unsuccessful strategy of offering a quasi-hermeneutic model to compete with Hempel's model for explaining events. Because of this strategy of alternative models of explanation, it is difficult if not impossible for neo-Wittgensteinians to recognize either the special causality of human intentions and choices of action or the possibility of a quasi-natural science of human action that treats the understanding of reasons, norms, and maxims simply as a heuristic aid for discovering causal effective dispositions and quasi-nomological regularities.

Consideration of the restrictions characteristic of the conceptual approaches of both adversaries in the third round of the E-V controversy is preliminary to what I now wish to accomplish. In what follows I shall recall an insight to which I have already referred. I shall attempt to show the validity of a transcendental-pragmatic expansion of the epistemological foundations of the theory of science as a way to resolve the problems we have discussed.[1]

We begin with the perspective of the logico-semantic method of explicating explanation as "scientific systematizations." In terms of semiotics and the logic of relations, one can characterize the approach of transcendental pragmatics as one that expands the two-place expression of a relation, "$x$ explains $y$" into the three-place expression "$x$ explains $y$ for the subject of knowledge $z$." This expansion, however, is not to be understood as an empirical pragmatics of the subjective context of cognitive achievements, so that, for example, one would have to discriminate between the different everyday explanations for schoolchildren, members of different professions, and social groups or cultures. Rather, the expansion is based, in principle, on the three-place character of the sign relation (Peirce), and thus on linguistically mediated acts of knowledge. Thus we go back to the subjective context in which explanations and other acts of knowledge are interpreted only insofar as they contain the subjective-intersubjective conditions of the possibility of constituting both the meaning of forms of human inquiry and, therefore, the possible meaning of cognitive achievements in general, as answers to forms of inquiry. In the present context it is important to note among meaning-constitutive conditions especially the "knowledge-constitutive interests" that can be presumed to be interwoven with language games and forms of ongoing practice in ideal-typical ways.[2] My argument is that these ideal-typical connections between cognitive interests, language games, and forms of ongoing practice can be considered the transcendental-pragmatic conditions of the constitution of the world of experience, and that they go beyond the forms or functions of the pure contemplation and pure understanding presupposed by Kant's transcendental idealism. This argument must be valid if the constitution of anything like "meaning" or of the categorial viewpoints for possible inquiries is to be made intelligible to human beings; a pure consciousness can win no meaning from the world. Nevertheless, although this consideration of the anthropologically contingent factors within the transcendental function goes beyond Kant's "transcendental psychology," it is not concerned with the causes that advance or impede cognitive enterprises; those are, rather, the subject of research for an external, empirical psychology or sociology of science. Instead, it is concerned with the internal reasons or grounds of the possibility of substantive and significant knowledge.

## 1.3 The Kernel of Truth in Post-Wittgensteinian New Dualism: The Complementarity between the Interest in the Theoretical Explanation of Events and the Interest in Coming to an Understanding

Introducing the pertinent context of transcendental-pragmatic conditions serves as an epistemologically relevant corrective to the abstract, logico-semantic explication of causal explanations. This argument can be illuminated as follows:

In the prescientific context of labor, interest in mastering objectified and controllable changes in the environment is tied to manipulative interference in nature. This interest takes the form of an experimental test of theoretical hypotheses in the service of scientific knowledge. To that extent it constitutes both the meaning of the categorial preconception of the why-question and the corresponding conception of the experienced world, in the sense of the causal necessity of changes in state. The idea that action is capable of bringing about changes in state by interfering in the environment is one that possesses certainty even on the prescientific level. In the framework of the natural sciences it gains precision as the concept of the capacity to manipulate objective state systems experimentally as long as they are sufficiently closed to external disturbances. In this way it becomes possible to overcome those neo-Humean elements in the neopositivist explication of causal explanation that make it impossible to distinguish between empirically well-confirmed regularities and real causal laws.

In the second chapter of *Explanation and Understanding*, von Wright develops a theory that shows in detail that the concept of causal necessity presupposes the concept of interventionist action. I interpret this theory in transcendental-pragmatic terms. I think it implicitly illuminates the possibility of a transcendental-pragmatic foundation for the well-documented New Dualism of causal explanation and the understanding of action. I also think this foundation differs in an epistemologically significant way from the foundation of the distinction between causal and teleological explanation von Wright himself presupposes and elucidates in Chapter III of his book. This thesis requires more precise elucidation if von Wright's book is to be evaluated critically.

Let us assume that on the level of experimental science, the notion that action can manipulate objective state systems in nature, provided they are sufficiently closed to outside disturbances, is a necessary premise for constituting the concept of the causal necessity of changes of state in nature. (This means it is necessary to constituting the categorial preconception of possible causal explanations as synthetic acts of knowledge.) If this is correct, the causal explanation of natural events presupposes an understanding of experimental action, which implies that the causal explanation of natural events presupposes agreement (*Sichverständigung*) among scientists as to the grounds (i.e., goals and assumptions) of experimental action.

In contrast to the situation of prescientific action, the case of experimental science involves the following complication.[3] The scientist's grounds and goals involve a desire for knowledge. They are not identical with the immediate reasons and goals of experimental actions that are placed in the service of knowledge. In other words, an experiment successful in the sense of testing hypotheses is not the same as an interventionist action successful in the prescientific sense—in terms of technology and labor. Rather, as an experiment with positive or negative results, the former always already presupposes the latter. This circumstance has implications for the categorial preconception of the causal necessity of state alterations that can be brought about in nature, that is, for the categorial presupposition that belongs to the preunderstanding of every experiment. It presupposes the possibility of a two-part agreement on the part of scientists with regard to aims and grounds. First, it presupposes that they can agree on the goal of interventionist actions that must be successful in technically "bringing about" natural effects if experimental questions are to be posed to nature (one could say, if such questions are to be translated into the language of nature in order to make nature answer human questions). Second, it presupposes that, given the goal of knowledge, they can agree on the assumptions to be made with regard to the causal behavior of nature (including that of the instruments employed in the experiment). This means, however, that they must be able to agree on the possible effect of actions that must be unequivocal and successful insofar as they "do" something, but that must remain undetermined insofar as they "bring something about" (in the words of von Wright).

This complication alters no aspect of the situation that results when nature gives the answers presupposed and expected by a theory. In this situation an experimentally mediated "bringing about of something" is made possible which—as a natural, scientifically mediated technique—forms a continuum with interventionist action that is successful on the prescientific level. For its part, if we exclude such basic actions as arm-raising, this interventionist action can already be mediated by quasi-experiments and a corresponding investigation of their success. For this reason one can simply say that scientific, causal explanation presupposes the purposive-rational understanding of technical interventionist actions in relation to nature. Moreover, because it is necessary to explicate the understanding of action linguistically, and because one person alone therefore cannot do experimental science (by, for example, making all virtual co-subjects into objects of causal explanation), one can claim the following: Something like a consensus with regard to technical action, and associated with symbolically mediated interaction, belongs to the subjective and intersubjective conditions of the possibility of causal explanation.

This presupposition of reaching understanding or agreement can be characterized as the transcendental-hermeneutic precondition of experimental natural science. Hence, in renewing the transcendental-pragmatic and transcendental-hermeneutic conditions of the language game in which natural events are causally explained, we discover as well the phenomenological horizon of the necessary premise of a complementary language game, that of the purposive-rational understanding of technical actions. This language game presupposes another type of action: communicative action and the nontheoretical, nonobjective form of communicative experience of symbols belonging to it. With Grice, we include under this type of action not only actions whose reasons co-subjects can understand but actions that can be constituted only in the reciprocal relation of subject and co-subject.

At this point I want to try to establish the relation between our transcendental-pragmatic explication and that of the neo-Wittgensteinians. The neo-Wittgensteinians conceive of the phenomenon of different language games or conceptual frameworks in purely language-analytic terms. Moreover, as far as I can see, they interpret them onto-semantically as different, theoretical object domains. My approach grasps the phenomenon from a unitary perspective, as the general phenomenon of complementary conceptual frameworks for aspects of the world, whereby *complementary* means that they both supplement and exclude one another. Only one of these aspects of the world can be the object of theoretical science; in contrast, the other necessarily possesses the value and function of a subjective-intersubjective presupposition of theoretical science, a presupposition to be seen in transcendental-pragmatic terms.

I think we can assume that this sketch of the situation of complementarity that transcendental-pragmatics considers necessary represents the absolutely fundamental situation of the categorial world understanding possible for human beings. In my view, among other things, this means: From the purely theoretical distance of pure observation, we can no longer presuppose any reflexive identification between the subject of knowledge, lived-bodily actions, and cognitive interests related to action. From this perspective, therefore, it is impossible for us to gain categorial meaning from the world. Hume attested to nothing else when he showed that if successive events are the objects of pure observation, there exists no formal-logical or categorial causal connection between them. The limit case of pure observation dissolves the connection between states of affairs in the life world that is always already preunderstood. For this reason, the science based on theoretical objectification of the world can no longer even begin to constitute the categorial meaning required to formulate questions and perform synthetic acts of knowledge. Moreover, because the modern logic of science abstracts from the transcendental-pragmatic dimension of the necessary categorial preunderstanding of knowledge and relevant theories, under its neo-Humean premises it would be hopeless to try to acquire an adequate explication of such synthetic cognitive achievements as explanation and understanding. (For example, as we have seen, it is impossible to distinguish between those general propositions of if-then statements that are relevant in causal-nomological terms and those that are not.)

The limit case of theoretical distantiation from the world, in which the tendency is to make even the bodily actions of knowing subjects into objects of observation, can claim the function only of a "switch point" in transcendental-pragmatic reflection on knowledge. For example, through its mediation, the "nonclassical theory construction" of physics is constituted; in it the categorial presuppositions of measurement and experiment indispensable for protophysics can be transcended and relativized anthropologically. (Hence, mathematically describable, functional relations can replace the causal relations to be presupposed for experiment.) Moreover, the switch point of radical transcendental-pragmatic reflection has the function of illuminating each of the different knowledge-constitutive interests, to ground the theoretical-explanatory, hermeneutic, and reconstructive or ideology-critical human or social sciences. Finally, this switch point of reflection (which replaces ontological and metaphysical "theoria") permits a dispensation from actions and practical interests that, precisely because it is no longer capable of constituting the meaning of the life world, permits argumentation and reflection or the legitimation and critique of all human theoretical and practical (ethical, juridical, and institutional) validity claims (by which I mean claims to meaning, truth, and normative appropriateness) on the level of philosophical discourse.[4]

I have indicated that by *meaning-constitutive cognitive interests* I mean such interests as that in causal explanation corresponding to the interest in manipulative experimental action and the interest in understanding that corresponds to integration with co-subjects. From the quasi-external standpoint of transcendental-pragmatic reflection on validity, the circumstance that we can act and, accordingly, have such meaning-constitutive cognitive interests can itself be considered contingent. That is, it can be seen as an anthropological fact which is the necessary condition of the possibility of the world of actors and its preunderstanding. In contrast, the a priori of reflection on validity, a reflection that itself remains linguistic and argumentative, cannot be considered contingent, for we cannot think a thought that could go behind the point of the transcendental reflection on validity. The conceptual attempt to suppose a different kind of thinking is, it seems to me, only apparently self-critical and "sceptical"; in truth, it is presumptuous and dogmatic.

Of course, it is equally dogmatic to confuse the possibility of transcendental reflection on the conditions of our interpretive (*verstehende*) being-in-the-world with the substantive, theoretical knowledge of science. Indeed, this confusion is a naive relapse into ontological metaphysics. It is important to see that there is no knowledge that is knowledge of things-in-themselves and that can therefore abstract from the complementarity of objective theory and subjective, transcendental-pragmatic reflection on action. Kant had to interpret this situation as a complementarity between the transcendental idealism of consciousness and the transcendental realism in which existing things-in-themselves affect consciousness. Hence, even he did not overcome the pre-Kantian paradigm of an ontological-metaphysical "theoria" situated outside the world.

Now, to the extent that we can see the different language games of causal explanation and the understanding of action as a conceptual articulation of the complementarity situation I have sketched, we can defend the complete disjunction of language games presupposed by the neo-Wittgensteinians. From the transcendental-pragmatic perspective, the logic of the situation of complementarity can be understood to be necessary. Moreover, this logic precludes the possibility of objectifying the action intention of the acting subject (or of its co-subjects, something I still must show). This intention must, rather, be presupposed or reflexively understood as the condition of the possibility of theoretical, causal explanations; hence, it cannot be objectified in the sense of a volitional-cognitive, causal complex for an intentional explanation functioning as a causal explanation of actions as events. To this degree, the transcendental-pragmatic interpretation of the situation of complementarity preserves the truth of post-Wittgensteinian New Dualism.

This does not mean, however, that it might not be possible to see actions themselves as events within the framework of a social science or psychology interested in theoretical explanation. Such explanations consider action events in their connection to natural events, and hence, explain their occurrence. Further, they can objectify previously understood reasons or intentions as dispositions to action, which can then be seen as causally effective factors. In this case one can view the explanation of motives as a causal explanation (under the restrictions elucidated above, with regard to the possible presupposition of natural laws). Precisely in this case, however, we can also see that, for transcendental-pragmatic reasons, the situation of complementarity with regard to the mutual presupposition and exclusion of causal explanation and the understanding of actions is necessary to the quasi-causal explanation of events of action. Indeed, it is just as necessary here as in the case of causal explanations of natural events; for this reason, as von Wright points out, the competition between the premises of natural causality and freedom of action must always be decided in favor of the latter.

We can use a thought experiment to show the impossibility of suspending either this complementarity situation or, therefore, the post-Wittgensteinian New Dualism and the Kantian dualism of theoretical and practical, or theoretical, object-related and transcendental reason. One need only imagine that two experimental psychologists introduce certain controlled, environmental stimuli in order to calculate the degree to which specific subjects can be causally motivated to express certain cognitive opinions and/or perform certain actions. Imagine further that they suddenly decide to forego their communication with each other over the grounds, goals, and hypothetical assumptions of their experimental actions, and to replace the communication with explanation of each other's causally effective motives. (We have already seen that good reasons or intentions interesting from a hermeneutic point of view can also be causally effective; this fact is, however, not to be confused with the desire to substitute explanation that is at issue here.) It is clear that, in this case, neither psychologist can any longer treat the other as a member of the communication community of scientists, but only as a scientific "object" (or, more precisely, as a "subject-object" he must encounter before restricting communication, to avoid such unwanted effects as self-fulfilling and self-destroying prophecies). Nevertheless, it is more important that, if the experiment is to be meaningful and to issue in possibly valid results, each psychologist must have automatic recourse to another communication community and to its language game of coming to an understanding over the foundations of action. Even if he were the last surviving human being, each psychologist would still have to refer to the community of the scientific tradition. Hence, the situation of complementarity reemerges.

## 1.4 Complementarity and a Concept of the Hermeneutic Geisteswissenschaften that Is Not Scientistically Restricted

Thus far, my analysis of the situation of complementarity has traced the kernel of truth in post-Wittgensteinian New Dualism back to its transcendental-pragmatic roots. This analysis, however, is still not sufficient to clarify how methodical-hermeneutic understanding can form an alternative to causal explanation that is relevant to the theory of science. Indeed, as we have seen, although the consequences of the situation of complementarity indicate the possibility of grounding both hermeneutic and quasi-causal analytic human or social sciences, as far as I can see, there is an influential scientistic prejudice obstructing recognition of these consequences at precisely this point. This prejudice admits the necessity of presupposing an understanding of action, as well as communicative agreement among scientists about the foundations of their activity. It considers these premises prescientific and even trivial, however, since the issue is that of methodologically relevant "science." The latter requires moving from a prescientific understanding of action to a scientific, causal explanation of actions as events to be accomplished by theoretical objectification of the actions. Indeed, it requires explanation of understanding as a possible "scientification" of hermeneutics.[5]

I think it is difficult to find an appropriate answer to this argument, for the same reason that it is difficult to overcome "scientism" even if one refers to a different theory of science. This was the paradoxical situation that was always confronted by philosophical attempts to ground the Geisteswissenschaften in the nineteenth century; if I am correct, it has continued until today to impede a solution to the E-V controversy. As happens so often in such cases, a terminological difference conceals a deeply entrenched difference in the delimitation of paradigms of rationality. If one uses the English or French word *science*, one cannot deny that the concept of what constitutes methodologically relevant science is essentially limited to the theoretical-explanatory approach of modern natural science, to an approach that first became possible through renunciation of the teleological, or "sympathetic," understanding of nature "from the inside" to which the natural philosophy of the Renaissance still adhered.

Ever since this *scientiae novae magna instauratio*, representatives of the "artes"—including the *ars interpretandi*—which since the seventeenth century has been called "hermeneutics"—have been faced with two alternatives: either undertake a scientification of their disciplines by adopting the natural scientific ideal of method, or expand the concept of science to include the methodological relevance of another approach, an approach in which the formulation of questions corresponds neither to the modern separation of theoretical and practical reason nor to the associated relation between subject and object characteristic of purely theoretical knowledge. The founders of the philosophy of the Geisteswissenschaften—in particular, Wilhelm Dilthey, the neo-Kantians Windelband and Rickert, in a certain sense, and even Max Weber—chose the second route, even though Dilthey tried to effect a compromise between German Idealism's concept of science and positivistic concessions, while the neo-Kantians attempted a similar compromise between Kant's alternatives of practical and theoretical reason. In the twentieth century, Heidegger revealed a deeper foundation to the problem of hermeneutics in the problem of world preunderstanding and its public "disclosedness." He was followed by Hans-Georg Gadamer, whose *Truth and Method* uncovered a convincing basis for the meaning of hermeneutic understanding in the practical context of reaching an understanding about a subject-matter (*Sache*) and in the mediation of historical tradition. Gadamer, however, also restricted the methodological claim of hermeneutics to the pre-Geisteswissenschaften status of "artes" based on authority and oriented toward pragmatic application. For this reason, it is possible to read his argument as confirmation of the scientistic monopoly on method.[6]

On the basis of the transcendental-pragmatic analysis of the theory of science that I have advocated, it seems both possible and necessary to free the concept of science from its scientistic limitations and to comprehend it in as expansive a manner as can be encompassed by the notion of a normative foundation on which acts of knowledge answer fundamental human questions in a methodical, disciplined way. From this perspective we can reconsider the thesis that, if one moves from prescientific communication about the reasons and intentions of actions to methodical science, the step must be identical in meaning to the move to the theoretical objectification of actions and their causal explanation as events—indeed, it must be a step toward the explanation and objectification of understanding. It can now be shown that this thesis involves a scientistic fallacy that simply overlooks a fundamental human interest in knowledge and the methodologically relevant dimension of possible acts of knowledge corresponding to it. Of course, this interest in knowledge is not legitimately applied to nature; but the scientistic fallacy can be traced back to the false assumption already elucidated: that in the language game of communicative understanding, the transition from speech in the first and second person to speech in the third must have the same meaning as the transition to the standpoint of observation or to the theoretical objectification of the other, together with the explanation of the other's actions. This assumption accords with the special version of the scientistic fallacy, according to which the methodologically relevant interest in understanding reasons for acting can be reduced either to the objective foundation or justification of action in terms of good reasons or to the causal explanation of actions as events. Still, to what extent is this a scientistic fallacy?

If the alternatives stated above were correct, we would have to deal with only two purely objective or intersubjectively valid contexts in science or the philosophy of science. We would deal, first, with the purely logical context in which actions and especially operations of knowledge are justified in a quasi-methodological way in accordance with normative standards that are to be presupposed. The limit case here would involve justifications in accordance with the standard of consistency in the sense of a (conventional?) system of norms that cannot be grounded further. We would deal, second, with the context of causal explanations of action as world events occurring in space and time. Such explanations can be empirically tested either inductively or by attempts to falsify them. The semantic explication of explanation, however, already assumes the empirical correctness of its premises. Hence, in this explication, the structure of the explanation refers back to the purely logical context, i.e., the structure of deduction in which the explanandum is deduced from the explanans.

Even today, the paradigmatic function of this basic premise of logical empiricism is scarcely to be overestimated. What, however, is its basis in the modern theory of science? In my view, it rests on a metaphysical idealization elaborated by the early Wittgenstein in a pure form in his *Tractatus*. In it, Wittgenstein ignores the conventional foundations of the rules or norms of logical justification to such an extent that ultimately he includes within the "*Tractatus* universe" only contingent facts and the logic of justifying descriptions and explanations of them that is assumed to lie in the deep structure of language. The problem of the reflexive agreement among subjects of science or language users thereby becomes superfluous. That they must come to an understanding about the rules of linguistic usage or the possible norms for justifying their language and world understanding is overlooked or, if you will, restricted to the unique transcendental-pragmatic or transcendental-hermeneutic "guiding" function of the *Tractatus*.

Actually, such an "architectonic"—in the sense of the metaphysics of logical empiricism and logical semantics—would be reasonable if a definitive agreement about the rules and norms for methodologically justifying human actions (including speech acts and acts of understanding) could be presupposed as a reality and not just as a "regulative idea" to which "nothing empirical can correspond." The "constructive semantics" of the late Carnap made pluralism in "semantical frameworks" dependent on conventions, and thereby left behind this metaphysics of logical empiricism. It would have had to lead to two expansions of the theory of science—first, to a philosophical-pragmatic reflection on the subjective-intersubjective conditions of the possibility of rule or norm conventions, to a reflection that was neither merely empirical-pragmatic nor formal-pragmatic but rather transcendental-pragmatic or transcendental-hermeneutic; and, second (and this is the point in the present context), to an empirically and normatively engaged hermeneutic reconstruction of the rules or normative standards for justifying validity claims. Such rules or standards are explicitly or implicitly transmitted in the general history of culture, philosophy, and science. Moreover, their reconstruction is already developed in the transcendental-philosophical and reflexive discourse on the justification of validity claims—for example, in the explicative discourse on the justification or critique of the validity of the linguistic meaning of theorems or forms of inquiry.

These considerations would establish the methodological relevance of the question corresponding to the hermeneutic interest in knowledge, namely, that as to those good reasons of others that may still be unknown: for example, the good reasons of the classics of the history of science or of members of alien cultures. This form of inquiry would have its place, so to speak, between the question of logico-semantic justification and that of the causal explanation of motives. The former already presupposes the normatively relevant understanding of normative standards and possible good reasons, in general, whereas the latter already presupposes the empirical, ostensibly merely heuristic understanding of the good or bad reasons assumed to be causally effective. From the conditions of the possibility of coming to an understanding, this discipline of transcendental hermeneutics would infer the normative premises or anticipations of an understanding of reasons that provided tentative justification. At the same time, it would be prepared to revise what it tentatively presumed to be good reasons for specific kinds of action in accordance with empirically acquired insights into better or different reasons. This would not involve deriving norms from empirical facts, however; rather, it would correct the presumed norms by replacing them with norms empirically and hermeneutically disclosed in accordance with the nondeductive "circle in understanding."

This analysis suggests an analogy between the reconstructive-hermeneutic discipline and the method of explication that is actually practiced—for example, in the explication of natural languages that uses artificial languages, which, in turn, presuppose a pragmatic interpretation helped by natural languages. Nevertheless, at least at the level of the analytic theory of science, the conception of such a discipline never arose. Instead, the theory of science continued to mistake the method of *Verstehen* for a merely heuristic prescientific aid to empirical, causal explanation and to see the latter as the sole empirical alternative to the objective grounding or justification of propositions in logical semantics. Accordingly, in connection with the discourse of justification, the theory of science simply identified the transition from reflexive speech in the first person to speech about the other or others in the third person with a transition to the theoretical standpoint of observation. In this way, the actions of others are now interesting only as world events to be explained.

In contrast, we must acknowledge the following:

1. The implicit identification of discourse about grounding or justification with the logico-semantic, deductive relation between sentences represents an abstractive foreshortening of the communicative situation. If one reflects in transcendental-pragmatic or transcendental-hermeneutic terms on the subjective-intersubjective dimension of dialogue that belongs to such discourse, it becomes clear that this discourse is critical and self-reflective. Therefore, if difficulties arise in understanding, the discourse can always be expanded into a hermeneutic discourse in which participants come to an understanding over meaning intentions and reasons for beliefs and actions.

2. This situation means that one can use the meaning intentions and reasons of others to question one's own in such a way that the latter becomes the theme of a reconstruction of self-understanding. One will consider the known or hypothetical action intentions and reasons of others—even absent others and dead representatives of the given tradition of discourse—and discuss them in the third person. That does not mean, however, that one assumes the theoretical standpoint of observation and causal explanation with regard to the intentions and reasons. Rather, one views their reasons or action intentions as those of virtual copartners in communication and incorporates them in the hermeneutic discourse. In other words, the intentions and reasons for action are seen as the beliefs and goal projections handed down by the tradition, for example, which, therefore, are relevant to grounding one's own actions; or they can appear in light of a "practical inference" as the hypothetically assumed premises of a purposive-rational understanding of actual actions. In any case, this incorporation of others' reasons and action intentions in the hermeneutic discourse attests to the possibility that a methodologically disciplined hermeneutic, cognitive achievement can arise from the knowledge-constitutive interest in intersubjective understanding. As I have said, possibly the best example of such a purely hermeneutic "Geisteswissenschaft" we have today is the empirical history of science and its normative reconstruction. Here, causal explanation itself becomes the theme of methodical understanding. This provides a pointed counterargument to the scientistically conceived and absolutized possibility of the psychologistic or psycholinguistic explanation of acts of understanding.

**1.5 The Complementarity of Causal Explanation and Hermeneutic Understanding in the Social Sciences**

This hermeneutic alternative to the interest in explanation is not contradicted by one's ability to integrate the actual actions of virtual partners in communication into the objectifiable structure of events in history, and thus pose the problem of explaining events. In the first place, the strictly hermeneutic interest in knowledge found in the philological interpretation of texts (and even in the history of science, for example) differs from interest in the hermeneutic interpretation of sources that helps establish and classify action events chronologically. The person who studies literature by interpreting texts is not interested primarily in Shakespeare's or Goethe's works because they can serve as sources for the reconstruction of chronologically objectified "real" history. Second, although the historical explanation of actions as events must also be a causal explanation even if it is an intentional explanation, it is still far from being a subsumption-theoretic causal explanation. As we have seen, history for us is not simply the totality of events or processes that can be explained in empirical-nomological terms. Rather, it is always already understood as that singular, irreversible, and innovative process which, in principle, we can continue through our actions. These actions are subject to nonfalsifiable, normative principles of rationality, which function as ideal laws of action that under circumstances can be successfully anticipated.

It is only in the limit case that an explanation of a historical event can change into a quasi-subsumption-theoretic, empirical causal explanation. As I have shown, this is possibly the case where epochal and regional sedimentations of a human "quasi-nature" are isolated and fixed in a nonhistorical though historically relative way. In this process they assume the form of institutionalized or habitualized rules or conventions that can be used as quasi-nomological regularities for strong or weak (statistical) causal explanations and placed in the service of social technology and its predictions. However, a transcendental-pragmatic reflection on the conditions of the possibility of constituting the thematic object of such a quasi-natural scientific social science shows that, here, the knowing subject's interest in knowledge and form of inquiry completes that transition, the necessity of which I have disputed. We move from the dialogic standpoint of hermeneutic discourse to the standpoint of the theoretical distantiation of subject and object—and, moreover, to the interest in the technologically relevant disposition of and control over events and processes.

This limit case of the explanation of events is represented by the "empirical-analytic social sciences," including psychology. The case is philosophically interesting because it demonstrates that, under certain circumstances, the ontic nature or quasi-nature of human beings or human society contradicts the suggestions of an onto-semantically interpreted neo-Wittgensteinianism. It permits actions to be the theme of a quasi-nomological natural science and thus to be controlled as events or processes that can be predicted conditionally. For this reason, the relationship between the ontic and the transcendental-pragmatic conditions of the possibility of valid acts of knowledge cannot be determined as easily on the level of the human or social sciences as it can on the level of natural science, or at least, that of physics. On the latter level, one must leave archaic magic behind; one has to come to terms with the fact that at least within inorganic nature, an interest in coming to an understanding corresponds to no ontic correlate in acts of knowledge that can be controlled methodologically. On the contrary, the resignation of understanding in favor of the law hypotheses appropriate to causal explanation opens the secure route of progressive science.[7] On the level of the human and social sciences, however, there are two fundamental, complementary interests in knowledge that correspond to two fundamental and complementary possibilities of man's practical attitude to man. Moreover, these two complementary interests also correspond to two methodologically relevant dimensions of scientific knowledge.

On the one hand, we must interact with human beings in both a strategic and a cooperative manner; we must therefore communicate with them as co-subjects of knowledge and action. Furthermore, this communication community must be historically expanded to include the mediation of tradition. The hermeneutic understanding of the Geisteswissenschaften thus arises in situations where crises emerge either in the process of understanding between human beings or in the mediation of tradition. On the other hand, we assume a theoretically distanced relation to human beings, that is, to the human quasi-nature that is fixed and objectified in actions as spatiotemporal events, as well as in social institutions and in psychosomatic dispositions to act. In the relation between subject and object, we suspend communication and focus on observation and data control. This allows us to abstract from the historically irreversible, sociocultural conditions under which the quasi-nature that is fixed at any given time arises and changes. Hence, the possibility emerges of quasi-nomological social sciences that can be used for social technology.

As I have noted, in the latter case, the possibility of prognostically testing explanatory hypotheses in repeatable social experiments is constantly threatened by such disturbances as self-fulfilling and self-denying prophecies. These disturbances illustrate the decisive function of the pragmatic conditions of the possibility of the quasi-natural scientific type of social science. Merton has described the "paradoxes" involved in social scientific predictions, paradoxes which, as far as I can see, have thus far not been taken seriously in an epistemological sense. Their basis apparently lies in the pragmatic circumstance that is connected to the quasi-natural social sciences, in which the virtual co-subjects of the knowing subject are viewed as objects. In those cases it is in no way self-evident that the separation of the subject and object of knowledge necessary in every theoretical-explanatory and experimental science can constantly be secured; rather, it is the interest of science and the social technology based on it to create and maintain this kind of quasi-natural scientific separation of subject and object by one-sidedly blocking communication between the subject and subject-object of science. In psychological experiments this can be effected over limited periods of time that are agreed upon by the parties involved. Viewed from a longer time frame, the participants retain reflexive control over the experiment, and by means of the quasi-natural scientific knowledge gained about themselves, are able to reckon with their own quasi-nature. A quasi-nomological sociology, however, can hardly deny that its unavoidable interest must lie in reifying the human subject-object of science in such a way that the science is not disturbed by the latter's reflection. Ceteris paribus, it thus lends support to the control of uninformed human beings by other human beings to whom knowledge has granted power. Indeed, if there has been an enormous development of such empirical analytic social sciences in the past few decades in the highly bureaucratized industrial countries of the East and West, this control seems to be its source; for these sciences are "value free" and are therefore a priori suitable for technological use.

Today, although these social sciences are well established and well accepted by the theory of science, they possess a peculiarly ambiguous characteristic, one that, it seems to me, consists in the following: On the one hand, it cannot be disputed that they possess an ontic basis in "things," and therefore lead to true or empirically correct results. On the other hand, they rest on an unreflective abstraction from the transcendental-pragmatic conditions of the constitution of the objects at their foundation. The moment one considers legitimate only this type of social science, its well-confirmed results tend to lead to a completely untrue and fatal view of the nature or essence of human beings and their capacity for moral determination.

I have already indicated that empirically well-confirmed results in such a science (i.e., causal explanations of behavior that are relevant for prediction) depend on establishing a quasi-natural scientific relation undistorted by the Merton effect. This allows formulation of an explanans that exploits the sedimentation and reification of habitual or institutionalized rules of action in the sense of an ahistorical but historically relative human quasi-nature. As we have seen, such rules can then be conceived of as quasi-nomological regularities. Suppose, however, that the presuppositions of object-constitution that are pragmatically determined by the technical interest in knowledge are forgotten. This occurs, for example, in a purely onto-semantic explication of "scientific systematizations." Then, at least the self-understanding of social scientists as members of human society becomes paradoxical.

The special status of social scientists is transcendentally and pragmatically determined. They are subjects of the explanatory social sciences, that is, members of a human community who cannot themselves be the object of motivational explanation and prediction, but who act as co-subjects of historically innovative deliberation, scientific planning, and social technology. Now, if, like B. F. Skinner, they ignore this status, they are ready to understand their own action "in terms of behavioral science." In that case, however, they succumb to the paradox of having to answer the question: Who should manipulate the manipulators? Conversely, social scientists can be conscious of their special status and even reflect on the fact that the pragmatic construction of a quasi-natural scientific subject-object relation with regard to society must work in their favor (by one-sidedly restricting information). This is necessary if the ontic reification of human action motives as dispositions is to be exploited for scientific and technological purposes. In this case, social scientists must be ready to affirm the social and political premises of a society led by experts and technocrats, a society in which the quasi-natural scientific subject-object relation of "behavioral science" is permanently established and corresponds to a division of society into the objects and subjects of science and social technology. However, precisely because the ways in which the human objects of science will then behave will confirm the empirical validity of quasi-nomological explanations and predictions, this behavior will not reflect the true nature of human beings or society. Instead, confirmation of empirical validity will rest on an artificial prevention of the reflexive effect of knowledge back on the ontic object of knowledge; but it is this effect that is characteristic of human beings and society as the dialectical subject-object of history.

We could, of course, claim that the true nature of human beings, in the sense of determining their possibilities, is represented by the expert who, as the subject of science, also participates in history. This supposition would be unrealistic even if one could credit the experts with a methodologically adequate consciousness of their situation; for the human subject-objects of science and social technology who constitute the greater part of society retain their creativity. Hence, their degradation to objects of repeatable experiments is not without consequences. In practice, for social science to secure a subject-object relation not disturbed by the Merton effect would require a system of political control so comprehensive that even the experts and their functionaries would be at least indirectly bound to it. Indeed, they would be bound so tightly to it that even on their side, the freedom of dialogic and cooperative actions could no longer be developed. In short, in its practical effect, both the naive, Skinnerian, scientistic self-understanding of the social scientist and the elitist, technocratic self-understanding encourages a situation Heidegger tried to illuminate in his metaphor of "en-framing" (*Gestell*).[8] Human beings first enframe nature in experiments, then the objectified quasi-nature of society. Finally, by enframing their scientific-technological thought, even as the subjects of research and technology, they themselves are enframed and thus objectified.

From this analysis of the consequences of absolutizing the technologically relevant, quasi-natural scientific conception of social science, it in no way follows that one could or should dispense with it in industrial or postindustrial society. Still, the analysis has consequences for the situation in which reflexive processes of coming to an understanding are controlled by the temporally delimited creation of a quasi-natural scientific relation between subject and object, something relatively easily achieved in psychological experiments. It means that, on the social scientific level, this situation must be compensated for by a critical and reconstructive social science which makes it the theme of its pragmatic interest in knowledge. That is, the situation of control must be made the theme of forms of inquiry and practical precautions that, if possible, secure communicative transparence in all sectors of the social system.

# 2

## Completion of the System of Knowledge-Constitutive Interests

### 2.1 The Difference between the Ideal and the Real Communication Communities

At this point it might appear that I have been concerned to ground a compensatory social science only in order to locate the transcendental-pragmatic origin of the interpretive social sciences within the situation of complementarity, and thus to view socialized human beings only as the virtual co-subjects of communication and interaction. From a transcendental-pragmatic point of view, that would merely contrapose the interest in coming to an understanding, an interest the communication community of scientists must itself presuppose in explaining behavior, to the interest in the quasi-nomological explanation of human behavior, an interest connected to social technology.

Such a conception of the complementarity between critical sciences would itself fall victim to the fallacy of a metaphysical idealization similar to that found in the alternatives of explanation and justification. Of course, this fallacy would not be the same as the "scientistic fallacy" examined above. It would not consist in completely ignoring the transcendental-pragmatic dimension of the constitution of objects, as logical semantics does; rather, the fallacy would lie in the fact that within the transcendental-pragmatic reflection on the conditions of the possibility of the social sciences, a necessary idealization is metaphysically hypostatized. In fact, in the transcendental-pragmatic analysis of the discourse situation of science one cannot avoid undertaking an idealization of possible modes of knowledge or methodologically relevant forms of inquiry in the sense of the situation of complementarity. As distinct from scientific objects and actions explainable as events, scientists must reciprocally view one another as co-subjects of an unlimited, ideal community in which they come to an understanding of meaning and form a consensus about truth. Moreover, as I elaborated, such Geisteswissenschaften as Lakatos's hermeneutic reconstruction of the "internal history" of science can be seen as historical expansions of the scientific discourse on meaning; but that means one must clearly distinguish empirical and normative reconstruction (e.g., texts and action intentions in the familiar sense of post-Wittgensteinian New Dualism) from the explanation of events. In other words, one must comprehend this methodological situation in terms of a complementarity, in terms of the reciprocal exclusion and supplementation of the cognitive interest in explanation by the interest in understanding thereby presupposed.

Nevertheless, the issue here is the project of critical-reconstructive social sciences in general as compensatory sciences of reflection. Whereas the counterfactual anticipation of the ideal communication community of acting subjects is necessary to methodological reflection on scientific discourse and to its expansion in the Geisteswissenschaften, with regard to this project it amounts to a purely metaphysical subreption of the reality of an ideal. In the case of the "scientistic fallacy" in the alternatives of explanation and objective justification, it is assumed that subjects already have come to a definitive understanding of meaning, so that the empirical-hermeneutic task of a science of understanding is ignored. In the same way, it is now assumed that the counterfactual, ideal conditions that are necessarily anticipated by the community of subjects of science are fulfilled absolutely. In other words, it is assumed that the ideal conditions of both the understanding and the intelligibility of the reasons or intentions behind the actions of the subject-objects of social history already exist. This assumption absolutizes pure understanding as the alternative to explanation and thereby commits the fallacy of a "hermeneutic idealism."[1]

This point can be made more precise. At this juncture, I am not questioning the possibility of quasi-nomological social sciences, but rather, claiming that the alternative to them is falsely determined. As long as the modes of behavior of historical subject-objects are not objectified as a quasi-nature and made the object of a quasi-natural scientific conception that is thereby restricted to epochal cross sections and regions, such modes of behavior must be assumed to be modes of action that can be understood in terms of good reasons alone (under the boundary conditions of the state of knowledge at any given time). That is, the actual historical and innovative achievements of human beings—achievements of a practical, cognitive, even artistic nature that transcend their objectification as quasi-nature—would have been considered fully intelligible, hence, as rationally justifiable under the conditions of the historical situation. Obviously this contradicts the insight of every historian, that political and social history is not the result of rational, intelligible action. It means that even if innovative human action transcends behavior that is simply determined by institutionalized and habitualized rules, that which it brings about is not the pure product of well-grounded action. If this has to be admitted, however, how can we more precisely determine that dimension in which political and social history can be made a theme and which "hermeneutic idealism" overlooks?

## 2.2 The Emancipatory Interest of Knowledge and the Critical-Reconstructive Social Sciences

Let us first try to determine why human history, in the narrow sense, cannot be seen as the product of well-grounded actions. It seems to me that there are two very different reasons (or causes). First, human beings are prevented from determining their actions by rational, intelligible reasons—even in the sense of formal purposive rationality—by the causal efficacy of dispositions to action deriving from first (inherent) and second (socially and historically sedimented quasi-) nature. Second, even if their actions are well grounded, they have consequences that they cannot foresee. This may be because they lack knowledge about the law-governed or quasi-law-governed possibilities of "bringing about changes in state" (von Wright), or because their action intentions are theatened by the action intentions of others with whom they cannot coordinate the effects of their action in either the sense of allowing the predictions of social technology or the sense of cooperating with one another according to an agreement.

These, then, are the reasons why hermeneutic idealism is inadequate as the methodological presupposition for the study of real history, though it remains legitimate as a reconstruction of the internal dimensions of intellectual history (*Geistesgeschichte*). If this statement is correct, however, it seems crucial somehow to combine the method of hermeneutic understanding with the method of the quasi-nomological explanation of events in a critical reconstruction of social history, in other words, to combine an understanding of intentional actions with the explanation of the unintended consequences of action, starting from the premise that the latter possibly are determined by natural laws or even by the regularities of an institutionally or habitually fixed quasi-nature. If, however, this combination of methods is to serve the reconstruction of social history, obviously, in contrast to the quasi-natural scientific social or "behavioral" sciences, it cannot consist in a heuristic conception of the understanding of (good or bad) reasons for acting; that is, it cannot view such an understanding simply as an aid to the quasi-nomological explanation of modes of behavior. This combining of methods would not explain the process of history as such, including the historical occurrence of determined regularities within epochs and regions. From the beginning, possible explanation would, rather, be restricted to the historically dependent, quasi-natural modes of behavior at any given time.

As I have shown, this procedure can only help expand the knowledge-for-control available to social technology. It cannot achieve a critical-reflective self-understanding of society that comprehends it as an interaction community and thus compensates for the kind of knowledge that serves domination. In the interest of such compensation, the process of history must be reconstructed critically as the modification or replacement of the intended consequences of action with explicable causal effects that follow from natural or quasi-natural laws. This leads to a deeper understanding of the historical process than can be reached on the basis of the pure understanding of action intentions.

The methodological crux of this indispensable combination of understanding and explanation becomes clearer if one considers a circumstance neglected thus far. The causal effects deriving from natural or quasi-natural laws codetermine not only the consequences of human action but that element of irrationality in action intentions which, one way or the other, affects their intelligibility. If the combination of hermeneutic and nomological or quasi-nomological methods of causal explanation can clarify even this development in intentions, then it must be the latter method that performs the merely heuristic function;

for the point here is to deepen the self-understanding of human actions from the inside, so to speak, by understanding their irrational and alien determinations, determinations that at first can only be explained. Two relatively transparent models for the combination of methods are at issue; both mediate a deeper understanding with heuristic methods of causal explanation and thus possess a scientific concept of the human sciences that is not scientistically restricted. With regard to the critical reconstruction of individual life histories, there is psychoanalysis, whereas, with regard to the critical reconstruction of social history there is the critique of ideology. In the present context, I do not think it either necessary or possible to go into the disputed details of these models or to restrict them to their Freudian or Marxist versions. It is also impossible to consider the interdependence of phylogenesis and ontogenesis reflected in the reciprocal relation between the object domains treated by each model.[2] In our context, it is enough to show that both models share the same methodological "figure": a partial hermeneutic mediation and deepening of reflexive self-understanding, and hence, of the understanding of modes of human action by a distanced causal explanation of objectified motives that, prima vista, evade understanding.[3] By means of this methodological figure, it seems possible to illuminate the way in which the critical-reconstructive social sciences compensate for the technologically relevant, quasi-nomological, social sciences.

The key to understanding this function lies in the methodologically relevant role of self-reflection. At this point it is useful to reflect that within the scope of modern scientism, self-reflection plays no role at all. The reasons for this can be clarified by looking at logical empiricism's paradigms of science and the philosophical theory of science from both sides. From a substantive point of view, the methodology of the natural sciences, in fact, does not need to take into account an empirically relevant self-reflection. In contrast, the cognitive achievements of the hermeneutic sciences, in principle, include the presupposition of possible self-reflection (either in Hegel's sense of finding oneself in the other or in Schleiermacher, Dilthey, and Mead's sense of the reciprocity between the deepening of self-understanding and the interpretive self-transposition (*Sichhineinversetzen*) into all humanity). Logical empiricism's characteristic lack of appreciation for this state of affairs can be seen in its failure to recognize that the internal reconstruction of the history of natural science is not itself a natural science.

Rather, insofar as it reflectively understands a human intellectual development, it forms the very paradigm of a "Geisteswissenschaft."

As I have noted, because of its fear of psychologism, logical empiricism banned the self-reflection of thought from philosophy, calling it an empirical-psychological matter. In addition, it substituted metalanguages and metatheories for the self-reflection of discourse that supposedly necessarily led to antinomies. For these reasons, it rejected the necessity of a nonempirically relevant, transcendental-philosophical self-reflection on the validity claims and conditions of the possibility of knowledge or forms of argumentation, though it subjected this rejection to no relevant reflection. The self-reflection of topical thought is the paradigm for the philosophical rationality of a final grounding; nevertheless, one could claim that, in the great expanse of contemporary philosophy, it has been silently suppressed by the mathematical paradigm of the metatheoretical theory of verification.[4]

Still, the special key that a methodologically relevant self-reflection offers to understanding the critical-reconstructive social sciences exceeds the functions of self-reflection, which scientism otherwise misjudges as well. The critical self-reflection of psychoanalysis or the critique of ideology, for example, differs from the formal transcendental self-reflection of thought and its validity claims in that it provides empirically relevant knowledge. It differs from the self-reflection implicit in hermeneutic understanding in that it constitutes a methodical depth hermeneutics and thus can supersede the limits normally respected by hermeneutics. By means of a detour into an initially causal-analytic analysis of the suppressed or otherwise objectified motives of our action intentions, this critical self-reflection is able to supersede the boundaries between reasons for acting that can be understood in rational terms and causes of action that cannot be understood, but rather, are determined by human nature or quasi-nature. Thus, for example, by provoking the reflexive, autobiographical self-understanding of the patient, psychoanalysis facilitates the appropriation of suppressed motives objectified as the causes of pathological symptoms. These then become reasons for acting that can be discussed rationally. The critique of ideology accomplishes a similar function with regard to broad social strata (which need not always represent the classes to which Marx refers) by provoking them to reflect on causally effective interests and motives (which need not always be economic ones). Generally these interests and motives are not directly articulated in the texts of tradition as they are normally interpreted by hermeneutics, but rather, are cemented in the quasi-nature of social institutions.

In relation to quasi-nomological social sciences that are technologically relevant, the compensatory function of such critical self-reflection lies in the opposition of two schema, which are methodologically relevant figures in the mediation of explanation and understanding. In the quasi-nomological social sciences, the prognostically relevant causal explanation of actions as events is mediated by an understanding of good or bad reasons for acting, which serves as a heuristic presupposition. Critical reflection by agents must, if possible, be prevented; that is, they must not reflect on the way the maxims of their action (internalized rules) and their reasons (goals and beliefs) function as quasi-laws (behavioral regularities) and causes (behavioral dispositions). Otherwise, one would have to expect the disturbances in predictions that arise from self-fulfilling or self-destroying prophecies. In contrast, in the critical-reconstructive social sciences, the heuristic mediation of the causal explanation of events of action by the understanding of good or bad reasons for acting is countered by precisely the reverse mediation. In this case, it is the depth-hermeneutic understanding of suppressed or otherwise objectified motives that is mediated by a prior analysis of pathological regularities and causal effects. This means that the critical self-reflection of the subject-object of science is not prevented as a potentially disturbing factor, but is mobilized as an indispensable factor—namely, as the vehicle for a possible appropriation of objectified motives, and hence, for a transformation of regularities and causes into maxims, rules, or reasons that can be understood from inside and discussed in a conscious, responsible manner.

In the context of the present investigation, this account of the methodological crux of the critical-reconstructive social sciences may suffice to raise the following question: What epistemological presuppositions are necessary to clarify this further differentiation of the social sciences, a differentiation that goes beyond the differentiation of hermeneutic and quasi-nomological methods?

## 2.3 The Relation of Onto-semantic and Transcendental-Pragmatic Conditions of Object Constitution

I have tried to show that the distinction between hermeneutic and quasi-natural scientific social sciences goes beyond the simple distinction between the natural sciences and the Geisteswissenschaften and that the former distinction is intelligible only on epistemological premises that go beyond both those of logical empiricism and those of an onto-semantically interpreted neo-Wittgensteinianism. As we have seen, logical empiricism absolutizes (strong or weak) causal explanation, whereas the neo-Wittgensteinians distinguish between the language game of the causal explanation of (natural) events and the language game of the teleological explanation or purposive-rational understanding of actions. Neither is able to make it clear that even within the social sciences, understanding of actions in terms of reasons must be distinguished from the quasi-subsumption-theoretic causal explanation of actions as events. In contrast, this necessity becomes clear under the epistemological premise according to which the ontological or onto-semantic distinction between the different, internally determined object domains of knowledge is to be conjoined with a transcendental-pragmatic distinction between different object-constitutive interests of knowledge. We begin with the onto-semantically and transcendental-pragmatically grounded complementarity between the language games of understanding action and that of quasi-nomologically explaining action events. Within the social sciences this corresponds to a complementarity between the interest in coming to an understanding and interest in controlling behavior on behalf of social technology. This is so because the transcendental-pragmatically grounded distinction and supplementation of aspects meets with an ontic ambiguity in the "nature" of human beings or society. The ambiguity involves the institutional or habitual sedimentation of human nature in a historically relative quasi-nature, on the one hand, and the transcendence of this quasi-nature, on the other, a transcendence certified in the ontic condition of the communicative understanding of the phenomenon of human quasi-nature itself—thus, for example, in the conditions of scientific discourse and its historical-hermeneutic expansion.

I have also tried to show that this ontic ambiguity in the "nature" of human beings or society[5] cannot be adequately formulated even if one assumes that the clear complementarity between those object domains that are subject to understanding in terms of reasons and those that are subject to quasi-nomological causal explanation is both onto-semantically and transcendentally pragmatically well grounded. In contrast to first nature, the quasi-nature of human beings is never clearly fixed but, rather, can be artificially fixed or transcended—with the help of the social sciences, for example. Precisely this circumstance decisively indicates the possibility of a wider dimension in the social scientific focus on human quasi-nature. Critical-reconstructive social sciences can and should correspond to the technologically relevant, indispensable quasi-nomological social sciences. Such sciences do not merely border on the latter in a complementary fashion, as do the purely hermeneutic sciences; rather, they compensate for their practically effective tendency to reify human quasi-nature. (In this way, the critical-reconstructive sciences show that empirically correct results in the quasi-nomological social sciences are not the plain expression of pure theoretical truth, as scientism supposes, but, like all human self-knowledge, are themselves indebted to a dialectical mediation of theory and practice.)

In reflecting on the conditions of the possibility of social-scientific knowledge, the question now arises whether an epistemological combination of ontological or onto-semantic and transcendental-pragmatic viewpoints can clarify this further differentiation of social scientific methodology, and, if so, how. The answer to these questions are positive and depend on introducing a third object-constitutive interest of knowledge, since the presuppositions of the critical-reconstructive sciences require supplementing both the hermeneutic interest in coming to an understanding and the technical interest of knowledge. This is so because, within actual human society the ontic conditions of neither quasi-nomological nor purely hermeneutic science agree with the regulative idea according to which principles of rationality (in the widest conceivable sense) are to permit a rational understanding of reasons and a quasi-nomological reliance on adherence to ideal laws. The ideal supplementation of understanding action and causally explaining action events is already anticipated in the complementarity situation of interaction in discourse; it is hampered, however, by the historically relative quasi-nature of human beings to the extent that this quasi-nature is not (yet) the pure expression of a rational determination of the situational boundary conditions of action, but, rather, in addition is always the expression of an alien determination by reified motives for acting. Accordingly, the third knowledge-constitutive interest of the social sciences can be characterized as follows: It is an interest in the constantly renewed, reflective opening of the way to the autonomous self-realization of human beings in the species (Kant). More precisely, as the self-reflection of argumentative discourse indicates, it is an interest in the ideal communication community that is always counterfactually presupposed in the empirical substrate of the species. Thus it involves the critical, explanatorily mediated unmasking of every tendency toward self-alienation and self-denial confirmed in the objectification of historically sedimented quasi-nature in the sense of a pseudo-nature, an objectification that is not only not reflected upon but is tendentially barred to reflection by the interest in technical control. In a conscious application of a legal or political metaphor, we can call this third cognitive interest the emancipatory interest of knowledge.

We have seen that the necessity of the emancipatory interest of knowledge derives dialectically from the fallacy of "hermeneutic idealism." This derivation indicates that postulating the third cognitive interest satisfies a specific need for the psychological (and, moreover, the social scientific) self-knowledge of human beings. For this reason, I think it completes the system or architectonic of the object-constitutive human interests of knowledge that are relevant to the empirical sciences. As I have emphasized, we are not concerned here with a transcendental-pragmatic system that provides the possibility of normatively grounding empirical interests of knowledge (they are the theme of the social sciences); rather, we are concerned with a transcendental-pragmatic system that provides the possibility of normatively grounding the internal cognitive interests that are a priori necessary and that must be presupposed in order to conceive of the constitution of possible social-scientific forms of inquiry. This does not preclude—but, rather, includes—the interest of philosophy and the empirical social sciences in the multifarious relations between empirically effective, external cognitive interests and the internal interests postulated by transcendental pragmatics. These relations must be admitted and can be found, for example, in the history of science. They are the particular theme of the critical-reconstructive social sciences.

Although interest in emancipation completes the system of cognitive interests constituting the objects of the social sciences, it does not constitute a systematic completion of the philosophical self-reflection of thought.[6] That is, the critical, emancipatory self-reflection of the history of the human species in the social sciences cannot replace the philosophical-epistemological reflection on the possible validity of knowledge. We can determine the meaning of the philosophical self-reflection of thought more precisely by using the categories of the current language-reflexive paradigm of philosophy. It thus refers to the transcendental pragmatic self-reflection on the validity claims of linguistically formulated arguments and on the conditions of their meaning constitution and intersubjective justification. That this self-reflection cannot be replaced stems from the fact that it alone can give the emancipatory interest of knowledge its necessary function. Ever since the ancient Greek "Enlightenment," however, the legitimate function of unmasking that belongs to the third interest of knowledge has repeatedly been absolutized so that even philosophical thought has been subjected to it and considered mere illusion or purely idealistic prefiguration. This absolutization leads unavoidably to a paradox with regard to the truth claim of the "unmasker." One must either disavow the truth claim of critical social science itself, or the critic who surpasses or replaces philosophy must grant himself the privilege of being the only one to have "gotten behind" things. In so doing he may refer either to the superiority of the "will" (to power)," a superiority not to be overtaken by reflexive reason, or to "material interests," the "libido," the logic of language, or anonymous, super-personal "structures" or functional, self-preserving "systems." In this, I do not think human thought will go beyond the position Hegel achieved in his critique of Kant (ignoring, for the moment, the burden imposed on it by a new metaphysical system)—namely, that of the self-reflection of the final truth claim of philosophy. All empirical-reflexive and transcendental-reflexive self-critique by philosophy must restrict itself to legitimate demonstration of the necessary mediating moments in thought. Here, I think the position of philosophical reflection that Hegel attained can be explicated only within the medium of a transcendental language pragmatics and, as a postmetaphysical position, is to be limited to a critique of knowledge grounded in the primacy of practical reason. This means we must revise Hegel's renewed pretension to a philosophical science in which historical experience is substantially incorporated in the concept. This now amounts to the claim that empirical science has a transcendental foundation, one which in Hegel achieves the reflexive certainty of its reflexive knowledge of foundations.

Having thus rejected a metaphysical and postmetaphysical absolutization of the critical social sciences, we must also dispel a further misunderstanding, and at this point I return to the immediate theme of the discussion. It seems to me that it would be wrong to understand the introduction of the third cognitive interest in the way logical empiricism understands the technical interest in a prognostically relevant, explanatory social science, that is, as a counterargument to the necessity of distinguishing between the explanation (of events) and (hermeneutic) understanding in the sense of the complementarity of corresponding cognitive interests and their ontic correlates.

It is true that an idealistic absolutization of the distinction between the ideal-typical language games of causally determined behavior and freely (rationally) determined action reflects an illusionistic estimation of the real freedom of motivations for human action, an estimation contradicted by every legal trial. Thus, in view of the narrower theme of this study, it is useful to distinguish between three or four possible kinds of methodologically relevant cognitive achievements: causal explanation, purposive-rational understanding, and the quasi-causal explanation in terms of motives that, depending on its combination with understanding, can serve either social technology (or technological self-control, as in the case of behavioral therapy) or the critique of ideology (and depth psychology). This terminological architectonic, in fact, provides the structure within which I want to place the results of my discussion of positivism-scientism and post-Wittgensteinian New Dualism, hence, my proposals for resolving the E-V controversy. That means I see an additional argument for the complementarity I have emphasized in the possibility and necessity of the emancipatory cognitive interest and the corresponding methodological mediation of reflexively deepened self-understanding by a causal explanation of the reified motivational process behind intentional actions that apparently are freely determined. In other words, both serve as an additional argument for the fact that the causal explanation of natural processes and the understanding of freely determined human actions exclude and complete one another.

On the one hand, the possibility or necessity of the third cognitive interest has implications for the ideal completion of rational understanding and the possible recognition that actions can be determined by rationally intelligible reasons. It attests to the fact that this completion represents an ideal or regulative principle that is anticipated in discursive interaction but to which social reality can never actually correspond. To this extent, presupposing the situation of complementarity reduces to a necessity of social scientific methodology that is not to be understood in a utopian manner. On the other hand, the possibility of critique in the interest of emancipation attests to the necessity of a counterfactual anticipation of the self-determination of human actions by reasons; for a critique of natural processes determined entirely by causes (whether this is a critique of ideology or something else) or, in other words, a reconstruction of social history committed to emancipation but which does not presuppose or anticipate freedom (in a partially counterfactual way) is just as absurd as a conception of causal-analytic, experimental natural science that does not presuppose the scientist's freedom of action, in von Wright's sense.

What I have said thus far constitutes a rejection of a naturalistic misunderstanding of the transcendental-pragmatic system of knowledge-constitutive interests and of the corresponding methodological dimensions of possible social sciences. I now want to characterize the idealist-conservative allergy to the postulate of the emancipatory interest of knowledge and the methodological conceptions corresponding to it. This is sometimes associated with a positivistic-pragmatist antipathy to the postulate in a peculiar alliance, and I want to distance myself critically from both.

If we compare the critical-reconstructive social sciences with the theme of unified science and the procedures for reaching understanding or mediating tradition, then the following must be admitted at the outset: In comparison with either the focus on causal processes in nature and human quasi-nature or the understanding presupposed and practiced without scientific or epistemological reflection, the critical, self-reflective focus of human society on itself presents something of a "scandal." The mediation of reflective self-understanding by the causal explanation of objectified motivations that I have sketched represents a methodological and conceptual "figure" of self-revelation. In its scientific-political aspects, however, its application is similar to the application of the reverse, technologically relevant mediation of explanation by understanding in the quasi-nomological social sciences; thus it typically is divided into two sides or parties—that of the subject of science and that of the subject-object of science, and one must reckon with an understandable resistance. In the sociological domain, this resistance is even more understandable, since, in this case, there can be no quasi-medical legitimation or institutionalization of the analyist's or critic's role. Moreover, the methodologically and ethically delicate claim of knowledge made by social criticism doubtless can be misused by fools, fanatics, or power-hungry cynics. For this reason, we must expect phases of "counterenlightenment"—whether legitimate or illegitimate—characterized by critical and skeptical appeals to modesty, by conservative affirmations of the binding character of substantive traditions or institutions that cannot be questioned, and, at the same time, by a concern for economic and technological efficiency that marks a quasi-progressive program of disenchantment. Indeed, it is not easy to dispute the prudence, even wisdom (*prudentia* and *sapientria*, in the sense of Cicero's union of philosophy and rhetoric) of the Dostoevskian Grand Inquisitor; this is the prudence to which the critique of the emancipatory interest of knowledge can appeal in the name of the quasi-natural security of those human beings who live in the shadow of traditions and institutions that have not been questioned or illuminated by the critique of ideology.

This conservative resistance, a resistance that is simultaneously motivated by pragmatic-technocratic concerns, objects to both the legitimate and the illegitimate subversive potential of the critical-reconstructive social sciences, as well as their pedagogical application. In the present situation, this resistance issues not only from defenders of freedom, whether qualified or not, but also from apologists of a social order in which progressive socialism is supposed already to have been definitively established. Hence, there are doubtless still other methodologically relevant figures of thought in the critical and meta-critical social sciences besides those we have considered. In the realm of the language of temporal and cultural criticism Hegel considered so intellectually rich, this circumstance must lead to constantly renewed complications and confusions in the domain of terminology, so that the result can be a paralysis of the self-articulation of the emancipatory interest of knowledge with regard to its classical "enlightenment" intentions.[7]

Although practically relevant, these complications and problems cannot affect the validity, and thus, the long-term practical relevance of the transcendentally grounded system of cognitive interests and their methodological consequences; nor can they affect the critical-reconstructive social sciences. With regard to the present treatment of the intended reflection on foundations, they offer indirect confirmation of something else. They show that, even as a problem in knowledge—i.e., abstracting from the explicit problem in application—the social sciences as a whole cannot be understood as a value-free knowledge based on the theoretical division of subject and object. This constitutes their difference, at least from the prebiological problem complex of the natural sciences.

## 2.4 Supplementary Remarks on Functional Explanation in Biological Systems Theory and in the Quasi-biological Theory of Social Systems

Another objection to the architectonic of a theory of science differentiated into cognitive interests must be taken more seriously. This objection arises from the circumstance that in reconstructing and resolving the E-V controversy, we did not consider one methodologically relevant cognitive act that lately has been central to biology and to a, so to speak, quasi-biological type of social science. I have in mind the form of knowledge of "functional explanation"; this has already been discussed in the logical semantics of logical empiricism under reductionistic auspices,[8] and is central to both biological-ecological systems theory and the theory of social-political systems.[9] This extremely complex problem cannot be treated adequately within the present discussion; nevertheless, I want at least to indicate the possibility of incorporating it in the architectonic of a transcendental-pragmatic theory of science.

An empirically identifiable organic or quasi-organic system, as such, constitutes an objective teleological structure for us. If I am correct, it is impossible to reduce this structure to one of causal explanation by appealing to the fact that system-stabilizing control systems can be technically and cybernetically controlled as correspondingly ordered causal chains.[10] Obviously, this kind of reduction can be justified only by the technical cognitive interest in manipulating the system by interfering in the causal chain necessary to its realization. Conversely, no matter how the causal chain has arisen, its understandable order—in the sense of an objective teleological, system-related structure—escapes such reduction. Of course, in the case of technological and cybernetic systems such as torpedos and thermostats, the instrumental subordination of causal mechanisms to the constitutive category of teleology is indisputable; but the cybernetic account of the self-stabilization of organic systems first became possible in its light. Thus the comparison that cybernetics itself suggests between organisms and automatons shows that the merely "objective teleology" of functional systems (which lacks the subjective goal intentions that hermeneutics can posit) does not yet fall outside the categorial framework of teleo-logical thought.[11]

If my remarks on the structure of the objective teleology of functional systems are sound, then a transcendental-pragmatic analysis of sub-jective forms of inquiry and meaning-constitutive cognitive interests may clarify the possibility or impossibility of validly reducing teleological to causal explanation in the case of biology as well.[12] It is only in the case of the technical interest in prognostically relevant explanations of events that biocybernetic regulation represents a chain of efficient causes that, in principle, can be manipulated by experimental action. However, interest in the genuine meaning of the function of control systems or of organs in the organism's system is analogous to the hermeneutic interest in understanding actions. Hence, the synthetic cognitive achievement is dependent on a categorial preconception, in the sense of objective teleology.

Even in this case, and in spite of the usual teminology, I prefer to speak not of a noncausal type of explanation but of a type of under-standing. That has the advantage of clearly excluding the idea of a metaphysical explanation in terms of an *effizienten causa finalis*, instead suggesting a partial analogy to the form of inquiry involved in the idea of understanding action intentions. (This analogy is especially plausible with regard to research in animal behavior [ethology]. Such research is constituted not by interest in a prognostically relevant knowledge of control but by interest in prehistoric comparisons for understanding human actions.) Here, as in the case of explaining action, one could concede to the post-Galilean causalists that, given the direction of their inquiry, no return to a pre-Galilean, Aristotelian method of explanation is possible. My theory of methodologically differentiated, cognitive achievements stands in opposition to meth-odological unity, but it is not proposed as a type of explanation that competes with ontologically or onto-semantically grounded theory. Rather, it derives from the premise that there are different possible correlations of ontic and transcendental-pragmatic conditions of the possibility of constituting the objects or meaning of different cognitively relevant phenomena.

Exactly opposite such a transcendental-pragmatic expansion of the epistemological horizon is the strategy of a purely logico-semantic explication of functional explanations. Such a strategy attempts to reduce their structure to one of causal explanation by following the

D-N model in presupposing that states of systems are antecedent conditions from which the existence of an organ or its mode of functioning is supposed to issue in a law-governed fashion. This involves either a formal reduction, as in the equation of causal explanation with the deduction of the explanandum from the explanans, or the beginning of a material reduction that is inadequate because of its formalistic restriction to the D-N model. The former alternative has nothing relevant to say about the synthetic cognitive achievement to be explicated; the latter presupposes precisely that which post-Galilean causalists have always correctly disputed, namely, that a goal to be achieved in the future could be the cause of an explanandum that precedes it.[13]

We now turn our attention to the application of functional understanding in the domain of psychology and the social sciences. There are two problems here. There is not only the problem on which I have focused, whether functional understanding as objective-teleogical understanding can be reduced to causal explanation, but also the question whether intentional (i.e., purposive-rational or, as regards goals, meaning-rational) understanding can be reduced to functional understanding. In the psychological domain the material issue is the possibility of a total depth-psychological and biological unmasking of the apparent autonomy and responsibility of human rational decisions by exposing the unconscious "magnificent rationality of the body" (Nietzsche) that determines them. This unmasking conflicts with the possibility relevant to the domain of social psychology and involves reducing all determinations of individual psychology to those of the control systems of collective living in small groups, such as married couples and families.[14] Moreover, within the sociological domain, the following question is crucial: Are social systems first to be defined on the basis of the identification (resting on consensus formation,, for example) of human beings with social groups and institutionally determined roles, so that the existence of such systems ultimately depends on whether they can be ethically and communicatively legitimated? Or, as self-generating systems necessary to life, must they, for their part, determine the preconsensual agreement and action conventions of human beings, so that the individualistic self-understanding of human subjects of action is reduced to an illusion?[15]

In my view, it cannot be doubted that a quasi-biological development of delimiting and self-generating systems is necessary to life, even on the levels of "subjective" and "objective spirit." To this extent, the corresponding methods of functional understanding are legitimate even as methods for the critical unmasking of the illusory self-understanding of individuals, groups, and entire societies. This has implications for the question concerning the total reduction of the purposive-rational and meaning-rational understanding of the intentional actions of persons to the functional understanding that concerns the teleological ratio of systems. It means that, here, the necessity reemerges of distinguishing between the historically sedimented quasi-nature of human beings and the ideal rational nature that is always, if more or less counterfactually, anticipated in the rationality claims of human actions and, above all, in the truth claims of human assertions.

Suppose we could at any time assume that the ideal nature of human beings that is always already anticipated were definitively realized in their historically realized nature. We would then have to postulate that, with regard to the functional understanding of actions in light of a teleological system ratio and with regard to the purposive- or meaning-rational understanding of action decisions in terms of subjectively sensible and responsible reasons, something like a mutual reduction of each to the other is possible. This is similar to the supposition made above with regard to realizing nonfalsifiable rules of reason in the sense of ideal laws. There is postulated a correspondence between purposive- or meaning-rational understanding and the prognostically relevant explanation of actions as events. Nevertheless, for the most part, the difference between the counterfactually anticipated rational nature and the historically sedimented quasi- or pseudo-nature is characteristic of the *condition humaine*; hence, for the claim of functional understanding to provide unmasking and reductive tasks, another more complicated situation emerges.

On the one hand, it is entirely conceivable that human quasi-nature qua pseudo-nature supplies the point of departure for replacing the communicative-hermeneutic understanding of reasons (which aids the processes of reaching understanding about meaning and of forming consensus over validity claims) with the functional understanding of surreptitiously effective system imperatives. This is often the case when a psychotherapist comprehends a patient's reason for acting as a "secondary rationalization" for a functionally determined behavior, for example, one determined by the pathological control system of the patient's relation to his partner. It is also the case when a politician at a conference that apparently permits a form of comunication open to all good reasons comes to see that the arguments of his opponents are determined by surreptitiously effective "reasons of state," in the sense of a limited equivalence class of functionally suitable problem solutions. On the other hand, it is not conceivable that the good or bad reasons behind human action, and especially communicative action, could be completely and functionally understood in terms of a limited self-generating system. This is demonstrated by an argument that theorists of reductionistic systems possibly regard as all too philosophical and pedantic: the normative validity claims of communicative actions or at least the truth claims of the systems theorists, are necessarily related, in principle, to the unrestricted system of possible consensus formation in an unlimited argumentation community. That is, they are necessarily related to a system which the classical metaphysics of Christian Platonism—thus the work of Malebranche and Leibniz— understood as one of the "intellectus divinus" that guarantees truth.

Accordingly, whereas the possibility and necessity of the functionalistic reduction of understanding is more or less plausible depending on the circumstances, in the situation of communicative understanding, it proves necessary to begin essentially with the more or less counterfactual anticipation of a communication community which refers to universally intelligible reasons. This is also true of the methodological situation of the hermeneutic understanding of alien cultures and one's own tradition, since this situation is to be grounded on that of communicative understanding. Hence, the "preconception of perfection" (*der Vorgriff der Vollkommenheit*) H.-G. Gadamer posits is, I think, the obligatory presupposition of the hermeneutic situation.[16] Nonetheless, obviously, the reason for the tension I have elucidated between the applicability of a hermeneutic understanding that refers to rational grounds and the applicability of a functionally reduced understanding again lies in the ambiguity of human quasi-nature. This is dependent on sedimenting itself in limited self-generating systems, as well as transcending all such systems in the direction of the unlimited system in which normative validity claims—and, above all, truth claims— can, in principle, be redeemed. Given this situation, it makes sense again to proceed from the interests of knowledge posited thus far, in determining the methodological position of the functional understanding of social system structures. In doing so, the following options emerge:

1. The case of the actions and institutions functionally determined by quasi-natural system structures is similar to that of the causal explanation of actions which, as events, are determined by quasi-natural dispositions. It is also possible in the former—indeed, for the interest of social technology in manipulation and control, it is advisable—to make the structures reified in the historically sedimented quasi-nature of human beings the object of functionally reduced understanding, and thus to abstract from the human claims and possibilities that transcend such reduction. Of course, here, the manipulative interference in functionally understood system structures will be connected to a further "reduction" of the functionally understandable control system to mechanisms that can be explained causally. Be that as it may, insofar as it abstracts from problems of legal and moral legitimation, functionally reduced understanding of system-determined modes of action and institutions can be interpreted as knowledge of control that is relevant to social technology. Even the purely functionalist understanding of actions and institutions in light of the ratio of social systems or subsystems must be interested in constructing and perhaps artificially maintaining in quasi-natural scientific subject-object relation in its knowledge of its object. This allows it to prevent those initiatives by human subject-objects that withdraw the object and hence, the ground from functional systems analysis by reflecting on their own determination by it. We thus encounter another analogy, this time one between preventing self-fulfilling and self-denying prophecies through the one-sided suspension of communication with the human subject-object of knowledge, and the functionally reduced understanding of social systems. In both cases, the community of informed scientists (and, perhaps, their employers) must reserve to itself the actual human status of subjects of knowledge with validity claims that can be redeemed only in an unlimited, open communication community. In short, just as a behavioral science interested solely in prognostically relevant causal explanations of events can be characterized as the quasi-physicalistic type of technologically relevant social science, a systems analysis interested only in functional understanding can be characterized as the quasi-biological type of technologically relevant social science. Both cases must reckon with a tendency toward technocracy that can be understood in terms of the cognitive interest in producing and maintaining sufficient division between subject and object.

2. For this reason, we must focus on the possibility and, given the emancipatory interest of knowledge, the necessity of a critical social science that effectively compensates for the technocratic tendency characteristic of the methods of both a functional, interpretive social science and a causal explanatory one. Thus we are led to the other alternative, the second possibility of a social scientific method that makes use of functional understanding. Illustrations are again offered by the methods of psychoanalysis and the critique of ideology, both of which waver between a scientistic and a hermeneutic self-understanding. And again, the emancipatory-compensatory crux of these methods lies in their opposition to the tendency of quasi-natural scientific methods to neutralize the self-reflection of the subject-object of knowledge on its own quasi-nature in favor of a subject-object split that is free of disturbance. Insofar as this quasi-nature is the object of scientific knowledge, the subject-object's reflection on it is placed in the service of a methodical deepening of self-understanding. This does not mean now that an already functionally reduced understanding must serve the prognostic, and thus technologically relevant, explanation of events; rather, in reverse, though functional understanding can itself still imply knowledge of the causal mechanisms presupposed in the realization of system functions, it must serve a nonreduced understanding. This consideration complicates the dialectical conceptual "figure" of a mediation of understanding by explanation that we have already discussed and which contrasts with the mediation of prognostically relevant explanation by understanding emphasized by Hempel and Max Weber. Here, the complication is that we must take into account a functional-analytic phase between the hermeneutic and the causal-analytic phases.[17]

3. In addition to social-technological and emancipatory-compensatory functions, however, the quasi-biological methods of understanding system functions can acquire a third function. We need not take either a technical interest or a critical, emancipatory interest in the objective teleology of the self-generating systems necessary to our lives. That is, we need not be interested in either controlling the means or transcending the system. Instead, our interest can be directed at a vital identification, and hence, preservation. This is as true for the psychic and social systems that constitute our second nature as it is for the biotic system on which we depend in the sense of our first nature. Here, nature and quasi-nature do not reflect only "the existence

of things, insofar as they form a necessary connection" (Kant), as they do for the physicalistic and quasi-physicalistic explanation of events; they are not simply the material for realizing our goals. Rather, they are a technologically relevant standard for our goal orientation, a standard to be obtained through consensual processes of coming to an understanding.

This fundamentally holds for all social systems with which we identify in the course of our lives. It holds especially, however, for a biotic-social, total system only recently developed as a unified, self-generating system for all human beings. I mean that total, socioeconomic and bioecological system of earthdwellers that has emerged in the expansion of industrial society and its exploitation and molestation of the planetary ecosphere. Today, if we look at the survival potential of all other human social systems, and of the bioecological systems of animals and plants, for the first time we must regard these systems as sub-systems of the total system and its determination by human initiative. It seems to me that the state of this system of first and second nature has become the most important standard to which long-term human goals must be made to conform.

Thus we have an especially illuminating example of the way in which functional understanding, as the quasi-biological method of social science, can, in principle, assume a function that differs from the quasi-physicalistic explanation of events. It does not merely offer—as always—an ambivalent knowledge of control, good for social technology, that should be subordinate and accessible to control by the communicative agreement of human beings over goals; it also contributes to the discursive determination of goals, insofar as it uncovers objective-teleological, self-generating systems with which human beings must identify if they wish to survive. In this sense, the task of maintaining and continuing social systems, hence, institutions of all kinds, can and must take on a systematic and restrictive function with regard to the long-term task of realizing those ideals of reason only in the light of which the communicative understanding of human beings is possible. This is especially true to the extent that these systems must be seen as subsystems of a biological-social total system of earthdwellers.

The following is also true: The state of the social system in which long-term human survival is to be guaranteed will be difficult to discover in abstraction from the needs of legal and moral legitimation, and that means from the possible redemption of the normative validity claims presupposed in all communicative understanding. For example, a social system that, over the long term, does not fulfill the needs of legitimating its institutions legally and morally may fall apart as a functional system.[18] This may also, and precisely, hold for the planetary social system I have indicated. Hence, the third function of functional understanding no longer involves an abstractive differentiation between actions that can be understood in light of system imperatives and actions understood only in light of universal norms of reason. Instead, it involves mediation still related to the long-term development of the system, namely, mediation between the system imperatives of biotic-social reality and the imperative to realize the ideal of reason always already anticipated in processes of coming to an understanding.

These highly preliminary, tentative remarks on functional understanding may suffice to elucidate the transcendental-pragmatic approach to a methodologically differentiated theory of science. To summarize: This approach goes beyond the abstractive, logico-semantic explanation of "scientific systematizations," accomplishing a transcendental-pragmatic reflection on subjective forms of inquiry and the meaning-constitutive cognitive interests that stand behind them. In this way, it attempts to clarify the categorial preconception of the synthetic acts of knowledge connected to causality, objective teleology, and subjective teleology (i.e., purposive rationality and the meaning rationality of situationally related goals).

# 3

# The Transformation of
# Transcendental Philosophy

At this point the question arises as to the fundamental, philosophical consequences of our attempt to resolve those problems within the theory of science that are connected to the E-V controversy. I believe these consequences could consist in overcoming the assumption of a theoretical subject-object relation in which the "subject" pole is considered the "limit of the world" and does not need to be made a reflexive theme. This is an assumption that—even and precisely— logical empiricism continues (following the antimetaphysical metaphysics of the *Tractatus*) and upon which it does not reflect. The claim I have made in this book, however, already points in the direction of an overcoming. As we have seen, it calls for an integrating supplementation of logical-semantic or onto-semantic interpretations of "scientific systematizations" in terms of a transcendental-pragmatic reflection on the subjective-intersubjective conditions of the possibility of valid cognitive achievements. In keeping with this approach, I want in the following at least to indicate what I would take as the fundamental philosophical implications of the epistemology of the social sciences I have outlined. At issue, it seems, is a transcendental-pragmatic transformation of Kant's transcendental philosophy. Therefore I shall try to illuminate the crux of the new approach in connection with Kant's characteristic and problematic distinction between the world of "appearances" and "things in themselves."

In my view, this distinction contains both a progressive and a regressive aspect. It is progressive insofar as it rejects the illusion of pre-

Kantian metaphysics according to which one could speak meaningfully of a world we could know without, at the same time, reflecting, as the subject of being-in-the-world, on two things: (a) the transcendental, subjective conditions of the possibility of constituting the objects or meaning of this world, and (b) the possible objective validity of the knowledge of experience. It is progressive in that it rejects the theoretical-ontological illusion that one can have meaningful experience as something resembling a pure spirit occupying a position outside the world of the world-in-itself. True, this is an unorthodox interpretation of the Copernican turn, and relies on the perspective of a transcendental-pragmatic reflection on being-in-the-world. It leads to the following criticism of Kant: The account of "things in themselves" is regressive insofar as it grants things-in-themselves real existence as well as causal functions in both affecting the sensuousness of subjects and, conversely, founding their spontaneity. These aspects of things-in-themselves are a function of the architectonic Kant establishes, of the "transcendental idealism," "empirical realism," and "transcendental realism" of things-in-themselves in whose sphere the reality of the intelligible I and the validity of the ethical "ought" are to be rooted. In granting reality to things in themselves, however, Kant contradicts the restriction of the use of categories to the phenomenal world, positing, instead, an "analogous," metaphysical schematism of categories.[1] This regressive feature of Kant's system is opposed by both metaphysical nostalgia and the progressive aspects of radically questioning metaphysical illusion. It must, nolens volens, rehabilitate the false assumption that one can know the world "as something" from a position of unengaged "theoria" outside of it.

The critical and metaphysical deep meaning of the Kantian system indicates why, despite repeated recognition of its inner paradoxes, constant, extremely shrewd attempts were made by interpreters to attribute these paradoxes to misunderstandings. I do not wish to associate myself with these attempts to renew Kantianism; rather, in connection with the resolution of the E-V controversy that I have outlined, I shall try to indicate how the progressive aspect of Kant's approach can be concretized within the framework of a conscious transformation of transcendental philosophy without retreating into the illusion of metaphysical-ontological "theoria."

The tenable critical thrust of the transcendental critique of reason is not that, in principle, we cannot know real, existing things as they are in themselves. The element of truth in this paradoxical teaching can be "sublated" under the proviso of fallibilism, in the sense of the Peircean distinction between the infinite knowable and what we can actually know.[2] The critical thrust of the critique of reason, rather, consists in radically abandoning a concept of knowledge that refers to things-in-themselves as its actual objects—that is, to things to be considered independently of not only actual knowledge but also possible knowledge. Our idea of possible knowledge must, instead, be related to real things, insofar as they can be considered experienceable under the subjective and intersubjective conditions of our being-in-the-world. In other words, we cannot understand the possibility of the categorially determined experience of the objects of the natural sciences (primarily of physics, in the sense of the proto-physics of measurement and experiment) unless we simultaneously reflect on the subjective and intersubjective conditions of both our bodily practical being-in-the-world and the linguistic processes of coming to an understanding of being-in-the-world.

This is exactly the thesis I have elucidated in this analysis and illustrated in the following series of three transcendental-pragmatic insights, or reflections.

1. The first insight followed from von Wright's argument that within a sufficiently isolated world system, the concept of the causal necessity of changes of state presupposes the concept of experimental action. This argument led to insight into an onto-semantically and transcendentally-pragmatically grounded complementarity involving the mutual exclusion, and hence supplementation, of language games and of phenomenal domains corresponding to them. Briefly, these domains comprise the description of objects of nature and the explanation of events, on the one hand, and, on the other, the understanding of action, an understanding that, in principle, does not concern objects but rather can be only a reflexive theme. Now, in my view, this insight does not imply merely that nature as "the existence of things insofar as they form a necessary connection" (Kant) presupposes the reality of actions that can be reflexively understood, grounded in purposive-rational terms, and hence, considered free; conversely, it implies that this concept of action presupposes the concept of a causally determined reality of sufficiently closed natural systems, which serves as the ex-perimentally manipulatable environment of human beings. (In fact, we assume such a comprehensive, natural law-governedness whenever

we refer to the "capability" of acting. If everything were possible, if the world surrounding us were governed by no causal laws, this notion would lose its meaning.)

Yet this mutual implication of the concepts of the freedom of action and causal necessity within closed natural systems certainly does not mean that, ontologically considered, the real world or the world that can be the theme of science must be subsumed under a Laplacean causal determinism. This conception (which Kant shared) results from an illegitimate theoretical-metaphysical extrapolation from the causal necessity within closed natural systems that acting subjects can manipulate to the world at large. The world at large, however, need not be identified within the world qua object of experimental manipulation. This is especially so, since the former can be the theme of a nonclassical physics that contains functional laws about mathematical probabilities instead of causal hypotheses to be tested in experiment. If nature were made a theme in this "distanced" sense, apart from the causal laws of classical physics, it could no longer be conceived of as the immediate complement to the comprehensible reality of experimental actions. Instead, it would have to be seen simply as the complement to the comprehensible reality of scientific actions (of knowledge) in general. To be sure, the indirect testability of corresponding theories must be guaranteed within the complementary domain of experimental manipulation; but that perhaps can be clarified by assuming that causal laws are approximated by probabilistic laws in the domain of the proto-physical world of measuring human beings.

I think that a conception of complementarity of this kind permits a transformation of Kant's solution to the antinomy of freedom and causal determinism. The theoretical-metaphysical differentiation of two worlds—that of the merely intelligible freedom (of the will) and that of the causally determined world of experience—is replaced by a phenomenological and linguistic complementarity. On the one hand, we have the perspicuously experienceable reality of natural laws and regularities of human quasi-nature, and, on the other, the reality of the subjective freedom of action, a reality that can be made the theme of reflexive understanding.

2. The second reflection consists in the insight that the purposive-rational understanding of subjective, nature-manipulating actions and their results must be linguistically articulatable even to be comprehensible to the individual subject of knowledge. This shows that re-

flexive, subjective understanding presupposes intersubjective, communicative understanding, hence, a model of communicative action or interaction that cannot itself be reduced to the model of nonreciprocal purposive-rational action on the part of the individual. This argument demonstrates the possibility of resolving the E-V controversy insofar as the central cognitive interest in hermeneutic understanding can be understood as complementary to, rather than competitive with, the scientific-cognitive interest in the causal explanation of objectifiable natural events. In this context the decisive argument involves distinguishing between two different kinds of transition — the transition from I-thou communication to communication with virtual co-subjects in the third person, and the transition to the observational standpoint of the theoretical relation between subject and object. This transcendental-pragmatic distinction discloses the conditions of the possibility of a distinction within the social sciences themselves between a quasi-natural, scientific, explanatory account of actions and a hermeneutic, interpretive one complementary to the first.

Given this resolution of the E-V controversy in terms of a transcendental-hermeneutic expansion of the thesis of complementarity, a further significant transformation of the Kantian architectonic becomes possible. The distinction between two worlds results in a distinction between the domain of "theoretical reason" within which, according to Kant, there can be no "constitution" of the object domain of the Geisteswissenschaften or social sciences and the domain of "practical reason," for which such an object domain can be a practical theme, though never a scientific one. We can now modify this distinction in terms of one that itself remains relevant to the theory of science.

It is true that, because of the prescientific prejudice in favor of the theoretical relation between subject and object, the possibility of a primary objectification of the world is restricted to what one could call "nature," in Kant's sense. To a certain extent, the distinction Kant and the early Wittgenstein make between the world that can be the theme of theoretical natural science and the transcendental-subjective "limit of the world" is confirmed by the situation of double complementarity, insofar as it refers to the transcendental-pragmatic presupposition of the concepts of first and second nature (i.e., the historically sedimented, social quasi-nature of human beings). It is still possible, however, to speak of a secondary constitution of the objects of the "historical-social" world, because it is possible to move from

I-thou communication to communication with virtual co-subjects in the third person and because hermeneutics can therefore make society and history its theme as the subject-object of scientific knowledge. Thus one aspect of the situation of double complementarity is clear. As we have seen, this situation arises from transcendental-pragmatic reflection on the subjective-intersubjective conditions of the primary objectification of the world, i.e., the constitution of nature. It is now clear that the situation of double complementarity can be interpreted neither in terms of the metaphysical dualism of two worlds nor in terms of a dualism of theoretical and practical reason that scientistically restricts the concept of science. Rather, as indicated by the neo-Kantian attempt to ground the "cultural sciences" by combining a quasi-natural scientific constitution of objects with a "value-relative" constitution of concepts, the problem of the secondary constitution of objects is the essential difficulty of the Geisteswissenschaften. In this context, the introduction of the concept of the "communicative experience of signs" seems epistemologically decisive. In principle, it cannot be reduced to the experience of "indices' (Peirce) that is constitutive of the encounter with nature but, rather, rests on a distinctive synthesis of "sensuousness" (in the sense of the "empathy" neopositivists identify with *Verstehen*) and the understanding of intentional or conventional "symbols" (Peirce and Royce). The concept of *communicative experience* I have introduced corresponds to the constitution of "historical-social reality" (Dilthey) as the comprehensible reality of subject-objects.

Thus the dimension of the hermeneutic understanding of "historical-social reality" is opened up between objectifiable nature and that dimension of the subjective-intersubjective conditions of objectifying nature which can be only a reflexive theme. This new dimension, however, implies not simply an expansion of the concept and theory of science but also a transformation of the concept of the "transcendental subject" that Kant presupposed as the condition of the possibility of objective knowledge of nature.

I do not mean that the Kantian concept of the identical subject of knowledge to be presupposed in all subjects of virtually universally valid knowledge conflicts with the possibility and necessity of hermeneutically mediated understanding with alien knowing subjects (i.e., alien cultures and one's own cultural tradition once it has become alien). Presently, neo-Wittgensteinians sometimes connect denial of an identical transcendental subject of knowledge with the idea of understanding alien and past forms of life in their "incommensurability" with one's own. Precisely in view of the philosophical reflection on the conditions of the possibility of hermeneutic understanding, however, this denial proves self-contradictory. Thus, for example, in the sentence, "In principle, we cannot abstract from the fact that we are individuals conditioned by different forms of life," the first part contradicts the second on the level of philosophical discourse. The first part implicitly views the "we" as the subject of the intersubjectively valid insight into the limits of the possibility of the abstraction; hence, it attributes to the "we" precisely that transcendental function disputed by the second part.[3] Suppose, for example, that, in view of the ontic diversity of alien (or dead) persons who can be identified by proper names, one regarded an interpretive self-transposition into this subject-object as possible without having to presuppose the "transcendental I." On the level of the epistemology of hermeneutic understanding, this would be completely paradoxical.[4] Hence, the conditions of the possibility of hermeneutic understanding cannot be conceived under the neo-Wittgensteinian premise that incommensurable language game monads (forms of life or social systems) could themselves guarantee an inter-subjective basis for the intelligibility of meaning. Rather, to the extent that the synthesis of hermeneutic understanding mediated between forms of life alien to each other (for example, in translating between languages), it would have to be grasped as the original manifestation of "communicative competence," thus of the hermeneutically relevant aspect of the unity of the transcendental subject of knowledge.

Nevertheless, in order to conceptualize this synthesis of understanding as an a priori mediation between empirical subjects of knowledge and forms of life in the synchronic and diachronic dimension, we must radically transform the classic concept of the transcendental subject. It can no longer be grounded in the prelingual and precommunicative synthetic unity of the consciousness of objects and self-consciousness. This unity in the coherence and evidence of data for a "consciousness in general" can no longer function as the sufficient condition of the possibility of the intersubjective validity of knowledge. In other words, the "methodological solipsism" of the "ego cogito" postulated by Hus-serl in his *Cartesian Meditations* can no longer be binding for the reflexive analysis of the transcendental subject as the condition of constituting the meaning of the world. Like the intersubjectively valid understanding of the meaning of something as something, the self-understanding of

the I must already be able to be linguistically articulated, hence, mediated by the hermeneutic synthesis of communication. Thus the
meaning of all thoughts must possess public validity, and therefore
cannot be understood as the noematic act of a solitary intentional
noesis.

This means that the concept of the transcendental subject can no
longer be conceived of in terms of the unity of a consciousness in
general, as self-sufficient and finished. Rather, it must accommodate
the thought of the communication community as the subject of processes of coming to an understanding about meaning. The possibility
of coming to an understanding about meaning in general, however,
already presupposes the possibility of forming a consensus about truth.[5]
Hence, the assent of other subjects of knowledge can no longer count
merely as the "subjectively necessary touchstone of the correctness
of our judgments," as it does for Kant; neither would the objective
validity of the form of our judgment be assured by the precommunicative "consciousness in general."[6] Instead, the possibility of creating
consensus in an unrestricted communication community must, in principle, be included among the conditions of the possibility of truth.[7] In
short, whereas the concept of the transcendental subject of knowledge
is indispensable for understanding the truth claim of any empirical
subject of knowledge, it requires a new explication. The definitive
subject of intersubjectively valid knowledge is identical with that ideal
communication community which is always already counterfactually
anticipated in every community that comes to an understanding about
meaning and truth and which, in addition, is, nonetheless, always to
be realized.

3. I believe the transformation of transcendental philosophy that is
most decisive for epistemology issues only from the third step of the
transcendental-pragmatic reflections. This is the step that questions
the complementarity between the nature or quasi-nature that can be
explained objectively and the social dimension of intersubjectivity that
can be understood reflexively or hermeneutically; for, in its view, this
is an anticipatory idealization.

I have already rejected the transcendental idealism of Kant that
corresponds to both an "empirical realism" and a transcendental realism of the thing-in-itself. In so doing, I appealed not only to a general
reinterpretation of the relation between natural laws and the subjective
conditions of the possibility of their constitution in the sense of the

thesis of complementarity, I also appealed especially to the corresponding complementarity between quasi-natural social "laws" and the subjective conditions of their possibility. On the one hand, the scientifically and theoretically relevant constitution of both nature and quasi-nature turns out to depend on subjective and intersubjective conditions, for example, on the underlying cognitive interest in a theoretical knowledge-for-control over objects. But we have seen that the transcendental-pragmatic understanding of these subjective conditions of constitution is not anchored in a transcendental-logical structure of a pure consciousness, since such a pure consciousness cannot be thought to constitute significance; rather, it is anchored ontically in the anthropological structure of knowledge-constitutive interests. Therefore, this understanding, on the other hand, includes the assumption that, to ground concrete differences in possible methodologically relevant types of science, the real ontic conditions of nature or of social quasi-nature must be set in relation to the transcendental-pragmatic conditions of modes of thematization. As we have seen, first nature cannot be made a scientific theme in terms of the interest in coming to an understanding. Conversely, the "ontic quasi-nature" of human beings can be made a scientific theme as the focus of a hermeneutic inquiry based on the interest in reaching understanding. Within certain confines connected with the measure to which dehistoricization or objectification is achieved, however, it can also be made the object of quasi-physicalistic or quasi-biological social sciences. This requires the assumption of appropriate subjective-pragmatic conditions of "positing" reified behavioral dispositions in the sense of a quasi-natural scientific subject-object relation undisturbed by Merton effects.

In the case of the emancipatory cognitive interest of the critical-reconstructive social sciences, this correlation of real-ontic and transcendental-pragmatic conditions of the possibility of scientific knowledge (a correlation that can be influenced practically) proves crucial for the successful constitution of objects as the presupposition of a methodologically relevant focus on them. At issue here is the possibility of compensating for the practical tendency toward objectification that is associated with "positing" the subject-object in the social sciences. The point is to provoke an empirically relevant self-reflection on the part of the social scientific subject-object by means of a "disclosive" causal or functional explanation of the nonconscious motivations and consequences of action for which the agent, nonetheless, is responsible.

That way, such sciences help "sublate" historically sedimented quasi-nature qua pseudo-nature. In this case, the necessity of correlating real-ontic and transcendental-pragmatic conditions of the possibility of scientific knowledge is expressed in the following circumstance: Human pseudo-nature is both the practical basis of the motivations and consequences of actions for which the agent cannot account, and the object of correct, empirical, quasi-nomological explanation and predictions. The interest in helping realize norms or reasons as "ideal laws" for human behavior, however, subjects this pseudo-nature to change by the human subjects of action and science. Hence, to the extent that human beings are successful in transcending their pseudo-nature, in the sense of the reflectively mediated emancipation I mean here (an extraordinarily delicate emancipation, given misuses—desired or not—and the bitter opposition of the counter-Enlightenment), they escape the positing grip of objectifying social technology and offer their assistance as co-subjects in a dialogical, deliberative form of planning.[8]

In changing the practically influenceable ontic conditions of the social sciences, emancipatory praxis brings about that dialectical mediation of theoretical and practical reason which the young Hegelians, and in particular the young Marx, postulated in connection with Hegel's speculative and theoretical sublation of the subject-object dialectic in the absolute knowledge of knowledge and its substantive content. In my view, as long as such emancipatory praxis can be postulated, it entails no "sublation of philosophy"; rather, within the framework of a transcendental-pragmatic transformation of philosophy, it indicates precisely the point at which a postulate of the theory of science becomes necessary: We must assume that the transition to the real praxis that forms the object of the social sciences can itself be derived from the critical-reconstructive social sciences. However, this transition can be programmed neither dogmatically nor hypostatized as a predictable, objective process. To this extent, the formal conditions of its scientific derivation and practical organization (in the sense of the political development of a consensus on proposals) remain to be subjected to the regulative principle of a transcendental philosophy that includes ultimate ethical foundations. To transcendental-pragmatic reflection, it is clear that at this point we have accomplished the mediation between the subject and object of science that Hegel anticipated and on which he reflected in an ex post way. It is accomplished as the transition from the practically influencable ontic conditions of social science to ethically responsible social praxis itself.

It seems to me that the transformation projected here from the perspective of a differentiation of the theory of science amounts to the establishment of a new paradigm for fundamental philosophy. Beginning with my transcendental-pragmatic expansion of the onto-semantics that constitutes the ascendant form of language-analytic philosophy at present, one could look for the new concept of first philosophy in a transcendental semiotics incorporating semantics and pragmatics.[9] On the level of philosophical methodology, language-analytic philosophy introduced the outline of a third paradigm of first philosophy, in addition to the pre-Kantian *Metaphysica generalis seu Ontologia* and the philosophy of transcendental consciousness. Nevertheless, despite the achievements of the neo-Wittgensteinians, it could not do justice to the level of reflection reached by classic transcendental philosophy from Kant to Hegel. Neither could it do justice to the dialectical and hermeneutic problems of the Geisteswissenschaften or social or cultural sciences discussed by Hegel, Marx, Dilthey, the neo-Kantians, and Max Weber. A transcendental semiotics does, however, integrate the methodological achievements of language-analytic philosophy (as well as those of the semiotic pragmatism of the American philosophy of "community" of C. S. Peirce, J. Royce, and G. H. Mead) with the idea of transcendental reflection as the paradigm of philosophical rationality. In this way, it is able to supply the fundamental philosophical framework for the required theory of science, a theory differentiated along both onto-semantic and transcendental-pragmatic lines.

# Appendix: Is the Controversy between Explanation and Understanding Obsolete?

Since the outbreak of the E-V controversy, there have been constant attempts to dismiss it as objectless, irrelevant to the theory of science, even ideologically determined. As far as I can see, there are three different motifs or types of argument for this tendency to consider the dispute obsolete.

1. Most important for the present investigation is a premise that has belonged periodically to the paradigm of analytic philosophy. The neopositivist logic of "unified science" argues that, although the dichotomy between explanation and understanding perhaps is warranted, it can be reduced to merely psychological and heuristic problems preliminary to the logic of scientific knowledge; that is, it precedes the structures of "scientific systematizations" (Hempel) that can be explicated within the "context of justification."

2. A second type can be understood as an amplification of this neopositivist distinction between features of knowledge that are relevant to the logic of science and those of interest simply from a psychological or pragmatic point of view. This is the ideological/anti-ideological topos, according to which the themes of the philosophy of the "interpretive Geisteswissenscahften" cannot be reduced pragmatically or psychologically; rather, they are to be attributed to "meaningless metaphysics," or worse, to be obscurantist ideology inspired in part by clerical reactionaries and in part by an anti-Western German romanticism directed against both scientific progress and the modern Enlightenment as a whole.

3. Prima facie very different from these first two topoi is a third, which representatives of a "hermeneutic phenomenology" have advocated in a characteristic way—to be sure, in a vague form not easily discussed. This topos starts with Heidegger's discovery of the "hermeneutic synthesis," in which something is understood "as something"; this is a discovery that forms the basic event of the "clearing of Being" in the projection of human being-in-the-world, which "philosophical hermeneutics" uses to deride as insignificant the older, methodologically relevant distinction between explanation and understanding. Still, the distantiation from a methodologically and epistemologically relevant hermeneutics in favor of a "philosophical hermeneutics" that begins from a deeper point may secretly be influenced by the kinds of argumentation topoi sketched above. This becomes clear in the following combination of suggestions by the late Heidegger, in which, with little reflection, he surrenders the modern theory of science to the neopositivist logic of science.

Heidegger is said to have shown the unitary "technical" character of the objectivizing science that has arisen from metaphysics in the modern era, which includes a history that explains events in chronological terms with an interest in controlling them. He is therefore said to have shown that the attempt to ground an alternative scientific methodology ultimately is hopeless, hence, antiquated. According to this conception, the philosophical primacy of hermeneutic understanding is not to be played off against the absolutization of the model of natural scientific causal explanation but, rather, against the modern absolutization of scientific "method" in general as the appropriate vehicle for the discovery of "truth."

It seems to me that these three topoi are suited only apparently (and this means only outwardly) to questioning the significance of the E-V controversy. At this point I want, first, to take a position with regard to the last topos. In my view, it rests on a mixture of noteworthy insights and misleading exaggerations or simplifications of the problem. The following seems to be essentially correct: Since its Greek beginnings, there has been a central tendency at work in Western metaphysics to develop and fix as paradigmatic the relation between subject and object that serves as the premise under which the world can be controlled theoretically. In modern times this subject-object relation became the foundation of mathematical natural science as a science that "posits" nature in experiment, and hence, is a priori related to technology. According to the fundamental character of this tendency, which Heidegger calls "enframing" (*Gestell*), human beings ultimately posit themselves and make themselves available to social technology under the same categories that first helped them dominate nature. In fact, nothing testifies to this tendency better than the belief that the epistemological relation between the subject and object of knowledge is no longer a reflective theme for contemporary analytic logic of science. That is, it is a theme neither for neopositivism nor for the latest tendency to reduce the object of the theory of science to the polytheism of more or less strong theories competing with one another. The relation is rather assumed to be all the more self-evident.

To this extent, one can, in fact, speak of an absolutization of the scientific-theoretical knowledge of control and of a technical interest in knowledge that is concealed and presupposed on the side of the subject. Both can be viewed as the result of Western metaphysics. Moreover, in the modern period, a general "rationalization" (Max Weber) of life practice accompanies the development in which the world is subjected to the control of science and technology. A more precise understanding of this general rationalization, however, discloses part of the subjective premises of the "enframing," subjective premises that can in no way be made accessible to causal and explanatory control and which, nonetheless, belong to the same life process of methodological standardization and discipline. Here, I mean the purposive action that, a priori, opens up the categorial horizon of a search for means, and hence, of a causal analysis of nature and possibly of social quasi-nature. As the ideal type for a rationalization of political and economic life practice, since the Renaissance and early capitalism, purposive-rational action has complemented the theoretical, causal explanation of the world (it is often identified with the mechanistic rationality of bodily movements that can be explained, as in Thomas Hobbes). Nevertheless, it is not primarily the object of nomological, causal explanation. As Weber recognized, it is, rather, the object of a social science involving rational understanding, first, and "interpretive explanation," only second.

In supplementing the Heideggerian perspective on the process of technicization with Weber's account of the process of rationalization, these comments make clear that it is inexact to equate methodical rationality with the rationality of objective, "controlling," and explanatory "science" (in the sense of natural science and quasi-nomological social science). Such an equation does not illuminate but rather obscures the complementary relation—i.e., a relation of mutual exclusion and supplementation—between the causal-analytic ratio involved in the theoretical explanability of the world and the means-end ratio that is an aspect of the capacity of human practice to be understood.

This leveling conflation of the scientistic and practical sides of the contemporary process of rationalization also conceals a central issue in the methodologically relevant controversy over explanation and understanding, and hence, considers it obsolete. This becomes clear if one reflects that, to understand the purposive rationality of human action, one must presuppose the rationality of the linguistic and communicative process of coming to an understanding between human beings. (The same is true for the rationality of strategic action, in which the purposive rationality of the action refers to and is measured by that of an opponent's action.) In turn, in the sense of the more or less counterfactual anticipation of an ideal, this process presupposes the ethical rationality of a communication community in which people mutually recognize one another's equal rights. This structure of the ideal-typical presuppositions of methodologically relevant types of rationality[1] is becoming transparent to philosophical reflection. In its light, I think we must consider it a capitulation of reason to surrender methodical rationality to the monopoly of the technical and scientific control of the world and, accordingly, to give up the claim of the hermeneutic Geisteswissenschaften or social sciences to autonomy in favor of a "happening" of truth or being that is no longer accessible to normative responsibility.[2]

Such a tendency, of course, becomes understandable when one considers the tendency exhibited by the paradigmatic complex of causal-analytic, scientific rationality and purposive-rational, practical rationality since the start of the modern period. This complex has tended to split off from the ideal types of rationality that are presupposed and, as a value-neutral, ideology-free complex of publicly recognized, procedural rationality, to disengage itself from the ethical-religious sphere in which, in the final analysis, norms and values are subjectively and privately grounded in ultimate decisions. This is precisely the disassociation Weber brought to consciousness in distinguishing "value-free science," on the one hand (including the purposive-rational understanding of actions) from irrational decisions of conscience founded on the polytheism of values, on the other.[3] He thereby helped ground the ideological complementarity system characteristic of the twentieth century, consisting in a public scientism or pragmatism and a private existentialism, a system that is considered by many to constitute the *ultima ratio* of a pluralistic, liberal-democratic social order.[4]

However, even in a social order that wants to ground itself on conventions ("agreements" through consensus-formation) free decisions of conscience norms, the validity of all final norms and truths can in no way be suspended or delivered to ultimate private decisions. This is the case simply because the rules and norms of communication serve as the condition of the possibility of conventions and agreement and are always already presupposed as intersubjectively valid.[5] Hence, it becomes clear that the monopolization of methodologically relevant rationality by the complex of causal-analytic, scientific rationality and purposive-rational, practical rationality is by no means to be accepted as fate or as the destiny of the "history of being." As already indicated, this process must, rather, be understood critically. It reflects the separation of a complex of scientific and technological rationality paradigmatic for the contemporary process of rationalization from ideally presupposed forms of communicative hermeneutic, on the one hand, and from ethical rationality, on the other.

If this assessment of the situation is correct, there is no reason to reclaim the fundamental prescientific domain of understanding qua "world-disclosure," together with the problem of practical reason, as the domain of a "happening of truth" that evades methodical standardization, and to contrapose them to the domain of a scientific method equated with that under which the world is made accessible to theoretical explanation. Instead, even within the complex of rationality that is paradigmatic for the modern era, the point is to distinguish between the causal-analytic ratio of scientific-theoretical world explanation and the purposive rationality of understanding it presupposes as its complement. This is necessary if we are to reconstruct this purposive rationality as a partial aspect or limit case of the intersubjective understanding that depends on the ratio of communicative experience.

Such an analysis is still supported by Heidegger's account of interpretive being-in-the-world (in *Being and Time*), insofar as it suggests a distinction between two complementary poles of interpretive being-in-the-world even within the prescientific domain of a phenomenology of the life world. These poles are: (1) the controlling objectification of the merely "present at hand," and (2) the communicative understanding in the sense of participation, of "being-with" other subjects of being-in-the-world. One can now see the explanatory natural sciences, on the one hand, and the interpretive Geisteswissenschaften, on the other, as methodical stylizations of the polar-complementary modes of interpretive being-in-the-world. This suggests that "philosophical hermeneutics" is not to be seen as a way of making the methodological interest of traditional hermeneutics obsolete; rather, it is to be viewed as a contribution to making good the (quasi-transcendental) grounding of hermeneutic methodology in the *Lebensphilosophie* that Dilthey attempted.

In contrast to the scientistic (and existentialist) absolutization of the methodical rationality in which the world is made accessible to theoretical objectification and causal explanation, we can develop a system of premises that reflects four different typical forms of rationality: (1) the scientific rationality of causal analysis presupposes, (2) the technological rationality of purposive-rational action that, for its part, presupposes (3) the hermeneutic rationality of understanding or coming to an understanding, and therein presupposes (4) ethical rationality.[6] If this analysis is correct, it already contains as well the decisive counterargument to the second type of argument as to the obsolete character of the E-V controversy, namely, the suggestion that interest in the dichotomy rests on nothing but a reactionary-romantic, anti-Enlightenment ideology.

That the theme of understanding in the Geisteswissenschaften is more susceptible to ideology than that of scientific explanation is easily understood, given Bacon's *natura nonnisi parendo vincitur*, which enforces the value-neutral approach of a rationality that is, a priori, related to by technology. Furthermore, the immunity of natural scientific rationality to ideology conforms to the possibility that it can serve any ideology or political power that is ready to acknowledge the factual authority of experts and to secure the margin of freedom necessary for their work. This consideration exposes the illusory or ideological character of the prejudice that tries simply to equate the scientistically absolutized rationality of explanation with the Enlightenment's idea of reason or progress. Conversely, the susceptibility of the theme of understanding in the Geisteswissenschaften to ideology corresponds to a possibility that exists only here, namely, that of contributing to the rational reconstruction and critique of the motivations of human actions and institutions, and hence, to the reconstruction and critique of the functional domain of possible ideology.

Hence, it is clear that, to show the irrelevance of the second topos of obsolescence, one need not deny that in the nineteenth and early twentieth centuries the German philosophy of the Geisteswissenschaften was in many ways determined by ideological, romantic, and naturalistic resentments. The questionable character of ideologies, however, whether on the level of lived cultural tradition or the level of their scientific reconstruction, cannot be exposed or critically destroyed with the help of causal-explanatory methods alone. It is decisive for the relevance of the E-V dichotomy that it, rather, requires the assistance of purposive-rational and meaning-rational interpretive methods. To this extent, the rationality of reconstructive understanding appears as the only possible way of continuing and expanding the Enlightenment beyond its natural scientific orientation into the sociocultural domain to which natural science itself, as a human activity, belongs.

Hence, as an objection to the relevance of the E-V controversy, only that of the neopositivist logic of science remains, according to which the problem of "understanding" can be reduced to a complex of questions external to the logic of explanation and which are interesting only from a psychological-pragmatic point of view. This objection, however, is neither exclusively nor primarily directed against the relevance of the E-V controversy; rather, it is the basic argument for the logic of explanation of unified science, and therefore constitutes a position *within* the controversy. In this book I criticize this position from a "transcendental-pragmatic perspective," offering an alternative to the paradigmatic argument of the logic of science.

# Notes

## Translator's Introduction

1. J. G. Droysen, *Grundriss der Historik* (1858/68), republished in Droysen, *Historik. Vorlesung über Enzklopädie und Methodologie der Geschichte*, ed. R. Hübner (Munich, 1957). L. von Ranke, *Aus Werk und Nachlass*, ed. Walter Peter Fuch and Theodore Schieder (Munich, 1964).

2. Dilthey, *Der Aufbau der geschichtlichen Welt in den Geisteswissenschaften* (Frankfurt, 1970).

3. C. Hempel, "The Function of General Laws in History," in Hempel, *Aspects of Scientific Explanation* (London, 1965).

4. Dray, *Laws and Explanation in History* (Oxford, 1957).

5. See, for example, P. Winch, *The Idea of a Social Science and Its Relation to Philosophy* (New York, 1958); "Understanding a Primitive Society," in Bryan Wilson, ed., *Rationality* (New York, 1971); A. T. Meldon, *Free Action* (London, 1961); C. Taylor, "Interpretation and the Sciences of Man," in *Understanding and Social Inquiry*, ed. F. Dallmayr and T. McCarthy (Notre Dame, Ind., 1977); G. H. von Wright, *Explanation and Understanding* (Ithaca, N.Y., 1971).

6. See M. Brodbeck, "Meaning and Action," in *Readings in the Philosophy of the Social Sciences*, ed. M. Brodbeck, 1968); and R. Rorty, "Method and Morality," in *Social Science as Moral Inquiry*, ed. N. Haan et al. (New York, 1983).

7. Taylor, "Interpretation."

8. Winch, *Idea of a Social Science*, p. 118.

9. Winch, "Understanding a Primitive Society."

10. Gadamer, *Wahrheit und Methode* (Tübingen, 1960). English, *Truth and Method* (New York, 1975).

11. Below, p. 82.

12. K.-O. Apel, "Szientistik, Hermeneutik, Ideologiekritik," in Apel, *Transformation der Philosophie* (Frankfurt, 1973); English translation in *Towards a Transformation of Philosophy*, trans. G. Adey and D. Frisby (London, 1980).

13. Habermas, *Erkenntnis und Interesse* (Frankfurt, 1968); trans. T. McCarthy (Boston, 1971), p. 271.

14. Below, p. 323.

15. A similar theory of cognitive, or "knowledge-constitutive," interests in the work of Habermas has been subjected to important criticisms; see, for example, T. McCarthy, *The Critical Theory of Jürgen Habermas* (Cambridge, Mass., 1978), pp. 92ff.

# Introduction

1. J. G. Droysen, "Grundriss der Historik" (1858/68), in *Historik, Vorlesung über Enzyklopädie und Methodologie der Geschichte*, ed. R. Hübner (Munich, 1937). On Droysen see E. Rothaker, *Mensch und Geschichte* (Bonn, 1950), pp. 49ff.; J. Rüsen, *Begriffene Geschichte, Genesis und Begrundung der Geschichtstheorie J. G. Droysens* (Paderborn, 1969), and "J. G. Droysen," in *Deutscher Historiker*, vol. 2, ed. H.-U. Wehler (Göttingen, 1971); H. Schnädelbach, *Geschichtsphilosophie nach Hegel* (Freiburg/Munich, 1974).

2. Droysen, "Grundriss," no. 9.

3. Ibid., no. 10.

4. See F. D. E. Schleiermacher, *Hermeneutik und Kritik*, ed. M. Frank (Frankfurt, 1977); A. Boeckh, *Enzyklopädie und Methodologie der philologischen Wissenschaften* (Leipzig, 1877); W. Dilthey, *Leben Schleiermachers*, ed. M. von Redeker, in *Gesammelte Schriften* (1914ff.; hereafter *GS*), vol. 14; H.-G. Gadamer, *Wahrheit und Methode* (Tübingen, 1960); English, *Truth and Method*, (New York, 1975); and H. Kimmerle, *Die Hermeneutik Schleiermachers in Zusammenhang seines spekulativen Denkens* (Heidelberg, 1957).

5. On the history of hermeneutics see W. Dilthey, "Die Enstehung der Hermeneutik" (1900), in *GS*, vol. 5; J. Wach, *Das Verstehen, Grundzüge einer Geschichte der hermeneutischen Theorie im 19. Jahrhundert*, 3 vols. (Tübingen, 1926-33).

6. Droysen, "Grundriss," no. 10.

7. Droysen, *Historik*, p. 25.

8. Droysen, "Grundriss," no. 12.

9. Ibid., no. 37.

10. See J. S. Mill, *A System of Logic Ratiocinative and Inductive* (London, 1843). In *Logik und Systematik der Geisteswissenschaften* (Munich, 1926), E. Rothaker claims that J. Schiel's translation of Mill's term *moral sciences* as *Geisteswissenschaften* first introduced the latter term into the German language. Moreover, he suggests that the translation was itself preconditioned by the tradition of the Geisteswissenschaft (singular) in the Hegelian school and especially by the work of Fr. T. Visher and K. Chr. Fr. Krause. On this terminology, see also A. Diemer, "Geisteswissenschaften," in *Historiker Wörterbuch der Philosophie*, vol. 3 (1974).

11. W. Dilthey, *Einleitung in die Geisteswissenschaften* (1883), in *GS*, vol. 1. On Dilthey, see O. Bollnow *Dilthey, Eine Einführung in sein Philosophie* (Stuttgart, 1936); Gadamer, *Wahrheit und Methode*, pp.

205ff.; English, pp. 195ff.; J. Habermas, *Erkenntnis und Interesse* (Frankfurt, 1968; English, *Knowledge and Human Interests*, Boston, 1971); Schnädelbach, *Geschichtsphilosophie*; M. Riedel, *Erklären oder Verstehen zur Theorie und Geschichte der hermeneutischen Wissenschaften* (Stuttgart, 1978).

12. Dilthey, *Ideen über eine beschreibende und zergliedende Psychologie* (1894), p. 1314; reprinted in *GS*, vol. 14, pp. 143ff.

13. Ibid., p. 1314.

14. Ibid., p. 1323.

15. Ibid., p. 1376.

16. W. Dilthey, *Der Aufbau der geschichtlichen Welt in den Geisteswissenschaften* (1910), p. 85, reprinted in *GS* vol. 7. Partial English translation in Rickman, ed., *Dilthey, Selected Writings* (Cambridge, 1976), p. 174.

17. Ibid., p. 146 (English, p. 191).

18. Ibid., p. 148 (English, p. 192).

19. Ibid., p. 86 (English, pp. 175-176).

20. On Vico's principle, see K.-O. Apel, *Die Idee der Sprache in Denken der Neuzeit von Dante bis Vico* (Bonn, 1963), pp. 321ff., Karl Löwith, "Vicos Grundsatz: verum et ractum convertuntur," in *Sitzungsberichte der Heidelberger Akadamie der Wissensschaften, Philos.-histor, Klasse* (Heidelberg, 1968); F. Fellman, *Das Vico-Axiom: Der Mensch macht die Geschichte* (Freiburg/Munich, 1976).

21. Dilthey, *Der Aufbau*, p. 259.

22. Ibid., p. 278.

23. Ibid., p. 148 (English, p. 192).

24. See J. Habermas, *Zur Logik der Sozialwissenschaften* (Frankfurt, 1967; English translation forthcoming in this series). Also K.-O. Apel, "Die Entfaltung der sprachanalytischen Philosophie und das Problem der Geisteswissenschaften," in *Philosophische Jahrbuch* (1965); English, *Analytic Philosophy of Language and the Geisteswissenschaften* (Dordrecht, Holland, 1967); "Szientistik, Hermeneutik, Ideologiekritik," in *Wiener Jahrbuch für Philosophie* I (1968); "Die Kommunikationsgemeinschaft als transzendentale Voraussetzung der Sozialwissenschaften," in *Neue Heft für Philosophie* (1972). The last two are included in *Transformation der Philosophie*, 2 vols. (Frankfurt, 1973; English, *Towards a Transformation of Philosophy* (London, 1980).

25. The discussion of the E-V controversy that post-Wittgensteinian action theory renewed cannot elucidate, for example, the hermeneutic question as to whether it is possible to understand empathetically (*nachverstehen*) the meaning intentions of authors and agents. Neither can it answer the related question as to the difference and the connection between the meaning intentions of texts or works and their binding meaning, or the question whether it is possible to understand meaning intentions hermeneutically—not to mention the meaning of texts or works—without evaluating normative validity claims (i.e., the truth claim of statements or the ethical claim to appropriateness of actions). The present investigation intends to make it clear that resolving the E-V controversy requires distinguishing between the causal explanation of events (and of actions qua spatiotemporal events) and the understanding of intentions, reasons for actions, or actions as entities that are internally determined by intentions or reasons. This distinction is a condition of recognizing strictly hermeneutic problems as scientific problems that can be discussed as such. To put it more pointedly, unless one has understood the

distinction between the quasi-natural scientific—psychological or psycholinguistic—project of explaining human understanding, on the one hand, and the understanding of explanation that goes on in Geisteswissenschaften such as the history of science, on the other, one will be unable to recognize that the peculiar problems of hermeneutics as they have been discussed in recent years by Gadamer, Betti, Hirsch, Habermas, and myself are methodological problems of the theory of science. Hence, the E-V controversy still requires resolution.

26. See the appendix on attempts to render the E-V controversy obsolete. This was part of the introduction in the original edition (trans.).

## Part I, Chapter 1

1. For the Dilthey school oriented toward his life philosophy, see the works of E. Rothaker, e.g.: *Einleitung in die Geisteswissenschaften* (Tübingen, 1920/1930), *Logik und Systematik der Geisteswissenschaften* (Munich/Berlin, 1926/1948), *Die dogmatische Denkform in den Geisteswissenschaften* (Mainz, 1954). For the neo-Hegelian direction, see the works of T. Litt, e.g., *Individuum und Gemeinschaft* (Leipzig, 1926), *Kant und Herder als Deuter der geistigen Welt* (Leipzig, 1930), *Die Befreiung des geschichtlichen Bewusstseins durch J. G. Herder* (Leipzig, 1946), *Denken und Sein* (Stuttgart, 1948), *Mensch und Welt: Grundlinien einer Philosophie des Geistes* (Munich, 1948/1961).

2. On Windelband and Rickert, see H. Seidel, *Wert und Wirklichkeit in der Philosophie Heinrich Rickerts* (Bonn, 1968), and H. Schnädelbach, *Geschichtsphilosophie nach Hegel* (Freiburg/Munich, 1974).

3. On Max Weber's theory of the types of *Verstehen* and *verstehende* explanation, see, in particular, "Soziologische Grundbegriffe," in *Wirtschaft und Gesellschaft*, 4th edition, ed. Joseph Winckelmann (Tübingen, 1956); English, "Basic Sociological Terms," in *Economy and Society*, tr. and ed. Guenther Roth and Claus Wittich (Berkeley, 1976), and "Über einige Kategorien der verstehender Soziologie," in Weber, *Gesammelte Aufsätze zur Wissenschaftslehre* (Tübingen, 1922/1951).

4. See the Introduction pp. 7ff. (trans.)

5. H. Rickert, *Die Grenzen der naturwissenschaftlichen Begriffsbildung* (Tübingen, 1902/13/21), p. 522.

6. Ibid; p. 560.

7. Ibid. pp. 562ff.

8. Ibid., p. 566.

9. Ibid., p. 578.

10. Hegel affirms this condition in his philosophy of the "sublating" (*aufhebende*) concept in which objective spirit is sublated in light of absolute spirit. That this problem has not, eo ipso, been resolved by the present philosophy of the empirical Geisteswissenschaften is manifested by the aporia that fluctuates between a normativist and an empiricist self-understanding of the history of science.

11. Weber's original approach was radicalized in phenomenological forms of sociology deriving from Husserl, for example, the work of Alfred Schutz. Actually, it builds a bridge to the "philosophical hermeneutics" of Heidegger's disciples, in whom the methodologically relevant distinction between an objectivizing understanding mediated by theory and a communicative understanding of "something as something" is occasionally lost.

12. Weber, "Über einige Kategorien der vertehender Soziologie," p. 427.

13. Ibid., p. 432.

14. Ibid., p. 436.

15. Ibid., p. 427.

16. Ibid., p. 436.

17. See K. Popper: "To give a causal explanation of an event means to deduce a statement which describes it, using as premises of the deduction one or more universal laws, together with certain singular statements, the initial conditions." *The Logic of Scientific Discovery* (New York, 1959), p. 59.

18. See C. G. Hempel, "The Function of General Laws in History" and "Studies in the Logic of Explanation," both in *Aspects of Scientific Explanation and Other Essays in the Philosophy of Science* (New York, 1965); "Explanation in Science and in History," in W. Dray, ed., *Philosophical Analysis and History* (New York, 1966); "Formen und Grenzen des wissenschaftlichen Verstehen," in *Conceptus* VI (1972), pp. 5–18.

19. The late Popper can hardly be used to support the position of a "methodological unity" if that involves rejecting the epistemological-methodological independence of the Geisteswissenschaften. On the contrary, in *Objective Knowledge* (Oxford, 1972), he developed de facto a model of cultural scientific understanding that refers to "objective mind" and thereby complements the D-N model of explanation. This form of understanding exhibits a structural affinity with the late Dilthey and even more with the neo-Kantian theory of understanding, in light of an "irreal," or binding, sphere of value relations.

Moreover, in *The Poverty of Historicism* (London, 1957/69), Popper supplies one of the strongest arguments I know of for the necessity of methodologically supplementing the explanatory natural sciences (and quasi-natural scientific social sciences) with *verstehende* Geisteswissenschaften, in other words, of supplementing sciences that produce specific predictions with sciences offering an "ex post" understanding of historical events. Popper argues against the possibility of predicting the progress of science itself, since to do so one would have to be able to replace innovative thinking with the prediction of its results. Thus, he provides a paradigm for the relation of our knowledge to historically relevant phenomena; moreover, he distinguishes it from the knowledge of natural phenomena to the extent that the latter are subsumable as instances under laws (as are the phenomena of historically sedimented psychosocial quasi-nature). This paradigm suggests that no phenomenon that forms part of the historical-social world can meaningfully constitute the object of a nomological (causal or probabilistic) explanation. Each is exclusively the object of an "ex post" understanding that examines good or bad reasons (as understood in the wider sense that Rickert tried to explicate by referring to an ideal realm of values and which Popper, following Bolzano and Frege, explains in terms of a third world).

I think it remarkable that many "critical rationalists" do not want to see that Popper's argument here fully confirms the interests of the representatives of the methodological independence of *Verstehen*. Hans Albert seems to believe that one could replace or improve the "understanding of explanation" that is relevant for the Geisteswissenschaften with the "explanation of understanding." (See "Hermeneutik und Realwissenschaft," in H. Albert, *Plädoyer für kritischen Rationalismus* [Munich, 1971], pp. 106–149; and *Transcendentale Träumereien* [Hamburg, 1975], p. 51.) He also believes one could substitute for methodical understanding, in the hermeneutic sense, a "descriptive and explanatory science of a general kind" (see Albert, *Plädoyer für kritischen Rationalismus*, pp. 48ff.) That this is impossible in principle, his teacher, Popper, among others, has already shown, whether Albert believes it or not. The same argument demonstrates that normatively relevant, internal (as opposed to external and empirical) cognitive interests are correlated with the cognitive goals of explanation, on the one hand, and of understanding, on the other. Windelband has already suggested this connection, and Albert, if he understands it correctly, can scarcely object.

20. Hempel, "Function of General Laws," passim.

21. W. Dray, *Laws and Explanation in History* (Oxford, 1957).

22. Hempel, "Function of General Laws," p. 5.

23. "Empathy, understanding and the like may help the research worker, but they enter into the totality of scientific statements as little as does a good cup of coffee which also furthers the scholar in his work." O. Neurath, *Empirische Soziologie* (Vienna, 1931); English, *Empiricism and Sociology*, ed. Marie Neurath and Robert S. Cohen (Boston, 1973), p. 357.

24. See F. D. E. Schleiermacher, *Hermeneutik und Kritik*, ed., with introduction, M. Frank (Frankfurt, 1977). On Schleiermacher and the history of hermeneutics, see J. Wach, *Das Verstehen, Grundzüge einer Geschichte der hermeneatische Theorie im 19. Jahrhundert*, vols. I–III (Tübingen, 1926–33), and H.-G. Gadamer, *Wahrheit und Methode* (Tübingen, 1960); English trans., *Truth and Method* (New York, 1975).

25. Hempel, "Function of General Laws," p. 239.

26. Ibid., p. 258.

27. Especially influential was the extensive development of the Hempelian argument by Abel in "The Operation Called *Verstehen*, in H. Feigl and M. Brodbeck, eds., *Readings in the Philosophy of Science* (New York, 1953). For criticism, see H. Skjervheim, *Objectivism and the Study of Man* (Oslo, 1959); K.-O. Apel, "Die Entfaltung der sprachanalytische Philosophie und das Problem der Geisteswissenschaften," in *Philosophische Jahrbuch* (1965), pp. 239–289; reprinted in *Transformation der Philosophie*, vol. II (Frankfurt, 1973); English, *Analytic Philosophy of Language and the Geisteswissenschaften*, Foundations of Language supplementation series, vol. 5 (Dordrecht, Holland, 1967); "Szientismus oder Transcendental Hermeneutik?" Zur Frage nach dem Subjekt der Zeicheninterpretation in der Semiotik der Pragmatismus," in *Hermeneutik und Dialektik*, ed. Bubner et al. (Tübingen, 1970); reprinted in Apel, *Tranformation der Philosophie* (Frankfurt, 1973); English, *Towards a Transformation of Philosophy*, trans. Glyn Adey and David Frisby (London, 1980). "Communication and the Foundations of the Humanities," in *Acta Sociologica*, 15; expanded version in *Man and World*, 5 (1972), pp. 3–37; D. Leat, "Misunderstanding *Verstehen*," in *Sociological Review*, 20 (1972).

28. Hempel takes into consideration neither empirical-hermeneutic methods of verification or correction nor the unique constitution of historical-hermeneutic data that is based on "individualizing" concept formation in Rickert's sense. Just as, in the former case, he demands a guarantee for the accuracy of interpretive hypotheses, in the latter he demands that "individualizing" concept formation in history helps make it possible "to grasp the unique individuality" of its "objects." (Hempel, "Function of General Laws," p. 233.) That the "individual is ineffable" is explicitly recognized by Rickert, as it is by the entire hermeneutic tradition. Rickert, however, intended his insight as a regulative idea in the Kantian sense: Even though the unique individuality of a person, historical event, or historical epoch can never be grasped definitively, nonetheless, a type of "characterizing" concept formation is possible in light of meaning generalities that fall under the regulative principle of the concept of the individual. Such, for example, are the concepts of Napolean, the French Revolution, the Renaissance, and even Western or human history. In *Theorie der Geschichtswissenschaft* (Munich, 1971), pp. 45ff.), K. G. Faber also misses this point, and argues in a way that is similar to Hempel.

29. Hempel, "Function of General Laws," p. 236.

30. Ibid, pp. 254ff.

31. Like Davidson in "Actions, Reasons, and Causes" (*Journal of Philosophy* [1963], pp. 685–700), Hempel seems to think that a methodologically relevant distinction between purposive-rational understanding (or rational explanation in Dray's sense) and mere rationalization is possible only insofar as one considers purposive-rational understanding a causal explanation of phenomena, and verifies it accordingly.

32. Hempel, "Aspects of Scientific Explanation," p. 471.

33. Ibid., p. 471.

34. See note 19 above.

35. Popper, *Poverty of Historicism*, pp. xi ff.

36. Dray, *Laws and Explanation in History*.

37. See Landesmann, "The New Dualism in the Philosophy of Mind," *Review of Metaphysics* (1965/66), pp. 324–349.

38. See R. Bernstein, *Praxis and Action* (Philadelphia, 1971), chap. 4; G. H. von Wright, *Explanation and Understanding* (Ithaca, 1971); A. Beckermann, ed., *Gründe und Ursache* (Kronberg/Ts., 1977).

# Part I, Chapter 2

1. Here and for the following, see K.-O. Apel, "Das Verstehen" eine Problemgeschichte als Begriffsgeschichte," in *Archiv für Begriffsgeschichte* (1955).

2. "In the explanation of given appearances, no things or grounds of explanation can be adduced other than those which have been found to stand in connection with given appearances in accordance with the already known laws of appearances." Kant, *Kritik der reinen Vernunft* (1781); English, *The Critique of Pure Reason* (1929, A772/B800). Also see "We are unable to explain anything unless we can bring it under laws which can have an object in some possible experience." A. Comte, *Grundlegung zur Metaphysik der Sitten* (1785; English trans. 1948), p. 127. A. Comte, *Cours de Philosohie Positive* (1830), Lecon I, section 2: "The explanation of facts is nothing more than the establishment of the connection between diverse particular phenomena and some general fact." J. S. Mill, *Science of Logic*, book III, chap. XII, sec. 1: "An individual fact is said to be explained by pointing out its cause, that is, by stating the law or laws of causation of which its production is an instance."

3. Cited in Apel, "Das Verstehen."

4. See, for example, Hegel: "Every understanding is an identification of the I and the object, a reconciliation of that which outside of this understanding is divided; what I do not understand remains something alien to and different from me." *Vorlesung über die Aesthetik*, in Glockner, ed., vol. XII, p. 448.

5. Here, I ignore Vico's *Scienzo Nuova* of 1725. See K.-O. Apel, *Die Idee der Sprache im Denken der Neuzeit von Dante bis Vico* (Bonn, 1963), chap. 12, and Apel, "Das Verstehen."

6. See G. H. von Wright, *Explanation and Understanding* (Ithaca, 1971), chap. 1, "Two Traditions."

7. Hobbes, *Leviathan*, I, 6, and *De Homine*, chap. 11.

8. Hume, *Inquiry into Human Understanding*, VII, part I.

9. In his *Treatise on Human Nature* (ed. L. A. Selby-Bigge [Oxford, 1888], p. 399), Hume characterizes the will as "nothing but the internal impression we feel and are conscious of, when we knowingly give rise to any new motion of the body or new perception of the mind."

10. See M. Riedel, "Das Erkenntnishtheoretische Motiv in Diltheys Theorie der Geisteswissenschaften," in *Hermeneutik und Dialektik, H. G. Gadamer zum 70. Geburtstag*, ed. Bubner et al. (Tübingen, 1970), vol. I, pp. 233–256.

11. For these reasons I cannot agree with Riedel's recommendation to return to Kant as an alternative to both the Hegelian dialectic and hermeneutics with regard to the problem of teleological explanation. (Riedel, "Causal and Historical Explanation, the Problem of Teleology in Analytic and Dialectical Philosophies of History," in *Essays in Explanation and Understanding*, ed. Manninen and Tuomela [Dordrecht, Holland, 1975].) To do so would merely be to return to the Kantian problem of the relation between theoretical and practical reason and would require revision of the Kantian foundation of transcendental philosophy.

12. If one considers Kant's work more closely, it is clear that the rehabilitation of the experience of the freedom of action within the framework of practical reason itself suffers under the premises of transcendental idealism. Even in ethics, Kant recognizes only the freedom and responsibility that belong to the inner intention of an action (the good or the bad will) and not the realization of freedom through the effect of action. Given the two assumptions of causal determinism in the world of experience and of the existence of a God who values the good will, Kant's position is thoroughly consistent.

13. The fundamental paradox in Kant's solution appears in altered form in Windelband's and Rickert's neo-Kantianism. Of course, they undertake a revision of transcendental philosophy at the level of its conceptual language: between Kant's "metaphysics of nature" and "metaphysics of morals" they create space for a transcendental theory of the historical world, for a metaphysics of culture. Nevertheless, on the wider ground of "transcendental idealism," they have to presuppose that the sensuously given phenomenon—or the material of the senses—is neutral with regard to the distinction between the natural and cultural sciences in constituting possible objects (Rickert's concept formation). In contrast to Dilthey's claim that the intelligibility of the individual phenomenon is also constituted by the possibility of sensuously identifying (*Einfühlung*) with a given expression, for Rickert, this intelligibility is constituted only by the value relation (*Wertbeziehung*) that the knowing subject assumes on the basis of practical interests. In this way he avoids the transition from Kant's transcendental idealism to a philosophy of identity as a foundation for understanding. There is a price for this evasion, however: the theoretically relevant circumstance that the Geisteswissenschaften involve objects (or subject-objects, in Bloch's sense) that themselves constitute meaning is not simply supplemented; rather, it is completely obscured or systematically replaced with the practical value relation of knowledge that the later Rickert conceived of in quasi-platonic, quasi-ontological terms as the relation of understanding to a realm of objective values or even to a realm of values existing in an irreal form. See H. Schnädelbach, *Geschichtsphilosohie nach Hegel* (Freiburg/Munich, 1974), para. 7.

14. Here, Apel uses the English (and French) word *science*, specifically noting that he has done so. (tr.)

15. On the Historical school, see E. Rothaker, *Einleitung in die Geisteswissenschaften* (Tübingen, 1920), and *Mensch und Geschichte* (Bonn, 1950), pp. 9–58.

16. With regard to the E-V controversy, the methodologically relevant point of the hermeneutic circle evidently lies in the following fact: as the spiral movement in which the understanding of meaning is expanded and revised, the process in which co-subjects of linguistic communication come to an understanding must be applied to that secondary subject-object relation in the knowledge of the Geisteswissenschaften in which the object must also be respected as the subject of meaning constitution. This means that the *circulus fructuosus* of the hermeneutic

explication of meaning can play a role only in those cognitive acts that involve establishing the meaning of an explicatum in the synthesis of *verstehende* interpretation, a synthesis that is also empirically informative. The hermeneutic circle can have no place, however, in those cognitive acts that already presuppose the fixed meaning of explicata, hence, in argumentations that can be logically formalized or in explanations that are systematizations of knowledge in Hempel's sense and can therefore be explicated in logico-semantic terms. In these cases, the circle must assume the logical form of a *circulus vitiosus*.

To this extent, the hermeneutic circle attests to the fact that the understanding with which the hermeneutic tradition is concerned cannot be equated with either explanation in the sense of the D-N model or with logical justification. Rather, it reflects a synthetic cognitive act that has its place, as it were, both between and behind (or this side of) the alternatives to which logical empiricism and Wittgenstein's *Tractatus* point. That is, it has the status neither of logical form nor of an empirical reality that can be accounted for in a formal-logical reconstruction that connects the data of observation. Whether we are concerned with empirical reality or a formalizable calculus, we must first come to an understanding as to meaning, be it the meaning of data, of operations, or the application of operations to the data. Therefore, hermeneutics can have transcendental status as part of a transcendental pragmatics in the framework of a transcendental semiotic. (See K.-O. Apel, "Transcendental Semiotics and the Paradigms of First Philosophy," *Philosophical Exchange* [2/4, 1978].) It can also serve, however, as the methodology of certain empirical interpretive sciences, the function of which is to be the critically reconstructive organon of processes of coming to an understanding about topical issues—for example, about the meaning of the problem situation in which we stand at any given time. The most contemporary example of such an organon is the history of science. This is not a natural science, since it tries to understand the theories of the natural sciences; but neither is it an empirical social science that would be interested in the contingent motives of scientists or a merely normative logic of science. As a hermeneutic Geisteswissenschaft, it must be able to expose a normative preunderstanding—for example, of good natural science or of good theories and explanations—to expansion or revision on the basis of the documents of the history of science that are to be understood empirically.

From this perspective it becomes clear that one need not use only the examples of empirical interpretation in the historical-philological disciplines to elucidate the hermeneutic circle. One can also refer to examples of conceptual or linguistic explication in Carnap's sense, as well as to theory interpretation and the "processing of theories" that is connected to their innovative application. For example, I have attempted to analyze the procedure for explaining significance that Peirce proposes in his "pragmatic maxims" as a limit case in which the hermeneutic circle is both presupposed and arrested. Here, the explanation of significance involves consideration of the experimental consequences of the primary understanding of concepts.

See K.-O. Apel, "Die Entfaltung der sprachanalytischen Philosophie und das Problem der Geisteswissenschaften," in *Philosophische Jahrbuch* (1965); English translation, *Analytic Philosophy of Language and the Geisteswissenschaften*, Foundations of Language supplementary series, vol. 5 (Dordrecht, Holland, 1967), p. 83, esp. pp. 137ff. Also see, Apel, "Szientismus oder Transcendental Hermeneutik? Zur Frage nach dem Subjekt der Zeicheninterpretation in der Semiotik der Pragmatismus," in *Hermeneutik und Dialektik*, ed. Bubner et al. (Tübingen, 1970); reprinted in Apel, *Transformation der Philosophie* (Frankfurt, 1973).

Nevertheless, this possibility speaks not against but in favor of distinguishing between the methods of nomological explanation and those of understanding meaning. The latter are always already presupposed and, more or less, methodically mediated. (See W. Stegmüller, "Der sogenannte Zirkel im Verstehen," in *Natur und Geschichte*, ed. Hübner and Menne, x, Deutscher Kongress für Philosophie, [Kiel, 1972], pp. 21–46.) These remarks are directed not against the examples but against Stegmüller's strategy of argumentation, in which he completely misunderstands the "interests" of the hermeneuticists.

17. See Karl Löwith, *Von Hegel zu Nietzsche* (Stuttgart, 1949); English, *From Hegel to Nietzsche, The Revolution in Nineteenth-Century Thought* (New York, 1964); Dietrich Böhler, *Metakritik der Marxschen Ideologiekritik* (Frankfurt, 1971).

18. Meineke, *Die Entstehung des Historismus*, Werke, vol. II (Stuttgart, 1936), and *Zur Theorie und Philosophie der Geschichte*, Werke, vol. IV (Stuttgart, 1959).

19. See Apel, "Types of Rationality Today, The Continuum of Reason between Science and Ethics," in *Rationality Today*, ed. T. Geraets (Ottowa, 1979) and "The Common Presuppositions of Hermeneutics and Ethics," in *Phenomenology and the Human Sciences* (Pittsburgh, Pa., 1979).

20. B. F. Skinner, *Beyond Freedom and Dignity* (New York, 1953).

21. Here I mean the elimination of that communication between the subject and subject-object of social science that hinders the possibility of repeating experiments and results in self-fulfilling and self-destroying prophecies.

22. Thus, for example, E. Topitsch, *Sozialphilosophie zwischen Ideologie und Wissenschaft* (Neuwied, 1961) and "Das Verhältnis zwischen Sozial und Naturwissenschaften," in *Logik der Sozialwissenschaften*, ed. E. Topitsch (Köln/Berlin, 1966).

# Part I, Chapter 3

1. It would be interesting to compare the philosophical premises and consequences of the different types of suspicion of psychologism that prevailed at the beginning of the twentieth century. One might, for example, compare the neo-Kantian suspicion of *Lebensphilosophie* in the name of Kant's transcendental logic with that of the early and late Husserl, and both with that of the more radical and influential modern logic of science that dates from Frege.

2. The original Kantian distinction was reformulated by Reichenbach and implicitly by Popper on the basis of modern logic. Today, as the difference between the context of discovery and the context of justification, it represents one of the most fundamental paradigms of the modern logic of science.

3. The practical extinction of the problem of nonpsychological epistemological reflection apparently is grounded in the Russell/Tarski axiom according to which the reflexivity of natural language must lead to semantic antinomies. Since then, philosophy has been incapable of redeeming its own validity claims, for example, those of metalogic, in reflecting on validity. This problem is not to be confused with that of a deductivist or metatheoretical "final grounding" or theory of proof.

Such confusion issues only under the premise of the Russell/Tarski axiom. See Apel, "Zur Idee einer transzendental Sprachpragmatic," in *Aspekte und Probleme der Sprachphilosophie*, ed. J. Simon (Freiburg, 1974), pp. 283–326; "Sprechakttheorie und transzendentale Sprachpragmatik zur Frage ethischer Normen," in *Sprachpragmatik und Philosophie*, ed. K.-O. Apel (Frankfurt, 1976); and "Types of Rationality Today, The Continuum of Reason between Science and Ethics," in *Rationality Today*, ed. T. Gereats (Ottowa, 1979).

4. Here and in the following, I follow Hempel's terminology in *Aspects of Scientific Explanation and Other Essays in the Philosophy of Science* (New York, 1965), pp. 174ff.; and that of W. Stegmüller, in *Probleme und Resultate der Wissenschaftstheorie* (Berlin, 1969), p. 161. According to these definitions, scientific systematizations are understood as all types of scientific argument "in which the occurrence of a past, present or future event is inferred."

5. Here, I have had to disregard the fact that a hermeneutically valid cognitive act of understanding is presupposed for the merely heuristic act of hypothesis construction to which Hempel refers. If historically determined maxims of behavior are to be applied as laws, they must first be understood correctly as maxims. The same holds for those grounds of action—that is, goals and appraisal of the situation—that are supposed to yield a volitional-cognitive causal complex.

That Hempel ignores these presuppositions accords with his neglect of the specific epistemological-methodological context of empathetic understanding, hence with his denial of the autonomous possibilities for empirical testing available to it. He emphasizes over and over again that the merely "intuitive" evidence of "empathetic understanding" can be checked only through observation in the context of the verification of falsification of causal explanations or the context of lawlike hypotheses presupposed in them. See W. Stegmüller, *Probleme und Resultate der Wissenschaftstheorie*, chap. IV, 5.

Discussion of the necessity of testing interpretive hypotheses by observationally testing corresponding causal hypotheses is misleading, for two reasons. Observation means either (1) the strict physicalistic and behavioristic notion of observation of the heroic period of logical positivism—but such observation *cannot* establish the facts with which the social sciences (both historical and behaviorist) are concerned, such as poor harvests, marriage settlements, and acts of buying and selling. These sciences already involve Weber's direct observational understanding (*aktuelle Verstehen*) of actions, as well as their intentions, motives qua reasons, and institutionally determined rules or norms; or—and this is indicative of scientism's present recession—by observation is meant (2) that any form of establishing facts empirically is to be admitted. To a certain extent, the quasi-nomological social sciences that abstract from the historicity of human actions can speak of an observational test here. One can no longer argue, however, as do Hempel and Abel, that the social scientific explanation of action is possible without the supposedly merely heuristic understanding of grounds, maxims, etc. Moreover, even in this case, discussion of an observational test is irrelevant for testing typical historical-hermeneutic hypotheses as, for example, the assumption that Cleopatra committed suicide by being bitten by a snake to avoid being taken prisoner by Octavius and to become immortal after death. If the notion of observation also includes the necessary hermeneutic procedure of attaining certainty here, then the original point of contrasting the empirical testing of explanatory hypotheses and the merely heuristic relevance of understanding is completely dissolved. This is commensurate with the present "immunizing" tendencies of such introductions to the "logic of the social sciences."

6. K. Popper, *The Logic of Scientific Discovery*, 2nd ed. (London, 1968).

7. See Stegmüller, *Probleme und Resultate*, and the introduction to "Der sogenannte Zirkel im Verstehen," in Hübner and Menne, eds., *Natur und Geschichte*, X, Deutscher Kongress für Philosophie (Kiel, 1972).

8. With regard to Goodman's paradox in "The Problem of Counterfactual Conditionals" (*Fact, Fiction and Forecast* [Cambridge, 1955]), Sellars writes: "Goodman's puzzle about contenability arises from a failure to appreciate the force of the verbal form of counterfactuals in actual discourse, and of the general statements by which we support them; and this failure stems, as in so many other cases, from too hasty an assimilation of a problematic of ordinary discourse to a formalism by reference to which we have succeeded in illuminating certain other features." Sellars, "Counterfactuals, Dispositions and the Causal Modalities," in Feigl, Scriven, and Maxwell, eds., *Minnesota Studies in the Philosophy of Science*, vol. II (Minneapolis, 1958). Also see A. Wellmer, "Erklärung und Kausalität," 1970, III (unpub. Habilitationsschrift).

9. Stegmüller, *Probleme und Resultate*, p. 760.

10. Ibid., p. 198.

11. In *Foresight and Understanding* (London, 1961), Stephen Toulmin clarifies the importance for the history of science of the distinction between real causal explanations that are guided by theories and prediction-techniques based on generalized symptoms, which often are very successful.

12. Stegmüller, *Probleme und Resultate*, p. 198.

13. See also A. Wellmer, *Erklärung und Kausalität*.

14. See P. F. Strawson, "Truth," in *Proceedings of the Aristotelian Society* (1950; reprinted in *Truth*, ed. G. Pitscher (Englewood Cliffs, N.J., 1964).

15. In practice it was assumed that the Hempelian ideal of context-free or "complete" explanation could at least be redeemed through reconstruction in the sense of the Hempel–Oppenheim model in such a way that the description of the explanandum could be deduced from the totality of laws and antecedent conditions. No natural scientific explanation has thus far demonstrated this, however. (See M. Scriven, "Explanations, Predictions, and Laws," in *Minnesota Studies in the Philosophy of Science*, ed. Feigl et al., vol. III (1962), pp. 201ff., 210ff.) The principal reason for this seems to be that the Hempel–Oppenheim model for the logical reconstruction of explanation presupposes an empiricist—that is context-free—language of description. Actual explanations in the natural sciences, however, always imply a description of the empirical world in light of theoretical and metatheoretical premises, so that the dynamic of possible progress in knowledge rests precisely on these premises. See Scriven, "Explanations"; S. Körner, *Experience and Theory* (London, 1969); M. Bunge, *Scientific Research* (Berlin, 1967); G. Radnitsky, *Contemporary Schools of Metascience* (Göteburg, 1970), pp. 30ff., 72ff., 112ff. For the transcendental-pragmatic consequences, see A. Wellmer, *Erklärung und Kausalität*; and R. Ruge, "Zur Logik wissenschaftlicher Erklärungen," part 3, Frankfurter diss. (1974).

16. On the methodological structure of deduction, induction, and abduction in Peirce, see K.-O. Apel, *Der Denkweg von Charles Sanders Peirce* (Frankfurt, 1975); English, *Charles Sanders Peirce, From Pragmatism to Pragmaticism* (Amherst, Mass., 1981). For an evaluation of Peirce's concept of abduction or "retroduction" with regard to a logic of explanation, see N. R. Hanson, *Patterns of Discovery* (Cambridge, 1958), "On the Symmetry between Explanation and Prediction," in *Philosophical Review*, 68 (1959), and "Notes toward a Logic of Discovery," in *Perspectives on Peirce*, ed. R. Bernstein (New Haven, 1965). Also see R. Ruge, *Zur Logik wissenschaftlicher Erklärungen*, part 3,2.1. On the distinction between types of abductive proof, see J. Habermas, "Erkenntnis und Interesse," *Merkur* (1968), 213, pp. 1139–1153.

17. For a report on Peirce's discovery of three forms of proof, see M. G. Murphy's analysis of an unpublished manuscript by Peirce in *The Development of Peirce's Philosophy* (Cambridge, Mass., 1961). Also see Peirce's "Memorandum Concerning the Aristotelian Syllogism," *Collected Papers*, II, pp. 792–807; cf. pp. 461–514 and *Collected Papers*, V, p. 144.

18. Peirce, *Collected Papers*, V, pp. 171, 191ff., and VIII, pp. 227ff.

19. See Hempel, *Aspects of Scientific Explanations*, pp. 425ff.

20. Radnitzky calls attention to this fact in his *Contemporary Schools of Metascience* (Göteborg, 1970).

21. On this and the following, see K.-O. Apel, "Programmatische Bemerkungen zur Idee einer transzendentalen Sprach-Pragmatik," in *Studia Philosophica in honoreum Sven Krohn*, ed. T. Airaksinen et al. (Turku); also in *Semantics and Communication*, ed. C. H. Heidrich (Amsterdam and London, 1973/74), pp. 79–108. Also see Apel, "Zur Idee einer tranzendentalen Sprachpragmatik," in *Philosophie und linguistische Theorie*, ed. J. Simon (Berlin/New York, 1971) and *Sprachpragmitik und Philosophie* (Frankfurt, 1976). As far as I can determine, the late Popper (*Objective Knowledge* [Oxford, 1972]) occupies a unique position between the paradigms of logical empiricism and the transcendental semiotics or pragmatics, the necessity of which I have postulated. On the one hand, in reconstructing the progress of knowledge, Popper emphatically emphasizes the necessity, in principle, of presuppositions with regard to questions, problem situations, prior knowledge, and the like. On the other hand, in his model of three worlds, he proceeds from a purely empirical conception of the subject of knowledge. The consequence of this is an "epistemology without a knowing subject," which, nonetheless, takes as its theme a domain

(the object domain of the "third world") in which there are problem situations, prior knowledge, and the like. But how is one supposed to uphold the meaning of these kinds of concepts—hence, the meaning of epistemology—if one abstracts not only from the empirical-pragmatic relation of knowledge to the knowing subject (an abstraction that is legitimate) but from the very existence of the knowing subject and thus from the normative relation between its validity claims and objectively valid knowledge?

It is not reflection involving empirical introspection, but rather transcendental reflection that allows us to transcend the domain of physical and psychic reality (worlds I and II, in Popper's terminology) and postulate a domain of objectively valid knowledge with its objectively valid problem presuppositions (Popper's world III). But this implies that the meaning absolutely valid knowledge and all corresponding idealizations have for us cannot be constituted on the basis of Popper's renewed Platonic *Chorismos* between the real and the ideal. Rather, its constitution is based on an identification that unavoidably is implicated in the truth claim of knowledge, namely, the identification of the actual knower with the transcendental subject of absolutely objective knowledge. Of course, philosophy no longer comprehends meaning and objective validity (truth) as Kant does, prelinguistically or in terms of methodical solipsism; instead, it understands that, in principle, both are mediated by language and communication. Hence, within the paradigmatic framework of this philosophy, talk of the necessary identity of the actual knower with the transcendental subject of knowledge means that every meaning claim and truth claim must, in principle, be subjected to an unconstrained discourse within an unlimited communication community. The identification of the knower with the transcendental subject thus refers to the redemption of meaning and truth claims in the consensus of this ideal communication community and thereby attains a regulative principle for the progress of science (from Kant to Peirce). By pursuing such a transformation of transcendental philosophy, I think Popper could have created a normative basis for the "critical conventionalism" of his philosophy of the "open society" (a philosophy that was at first anti-Platonic) without the abrupt recourse to Platonism. See K.-O. Apel, "C. S. Peirce and the Post-Tarskian Problem of an Adequate Explication of the Meaning of Truth," *The Monist* 63/3 (1980).

22. Thus, perhaps it might be possible, with Strawson (*The Bounds of Sense* [Norwich, 1966]), to overcome both Kant's "transcendental idealism" and the two-world metaphysic it grounds without also giving up the idea of the Copernican turn in the sense of placing nature under transcendental conditions of knowledge.

23. Kant, *Kritik der reinen Vernunft* (1781/1789, B XII–XIV; English, *The Critique of Pure Reason*).

24. On the reinterpretation of the schematism of Kant's categories from the perspective of experimental action, see F. Kambartel, *Erfahrung und Struktur* (Frankfurt, 1968).

25. Strictly taken, a pure spirit or pure consciousness can acquire no notion of the significance of the world. This basic intuition leads from Dilthey's conception of "life relations" to E. Rothaker's supplementing the "principle of consciousness" (into which K. L. Reinhold wanted to integrate the point of Kantianism) with the anthropological "principle of significance" (*Bedeutsamkeit*). For me, this is one root of the anthropological postulate that there are internal cognitive interests, that is, categories as points of view for inquiry. See E. Rothaker, *Geschichtsphilosophie* (Munich, 1934), pp. 98ff., *Philosophische Anthropologie* (Bonn, 1964), pp. 77ff. Also: K.-O. Apel, "Die Entfaltung der sprachanalytischen Philosophie und das Problem der Geisteswissenschaften," in *Philosophische Jahrbuch* (1965), pp. 239–289; reprinted in *Transformation der Philosophie*, vol. II (Frankfurt, 1973; English, *Analytic Philosophy of Language and the Geisteswissenschaften*, Foundations of Language Supplementation Series, vol. 5 (Dordrecht, Holland, 1967); "Szientismus oder transzendentale Hermeneutik? Zur Frage nach dem Subjekt der Zeicheninterpretation in der Semiotik des Pragmatismus," in *Hermeneutik und Dialektik*, ed. Bubner et al.; "Types of Social Science in the Light of Human Interests of Knowledge," *Social Research* 44/3 (1977), pp. 425–470; reprinted in *Philosophical Disputes in the Social Sciences*, ed. S. Brown (Amherst, Mass., 1979).

26. In *Vorlesungen über die Metaphysik* (Darmstadt, 1964) and in the *Prolegomena*, #39, Kant speaks of a "transcendental grammar." He thinks, however, that it lies supralinguistically "in our

understanding" and is preordered "to every language." See J. Simon, *Philosophie und linguistische Theorie* (New York/Berlin, 1971).

27. Such a reconstruction of Kant is suggested, for example, by J. Piaget's "épistémologie génétique."

28. It must be admitted that an argument of the form:

$$\frac{(x) \quad (FxGx)}{Fa \qquad Ga}$$

Thus, for example, an ad hoc generalization such as "all ice floats in water"—as an answer to the question "Why does this ice cube float in water?"—does not represent an explanation even in the sense of the syntactic-semantic explication of the D-N model. To this extent, my argument ("Programmatische Bemerkungen zur Idee einer transzendentalen Sprach-Pragmatik," pp. 24, 95 [based on Radnitsky, *Contemporary Schools of Metascience*, p. 169]) is mistaken, as I. Niinoluota correctly established in "Inductive Explanation, Propensity and Action" (in *Essays on Explanation and Understanding*, ed. Manninen and Tuomela [Dordrecht, Holland, 1975], p. 364n10). Only by considering "pragmatic presuppositions" on the basis of a "logic of questions" can Niinoluoto show the extent to which the argument,

$$\frac{\text{All ice floats in water.}}{\text{This is a cube of ice.}}$$
$$\text{This object/thing floats in water.}$$

can be a suitable answer to a why-question (that is, the question why the object/thing floats in water). Hence, it seems to me, Niinoluoto confirms my general thesis that, as a model of syntactic-semantic explication, the D-N model is insufficient to explicate the meaning of explanation. More essential, I believe, is Niinoluoto's inability to use his pragmatic reflections to distinguish a scientific-causal explanation from the mere grounding of judgments. Even if the argument just presented represents a relevant answer to the corresponding why-question under empirical-pragmatic perspectives, from the perspective of the theory of science it is at best merely a prognostically relevant ground for the perceptual judgment that "This object/thing floats in water." For this reason I agree with von Wright's argument (in "Replies to Commentators . . . ," in *Essays on Explanation and Understanding* ed. Manninen and Tuomela) in which he doubts that "mere subsumption under a hypothetical universal sentence ever "explains" anything, whatever the context may be in which we ask for an explanation and whatever the state of knowledge or lack of knowledge of the asker may be."

29. See H. Hoppe, *Kant's Theorie der Physik* (Frankfurt, 1969).

30. Kant, *Reflexionen zur kritischen Philosophie* (1882–84), ed. B. von Erdmann, no. 395. On the prehistory of this theme, see Apel, *Die Idee der Sprache im Denken der Neuzeit von Dante bis Vico* (Bonn, 1963).

31. On the following, see F. Kambartel, *Erfahrung und Struktur* (Frankfurt, 1968); J. Habermas, *Erkenntnis und Interesse* (Frankfurt, 1968), pp. 164ff.; English, *Knowledge and Human Interests* (Boston, 1971), pp. 128ff.; and especially von Wright, *Explanation and Understanding* (Ithaca, N.Y., 1971), II, 7–9.

32. It appears that these reflections vitiate Peter Winch's objection to von Wright's theory of interventionist causality in "Causality and Action," in *Essays on Explanation and Understanding*, ed. Manninen and Tuomela.

33. On this and the following, see von Wright's grounding of his distinction between actions and basic actions, *Explanation and Understanding*, p. 68.

34. Ibid.

35. Such a theory of the dependence of higher levels of being on lower levels is proposed by Nicolai Hartmann in his ontology of real being.

36. Habermas has already made this clear in his interpretation of Peirce, in *Erkenntnis und Interesse*, pp. 162ff.; *Knowledge and Human Interests*, pp. 127ff.

37. See P. Bernays, "Reflections on Karl Popper's Epistemology," in *The Critical Approach to Science and Philosophy, Essays in Honour of Karl Popper* (London, 1964); and A. Wellmer, *Methodologie als Erkenntinistheorie. Zur Wissenschaftslehre K. R. Poppers* (Frankfurt, 1967).

38. See Kant, *The Critique of Pure Reason*, pp. B476ff.

39. Ibid., pp. B478ff.

40. On the self-differentiation of levels of transcendental reflection in a systematic sense relevant to the theory of science, which reaches its conclusion in the self-knowledge of philosophical knowledge, see T. Litt, *Mensch und Welt: Grundlinien einer Philosophie des Geistes* (Munich, 1948).

41. The purely ideal-typical status of this architectonic does not take into consideration the fact that the structures of rationality presupposed in the sense of ideal intelligibility are never reached in the concrete social-historical reality of human culture. Nevertheless, although the latter always represents a quasi-nature, these structures of rationality must always form the goal of struggles for enlightenment and emancipation. Out of the ideal-typical complementarity between explanation and understanding, the *condition humaine* yields its own cognitive interest, the particular object of which is the reconstruction of history. As will be demonstrated, the issue here refers to the task of a critical reconstruction of the dialectic between Hegel and Marx, so to speak, in light of the transcendental-pragmatic transformation of Kantian epistemology.

# Part I, Chapter 4

1. Landesman, "The New Dualism in the Philosophy of Mind," *Review of Metaphysics* 19 (1965/1966), pp. 329–349.

2. In the following ideal-typical reconstruction, I am relying on such texts as Charles Taylor's *The Explanation of Behavior* (London, 1964) and "Interpretation and the Sciences of Man," in *Understanding and Social Inquiry*, ed. F. Dallmayr and T. McCarthy (Notre Dame, Ind., 1977). On von Wright's somewhat different application of the Logical Connection argument, see Part II, Chap. Three, Sec. 2 of the present work.

3. This also shows that the categorial distinctions between language games to be exhibited here are more fundamental than the distinctions between interpretive *theories* the methodology of unified sciences recognizes as ultimate.

4. See F. Stoutland, "The Logical Connection Argument," *American Philosophical Quarterly* 7 (1970).

5. The normal conditions under which a subjective teleological system as such (that is, a system set by a volitional-cognitive complex) stands are to be confused neither with the normal conditions under which a closed causal system can be conceived nor with the conditions under which an objective teleological system such as an organism can maintain its existence. In the latter case, causal laws are presupposed for the normal fulfillment of the necessary conditions of the system's functioning. In the case of closed causal systems, the existence of the system

itself is the normal empirical condition of the possibility of successful experimental actions, hence of the discovery of anything resembling the structure of causal laws. In the case of subjective teleological systems set by the actor himself (on the basis of goal intentions that either can or cannot be realized, and on the basis of appropriate or inappropriate assumptions with regard to suitable means), the normal conditions do not consist in the causal laws grounding the substantive adequacy of the means-end relation. Rather, they consist in the absence of contingent external and internal obstructions to the realization of teleological intentionality, whereby lack of rationality may be counted as an internal obstruction.

6. See especially P. Winch, *The Idea of a Social Science and Its Relation to Philosophy* (London, 1958); and J. R. Searle, *Speech Acts* (Cambridge, 1969).

7. See H. Freyer, *Theorie des objektiven Geistes* (Leipzig, 1923; repub., *Urmensch und Spätkultur* (Bonn, 1956).

8. See especially P. Winch, *Idea of a Social Science*; and Apel, "Die Entfaltung der sprachanalytischen Philosophie und das Problem der Geisteswissenschaften," in *Philosophische Jahrbuch* (1965); English trans., *Analytic Philosophy of Language and the Geisteswissenschaften*, (Dordrecht, Holland, 1967); pp. 72ff., and *Transformation der Philosophie* (Frankfurt, 1973), vol. II, pp. 258ff.

9. But see chap. 1, note 19 of the present work.

10. See P. Winch, *Idea of a Social Science*, and "Understanding a Primitive Society," *American Philosophical Quarterly* I (1964); also see T. S. Kuhn, *The Structure of Scientific Revolutions* (Chicago, 1962), which transfers the neo-Wittgensteinian relativism to the understanding of the history of science. For criticism of Winch's relativism, see Apel, *Transformation der Philosophie*, vol. II, pp. 250ff.

11. Dilthey attempted to avoid this problem by means of the conception of a "philosophy of philosophy" that could be reduced to a Geisteswissenschaft, whereas Wittgenstein turned to the paradoxical conception of the critical-therapeutic function of philosophy in resolving problems, a function, nonetheless, that is supposed to include no systematic-theoretical validity claim.

12. See my criticism of Wittgenstein in Apel, *Transformation der Philosophie*, vol. I, pp. 272ff., 356ff.

13. In my discussion of Searle, *Speech Acts*, I attempt to move in this direction; see Apel, ed., *Sprachpragmatik und Philosophie* (Frankfurt, 1976), and *Transformation der Philosophie*, vol. II, pp. 358ff. See also J. Habermas and N. Luhmann, *Theorie der Gesellschaft oder Sozialtechnologie* (Frankfurt, 1971); J. Habermas, "Wahrheitstheorien," in *Wirklichkeit und Reflexion*, ed. H. Fahrenbach (Pfullingen, 1974), pp. 211–265, and "Was heisst Universalpragmatik," in *Sprachpragmatik und Philosophie*, ed. K.-O. Apel; in English in J. Habermas, *Communication and the Evolution of Society* (Boston, 1978).

## Part II, Chapter 1

1. Von Wright has elaborated this approach in a later book, *Causality and Determinism* (New York, 1974).

2. By the term *onto-logic* I want to distinguish von Wright's assumption of logical atomism from a naive metaphysical ontology. On the details of von Wright's theory of causality, see the penetrating studies of H. J. Schneider, "Die Asymmetrie der Kausalrelation," in *Vernünftiges Denken: Studien zur praktischen Philosophie und Wissenschaftstheorie*, ed. J. Mittelstrass and M. Riedel

(Berlin and New York, 1978); and A. Wellmer, "Georg Henrik von Wright über Erklären und Verstehen," in *Philosophische Rundschau* (1978–79).

3. Von Wright uses the terms *manipulative*, *actionist*, and *experimentalist* for his concept of causality. See *Explanation and Understanding* (Ithaca, N.Y., 1971), II, p. 9, and 1974, pp. 57ff. The term *interventionist* is used by R. Tuomela, "Explanation and Understanding of Human Behavior," in *Essays on Explanation and Understanding*, ed. J. Manninen and R. Tuomela (Dordrecht, Holland, 1975).

4. Von Wrignt, *Explanation and Understanding*, pp. 190–191n4.

5. Ibid., p. 190.

6. Ibid., p. 190n4.

7. Ibid., p. 73.

8. Following Paul Lorenzen, one can give Wittgenstein's notion of learning a language game a normative-constructivist interpretation. (For a constructivist interpretation of Wittgenstein's concept of language games, see Kuno Lorenz, *Elemente der Sprachkritik* (Frankfurt, 1970)). Accordingly, one could interpret the hierarchy of learnable language game-paradigms as the methodical a priori for the construction of science. H. J. Schneider, "Die Asymmetrie der Kausalrelation," in *Vernünftiges Denken*, has confirmed and made fruitful the affinity between von Wright's approach and that of Lorenzen's constructivism of protophysics.

9. See K. Popper, *Objective Knowledge* (Oxford, 1972); Konrad Lorenz, *Die Rückseite des Spiegels: Versuch einer Naturgeschichte des menschlichen Erkennens* (Munich and Zurich, 1973); and N. Chomsky, *Reflections on Language* (New York, 1975).

10. In *Causality and Determinism*, von Wright attempts to gather "the facts of the world" which, aside from the sociocultural assumptions internal to the language game, are presupposed by the conceptual framework of experimental science.

11. Habermas has developed this point clearly in connection with Peirce. See *Knowledge and Human Interests* (Boston, 1971). In *Methodologie als Erkenntnistheorie. Zur Wissenschaftslehre K. R. Poppers* (Frankfurt, 1967), Wellmer stresses that the transcendental-pragmatic framework of experimental action is presupposed in Popper's theory of falsification, though it is not considered sufficiently. I think the point can be generalized and used against the universalization of falsification in "critical rationalism." If this position argues that the traditional postulate of grounding (as well as the postulate of the transcendental grounding exhibited in the conditions of the possibility of intersubjective validity) can be replaced with the postulate of unlimited criticism, then an objection must be made: Just as the possibility of valid falsification depends on the transcendental-pragmatic framework of repeatable experimental action, in the same way, the possibility of valid criticism depends on the transcendental-pragmatic framework of critical discourse. Whoever holds everything to be criticizable, in principle cannot introduce any notion of criticism. In other words, whoever disputes the transcendental-pragmatic framework of possible falsification or possible criticism cannot distinguish his position from that of skepticism; this is a distinction Popper intends to make. See my essay, "Das Problem der philosophischen Letztbegründung im Lichte einer transzendentalen Sprachpragmatik: Versuch einer Metakritik des 'Kritischen Rationalismus,'" in *Sprache und Erkenntnis, Festschrift für G. Frey*, ed. B. Kannitscheider (Innsbruck, 1976), pp. 55–82.

12. Von Wright, *Explanation and Understanding* (Ithaca, 1971), p. 73.

13. See C. S. Peirce, "The Grounds of Validity of the Laws of Logic," *Collected Papers*, vol. V, pp. 318–356; as well as Habermas, 1971, II, 6. I disagree on only one point with Habermas's

impressive interpretation of Peirce's "transcendental pragmatism" (which I call transcendental pragmatics). Whereas Habermas rejects Peirce's theory of reality as uncritical ontology, I interpret it and its semiotic premises as "meaning-critical realism." Hence, I consider it a component of a transcendental-pragmatic transformation of Kant which overcomes his "transcendental idealism." See my *Der Denkweg von Charles Sanders Peirce* (Frankfurt, 1975), III and pp. 257, 339ff.; trans. as *Charles S. Peirce: From Pragmatism to Pragmaticism* (Amherst, Mass., 1979). This point appears decisive for disputing Albert's thesis that, with regard to the validity of natural scientific knowledge, a transcendental-pragmatic position must disintegrate into a reductionistic pragmatism or instrumentalism resembling that of William James, John Dewey, or even Nietzsche, Bergson, or Max Scheler.

14. Von Wright, *Causality and Determinism* (New York, 1974, p. 136.

15. B. Stroud, "Transcendental Arguments," *Journal of Philosophy*, no. 65, p. 255.

16. See esp. von Wright, *Causality and Determinism*, IV, para. 8.

17. Von Wright, *Explanation and Understanding*, p. 199n39.

18. J. Bogen makes this claim in "Physical Determinism," in *Readings in the Philosophy of Action*, ed. Norman S. Care and Charles Landesmann (Bloomington, Ind., 1968), p. 152. Also see A. Beckermann, ed., *Analytische Handlungstheorie*, vol. II: *Handlungserklärungen* (Frankfurt, 1977). Nevertheless, this claim and the concomitant distinction between the actor's initiation of a movement and its causation seems to imply that Bogen seeks a solution considered by the neo-Wittgensteinian differentiation of language games. Hence, unlike Beckermann, I do not think Bogen raises arguments against the neo-Wittgensteinian distinction, but instead, begins to supplement it. In this regard, see also von Wright's debate with Chisholm, in von Wright, *Explanation and Understanding*, pp. 191ff. and note 44.

I also find unilluminating the other argument that Beckermann, following Davidson ("Agency," in *Agent, Action and Reason*, ed. R. Binkley et al. [Oxford, 1971]), raises against the New Dualism. It is correct that the object of reference in the interpretation of an event as an action is "numerically identical" with the object of reference in the natural scientific apprehension of the event, in spite of the difference in language games. But it is a category mistake or *petitio principii* to draw the conclusion that the object of reference has the status of a causally determined event and thus that "the causes of the movement of the physical body corresponding to an action must be the causes of this action." Beckermann, "Agency," p. 32. As the sketch of the transcendental-pragmatic principle shows, it is, a priori, meaningless to want to state anything about the numerical identity of objects of reference independent of the horizon of a specific language game. This means, however, that a statement meaningful in the context of one language game—for example, concerning the natural causes of bodily movements—need not be meaningful, eo ipso, in the other—for example, concerning intentional action.

19. See A. Podlech, *Der Leib als Weise des In-der-Welt-seins* (Bonn, 1956).

20. Von Wright, *Explanation and Understanding*, p. 70.

21. Ibid., p. 68.

22. Ibid., p. 89.

23. Ibid., p. 71.

24. G. E. M. Anscomb, *Intention* (Oxford, 1957).

25. Arthur Danto, "What Can We Do," *Journal of Philosophy* 60 (1963); von Wright, *Explanation and Understanding*, p. 199n38.

26. As far as I can determine, the interpolation is confirmed in von Wright's new and more precise treatment of the problem, in *Causality and Determinism*, IV, para. 8; von Wright, *Causality and Determinism*, p. 81.

27. Von Wright, *Causality and Determinism*, pp. xxi, 124ff. One can question whether the notion of coproducing the causes of the results of action that belong to one's own physical body cannot also be conceived of without the idea of a retroactive causality. Essentially, its apparent unavoidability arises from the circumstance that the actor, by acting, cannot set in motion the causal system of his physical body (the stimulation) that is integrated in a basic action in the a priori of the lived body. The actor cannot know the effectiveness of the antecedents of his action belonging to his own physical body in the sense of an immediate understanding of action. Nonetheless, through the athletic training of corporeal dexterity, not to mention autogenic training and yoga, the actor can receive a vivid feeling that his own lived body can be treated as an instrument even if it can never be reduced to a component of the objectifiable, material world. This feeling results from the fact that the lived body forms a continuum with the causal systems of the external world and that one can set these systems in motion as a means in the framework of purposive-rational action on the basis of insight into their nomological character. To this extent, it is not difficult to conceive of the coproduction of those causes of the results of action that belong to one's physical body as an unconscious activity—meaning the setting in motion of a causal system in accordance with the normal temporal direction of causes and effects.

28. See Manninen and Tuomela, *Essays on Explanation and Understanding* (Dordrecht, Holland, 1975).

29. Thus C. S. Peirce could sometimes expect that the universe would be rationalized by habits resulting from understanding natural laws in light of conditional modes of behavior following the "pragmatic maxim." Later he recognized that the idea of such a rationalization presupposes a still higher degree of conceptual clarification than can be achieved through the pragmatic maxim, requiring, as it does, the conception of a summum bonum which, as the final goal that can be pursued "in the long run," can also ground those ends of action whose function as means in the conditional sentences of the pragmatic maxim is explicated. See Peirce, *Collected Papers*, vol. V, para. 3, and my interpretation, *Der Denkweg von Charles Sanders Peirce* (Frankfurt, 1975), pp. 164ff.

30. For a still inadequate—and, in detail, problematic—introduction of the a priori of the body as the condition of the possibility of scientific knowledge, see K.-O. Apel, "Das Leibapriori der Erkenntnis," in *Archiv für Philosophie*, 12, pp. 152–172; reprinted in *Neue Anthropologie*, ed. Gadamer and Vogler, vol. 7 (Stuttgart, 1963), pp. 264–288.

31. C. G. Hempel, "Reasons and Covering Laws in Historical Explanation," in *Philosophy and History*, ed. Sidney Hook (New York, 1963), p. 146.

32. William Dray, *Laws and Explanation in History* (Oxford, 1957), chap. 5, and "The Historical Explanation of Actions Reconsidered," in Hook, *Philosophy and History*.

33. See K.-O Apel, "Szientismus oder tranzendentale Hermeneutik, zur Frage nach dem Subject der Zeicheninterpretation in der Semiotik des Pragmatismus," in *Hermeneutik und Dialektik*, ed. Bubner et al., vol. I.

## Part II, Chapter 2

1. Georg Henrik von Wright, *Explanation and Understanding* (Ithaca, 1971), p. 27.

2. A distinction and combination differentiated at the level of the human "subject-object" of science.

# Part II, Chapter 3

1. G. H. von Wright, *Explanation and Understanding* (Ithaca, N.Y., 1971), p. 27; emphasis mine.

2. Ibid., p. 96.

3. Ibid., p. 107.

4. Ibid., p. 27.

5. Ibid., p. 198n33.

6. Ibid., p. 198; emphasis mine.

7. See ibid., p. 107.

8. Ibid., p. 196n21.

9. Von Wright, "Practical Inference," *Philosophical Review* (1972).

10. Von Wright, *Explanation and Understanding*, p. 25.

11. Ibid., p. 117.

12. Ibid.

13. F. Stoutland, "The Logical Connection Argument," *American Philosophical Quarterly* 7 (1970); von Wright, *Explanation and Understanding*, p. 94.

14. Von Wright, ibid.

15. Ibid.

16. Ibid., p. 116.

17. Von Wright employs a curious argument in showing that both linguistic communication with a person and an inference based on observation of an action represent only a "hypothetical" and "provisional" verification of an intention. He begins with the premise that one must consider communication by the other as "verbal behavior" and this behavior itself as the object of an intentional-teleological explanation. Thus he arrives at the thesis: "Verbal behavior does not in principle afford more direct access to the inner states than any other (intentional) behavior." (Ibid., p. 113.) Here, it seems to me, von Wright commits the same scientistic fallacy he commits in identifying the transition from the first to the third person with the transition to the "point of view of the spectator." To be sure, he commits this fallacy not on a strictly behavioristic level but, rather, on the analogous level of the theoretical-observational attitude. In this case, however, it is even easier to show that he overlooks the hermeneutic dimension of understanding.

If von Wright's thesis were in principle correct, it would have to be possible to inquire after the intentions of others simply by observing them, without presupposing a functioning understanding with them; for, if knowing subjects (von Wright or his readers) wanted in any way to experience the meaning intentions of others, they would have to be required to make all possible partners in communication objects of explanatory inferences or explanatory hypotheses. In this case, though, they would have to be capable of understanding at least their own thoughts as prelinguistic "noemata," in Husserl's sense; and that means as the correlate of their own intentions ("noeses"). Otherwise, they would be able to form no hypotheses whatsoever. I would call this the position of "methodological solipsism." In Husserl's *Cartesian Meditations* it is considered the starting point of the "honest thinker," but it seems to me also characteristic of almost all the classical thinkers of modern times since Descartes, and thus of von Wright as well.

The alternative to this position would consist in starting from the understanding that the meaning of one's own thoughts, hence, that of all explanatory hypotheses about the intentions of others, are, in principle, already linguistically mediated. This seems to imply that all hypothesis formation (whether about natural things or the actions of others) already presupposes that, normally, we do not first understand the communications of others on the basis of explanatory hypotheses about intentions. Understanding the communications of others, rather, seems to be the condition of the possibility of intentional explanations, just as understanding one's own interventionist actions is the condition of the possibility of causal explanation. If, in critical cases, I find the communications of others unintelligible or have grounds for doubting their honesty, I must assume that, normally, I have no difficulty receiving trustworthy, intelligible information from others. The hypotheses (formed hermeneutically or by the critique of ideology) that I construct in the former instances cannot, for example, proceed from the assumption that, in principle, it is possible to attain certainty about others' intentions only because one can observe the actions they intend. Instead, these hypotheses must proceed from the assumption that such certainty is possible, in principle, even when the intended action does not occur; and this means that, in principle, it must be possible to verify the hypotheses that I must construct to deal with crises in communication by relying on the assistance of a functioning understanding. This assumption obtains even in the case of the critical evaluation of the quasi-communicative transmission of tradition. For example, in evaluating sources, a historian assumes that, given a sufficiently trustworthy tradition, it is, in principle, possible to do history and thus evaluate these sources on the basis of others. In any case, the historian cannot recur to an observation of the actions, the intentions of which he wishes to understand.

Von Wright's failure to recognize the certainty adhering to the preexplanatory process of understanding in this context seems to form a deeply rooted foundation for his failure to pinpoint the uniqueness of hermeneutic hypotheses, including those of the purposive-rational understanding that is based on the "practical inference"; it is also the foundation of his failure to distinguish them clearly enough from the function of a theoretical explanation of events, including events of action. In contrast, I want to see the alternative position I have elucidated as a transcendental-pragmatic (or transcendental-hermeneutic) radicalization of that reflection which von Wright pursues in Chapter 2 of *Explanation and Understanding*, in his ingenious explication of the premises of the certainty of action. Like any other concept, the concept of an action as bringing about something by doing something else presupposes the concept of the linguistic process of understanding, that is, of communication qua symbolic interaction.

It also seems to me that this is the way we must interpret the point of Wittgenstein's argument against the possibility of a private language, an argument I view as a way to overcome modern "methodological solipsism." As long as one understands this argument as the transition from an introspectionist standpoint to a version of behaviorism, as much of the literature continues to do, one remains locked within the paradigm of this modern "methodological solipsism"; thus, John Locke was a methodological solipsist in attempting to build the bridge from a subject's own "private ideas" to the "private ideas" of others, as was Rudolph Carnap when he assumed the standpoint of a physicalistic behaviorism after rejecting Locke's introspectionism. In Carnap's view, the subject of knowledge would have to make fundamentally all co-subjects (even, for example, the verifiers of scientific theories) the objects of observation and behavioral description.

The obstacle that makes it difficult for von Wright to break out of this conceptual paradigm becomes clear in that passage where he sees reflections as self-observation or the "observation of my inner states." This form of knowledge he correctly calls "just as 'external' and 'indirect' as that of another observer." (Ibid., p. 114.) In fact, I would not equate reflection in this sense— that is, as the correlate to communicative understanding in the self-certainty of the actor— with self-observation. Neither would I let the self-certainty of action be absorbed in the "intentionality of my behavior" (ibid.), which is present and can therefore simply be observed. The intentionality in question must first be identified; hence, it seems to me, the relevant type of reflection instead becomes clear in Austin's discovery of the linguistic possibility of "performatives," more precisely, in the possibility of "illocutionary acts" to which such performatives bear witness. These acts serve as the paradigm for actions that understand and, at the same time, can communicate themselves. Now, one may not wish to take this type of reflection seriously as evidence of intentions; but, then, ultimately one cannot take human validity claims (such as the truth claims of arguments) seriously either, for that type of reflection accompanies all acts (Fichte), and it can be articulated in self-referential discourse. See J. Habermas, "Vorbereitende Bemerkungen zu einer Theorie der kommunikativen Kompetenz," in Habermas and Luhmann, *Theorie der Gesellschaft oder Sozialtechnologie* (Frankfurt, 1971), and "Wahrheitstheorien," in *Wirklichkeit und Reflexion*, ed. H. Fahrenback (Pfullingen, 1974). Also see W. Kuhlmann, *Reflexion und kommunikative Erfahrung* (Frankfurt, 1975).

18. Ibid., p. 116.

19. Ibid., p. 117.

20. Ibid., pp. 160ff. Actually, for Popper, as well, innovative cultural achievements—thus, all historically relevant actions—in principle, cannot be explained nomologically. That is, they cannot be explained in terms of possible predictability, but only "ex post understood." Here, we can clearly see a convergence of Hegel, those attempting to ground the Geisteswissenschaften, and Popper and von Wright with regard to the special epistemological-methodological status of historical understanding and explanation, correctly conceived.

21. Von Wright, *Explanation and Understanding*, p. 120.

22. D. Davidson, "Actions, Reasons and Causes," *Journal of Philosophy* 60 (1963).

23. W. Dray, *Laws and Explanation in History* (Oxford, 1957).

24. Von Wright, *Explanation and Understanding*, pp. 193n4, 195n19.

25. Ibid., p. 81.

26. Ibid., p. 100n39. Emphasis mine.

27. Ibid., p. 130.

28. Under Kantian premises, discussion of a "citizen of two worlds" is already difficult enough, since it presupposes a third standpoint on the part of the philosopher. Under post-Wittgensteinian premises, one must speak of human beings as "objects" of two language games. To do so, however, one needs not only a reflective standpoint that focuses on the difference in language games but, it seems, a third language game, one containing the concept of human causal agency.

29. I. Kant, *Critique of Pure Reason*.

30. Von Wright, *Explanation and Understanding*, p. 129.

31. Ibid.

32. N. Hartmann calls this the coexistence of the freedom and dependence of higher levels on lower levels, which themselves are also independent of the higher levels and, for example, are causally effective.

33. Von Wright himself admits that his point is close to Chisholm's. Chisholm, "Freedom and Action," in *Freedom and Determinism*, ed. K. Lehrer (New York, 1966). Chisholm distinguishes

"transeunt" natural causality from the "immanent" causality of action and thereby resolves the problem he discovers, of the inner connection between "counterfactuals," causality and the freedom of action. For von Wright, the concept of "immanent causation" is "connected with insurmountable difficulties"; nevertheless, he continues, "perhaps one could say that my notion of '(transeunt) causation,' because of its dependence on the notion of action, has a notion of 'immanent causation' already built in" (von Wright, *Explanation and Understanding*, pp. 191–192 and note 44).

34. Ibid., pp. 123–124.

35. Ibid., p. 134.

36. Ibid.

37. A demand found in Peter Winch's *The Idea of a Social Science and Its Relation to Philosophy* (London, 1958). See my critique in *Analytic Philosophy of Language and the Geisteswissenschaften*, Foundations of Language Supplementary Series, vol. 5 (Dordrecht, Holland, 1967), and Apel, *Transformation der Philosophie* (Frankfurt, 1973), vol. 2, pp. 250ff.

38. Von Wright, *Explanation and Understanding*, p. 135.

39. This would also be my objection to Nordenstam's objection to my interpretation of von Wright. See T. Nordenstam, *Explanation and Understanding in the History of Art* (Bergen, 1978), Stensilserie No. 43; and K.-O. Apel, "Causal Explanation, Motivational Explanation and Hermeneutical Understanding," in *Contemporary Aspects of Philosophy*, ed. G. Ryle (London, 1977).

40. See K.-O. Apel, "Types of Rationality Today: The Continuum of Reason between Science and Ethics," in *Rationality Today*, ed. T. Geraets (Ottawa, 1979), and "The Common Presuppositions of Hermeneutics and Ethics," in J. Sallis, ed., *Phenomenology and the Human Sciences* (Pittsburgh, Pa., 1979).

41. Here, I refer to the grounding of norms that Habermas and I have attempted. See J. Habermas, *Legitimation Crisis* (Boston, 1975), part 3, "Wahrheitstheorien," in *Wirklichkeit und Reflexion*, ed. H. Fahrenbach (Pfullingen, 1974), and "What Is Universal Pragmatics," in *Communication and the Evolution of Society* (Boston, 1975). See K.-O. Apel, *Transformation der Philosophie* (Frankfurt, 1973), vol. II, pp. 358ff., "Sprechakttheorie und transzendentale Sprachpragmatik zur Frage ethischer Normen," in *Sprachpragmatik und Philosophie*, ed. K.-O. Apel (Frankfurt, 1976), and "Types of Rationality Today," in *Rationality Today*, ed. T. Geraets. See also W. Oelmüller, *Materialen zur Normendiskussion* (Paderborn, 1978). P. Lorenzen and O. Schwemmer have attempted something which in many ways is similar. See P. Lorenzen, *Normative Logic and Ethics* (Mannheim, 1969); O. Schwemmer, *Philosophie der Praxis* (Frankfurt, 1971); and P. Lorenzen and O. Schwemmer, *Konstructive Logik, Ethik und Wissenschaftstheorie* (Mannheim, 1973). Finally, see F. Kambartel, ed., *Praktische Philosophie und konstructive Wissenschaftstheorie* (Frankfurt, 1974).

# Part II, Chapter 4

1. A. Beckermann, *Gründe und Ursachen* (Kronberg, 1977); and R. Tuomela, "Explanation and Understanding of Human Behavior," in *Essays on Explanation and Understanding*, ed. J. Manninen and R. Tuomela (Dordrecht, Holland, 1976), and *Human Action and Its Explanation* (Helsinki, 1974).

2. D. Davidson, "Actions, Reasons and Causes," *Journal of Philosophy* 60 (1963); P. M. Churchland, "The Logical Character of Action-Explanations," *Philosophical Review* 79 (1970), pp. 214–236; R. Brandt and J. Kim, "Wants as Explanations of Actions," *Journal of Philosophy* 60 (July 1963), pp. 425–431.

3. Beckermann, *Gründe und Ursachen*, p. 151n8.

4. Ibid., and Davidson, "Actions."

5. Beckermann, *Gründe und Ursachen*, p. 48.

6. See G. H. von Wright, *Explanation and Understanding* (Ithaca, 1971), pp. 86ff.

7. Ibid., pp. 66ff.

8. See Beckermann's critique of von Wright in *Gründe und Ursachen*, pp. 165ff. and note 55.

9. Ibid., p. 157n32.

10. Ibid., p. 135.

11. Ibid., p. 138.

12. In this instance, I am interested in why (for what reasons anyone would find rationally intelligible) Beckermann draws this conclusion, not why the corresponding event occurred at some point in recent history.

13. Beckermann, *Gründe und Ursachen*, p. 136.

14. The reflective perspective of dialogue both distinguishes communicative actions in the narrower sense—that is, speech acts—from intelligible human actions and places them in relation to one another. As we know from Grice's investigations ("Meaning," *Philosophical Review* 66 [1957], pp. 377–388), the latter are distinguished from the former insofar as they can succeed as actions without being effectively understood by other agents, whereas it is precisely by being understood that the former succeed: In dialogue human beings are forced to take over the role of the other (Mead), hence, to engage in self-reflection. This self-reflection, however, is not connected only to the communicative actions that effectively anticipate the understanding of one's partner; it is connected as well to virtually all actions that should be understandable and that should be accounted for by their subjects. In other words, if no communicative actions were constituted by the intention to demand understanding and thus self-reflection, there would be no intelligible human actions at all. Similarly, if there were no reflective perspective of dialogue, there would be no possibility of the hermeneutic Geisteswissenschaften.

We can pursue a still more radical reflection. The distinctive feature of the relation of human language to the "logos" is not exhausted by the representational function of propositional sentences qua "bearers of truth," as was long assumed. Since Habermas's "universal pragmatic" interpretation of speech-act theory, it has become clear that it also rests on the performative-propositional double structure of self-reflective speech acts. (See Habermas's "Vorbereitende Bemerkungen zu einer Theorie der kommunikativen Kompetenz," in *Theorie der Gesellschaft oder Sozialtechnologie*, ed. J. Habermas and N. Luhmann [Frankfurt, 1971].) It has become particularly clear since Habermas has shown that the metalinguistic predicate " . . . is true" can be considered redundant only on the level of unproblematic communication. It can be a meaningful predicate insofar as it opens up the possibility of mobilizing a reflection on the truth claim of a proponent's proposition and making this reflection performatively explicit. (See Habermas, "Wahrheitstheorien," in *Wirklichkeit und Reflektion*, ed. H. Fahrenbach [Pfullingen, 1974].) I would say the possibility of the metalinguistic level of metalogic and semantics (including the theory of types and Tarski's theory of a metalinguistic hierarchy) is transcendentally-pragmatically grounded in the performative-propositional double structure of topical self-reflective discourse. See K.-O. Apel, "C. S. Peirce and the Post-Tarskian Problem of an Adequate Explication of the Meaning of Truth," *Monist* 63/3 (1980), and "Zwei paradigmatische Antworten auf die Frage nach der Logos-Auszeichnung der Menschlichen Sprache," in *Perspectiven der Kunst- und Kulturphilosophie*, ed. Pfafferott and Strohmeier (Bonn, 1980).

15. The debate between Thomas Kuhn and the Popperians over the philosophical significance of the history of science offers an illustration of this situation. (See I. Lakatos and A. Musgrave, eds., *Criticism and the Growth of Knowledge* [Cambridge, 1970]; and W. Diedrich, ed., *Theorien der Wissenschaftsgeschichte* [Frankfurt, 1974].) For a long time this debate was guided by the assumption, held to be self-evident, that the issue concerned the opposition between the (normative) logic of science and the history of science as an empirical-analytic social science. According to his own, original self-understanding, Kuhn wanted to see how far it was possible to view the actual motives of scientists as the causes of both their research strategies and the acceptance or rejection of theories. From the point of view of formal logic, by contrast, the Popperians could correctly deny that the empirical facts with regard to researchers' motivations could, in principle, be used to contradict the normative rules of methodology. Actually, the much discussed "challenge to the theory of science by the history of science" can in no way be understood under these premises. In truth, Kuhn was *not* interested primarily in an exhaustive description of the facts of the history of science or in their explanation in terms of the causally effective actual motives of researchers. He was at least equally interested in finding examples relevant to the theory of science to show that the classics often had good reasons for acting contrary to the way prescribed by the normative logic of science. Indeed, his point was that, under the conditions of these normative standards, the classic achievements of the natural sciences that are considered the landmarks of progress would not have been possible.

In the present context I am concerned not to judge the merits of Kuhn's—partially questionable—thesis but to clarify the theoretical premises in terms of which the debate between logicians and historians of science can be discussed meaningfully. Among these premises is an appropriate conception of the methodological status of the history of science. Such a conception cannot be attained as long as the history of natural science is either methodologically equated with natural science itself (as actually happens), or is confused with an empirical social science interested in explaining events in terms of (good or bad reasons qua) effective motives. In my view, the history of science is, rather, the most instructive contemporary example of a hermeneutic Geisteswissenschaften. The history of science is not concerned with a purely normative justification of methodically relevant actions or strategies of action, as is the "logic of inquiry"; neither is it concerned with an explanation of events that can be verified empirically. Rather, its concern is an empirically appropriate understanding of the relevant achievements of leading scientists in light of "good reasons" or normative standards. The latter can differ partially from those presently acknowledged, and hence are themselves indebted to the efforts of historical understanding. Lakatos has taken a step in the right direction by distinguishing between reconstructing the internal history of science and reconstructing its external history. It seems to me, however, that even he fails to illuminate the "hermeneutic circle" that exists between empirical and normative reconstruction, a circle that remains a stumbling block under standard scientistic premises. Nevertheless, unless we recognize the "hermeneutic circle" (or the "spiral" of better understanding what we must have always already understood), we cannot grasp the specific purpose of methodical understanding—namely, the expansion of our knowledge of the rational standards (rules, norms, goals, and beliefs) that, in grounding or justification, we always take to be valid and which, in the quasi-causal explanation of actions, we still heuristically assume as possible regularities (Hempel).

16. Beckermann, *Gründe und Ursachen*, p. 141.

17. Ibid., p. 146.

18. Ibid.

19. Martin, "Explanation and Understanding in History," in *Essays on Explanation and Understanding*, ed. J. Manninen and R. Tuomela (Dordrecht, Holland, 1975), pp. 310ff.

20. Von Wright, "Replies to Commentators," in *Essays*, ed. Manninen and Tuomela, pp. 411ff.

21. Martin, "Explanation and Understanding," p. 310.

22. Ibid., p. 311.

23. W. Dilthey, *Der Aufbau der geschichtlichen Welt in den Geisteswissenschaften*, reprinted in *Gesammelte Schriften*, vol. 7 (Leipzig and Berlin, 1914), pp. 146ff., 206ff.

24. Von Wright, "Replies to Commentators," p. 124.

25. At this point I ought to engage in a critical evaluation of O. Schwemmer's new book, *Theorie der rationalen Erklärung: Zu den methodischen Grundlagen der Kulturwissenschaften* (Munich, 1976); within the framework of the present work, however, that is not possible.

26. That this is not satisfactory I hope to have shown in my discussion of Winch as the representative of the post-Wittgensteinian new relativism, in K.-O. Apel, *Transformation der Philosophie* (Frankfurt, 1973), vol. II, pp. 250ff.

27. As, for example, the history of science viewed as the hermeneutic reconstruction of its "internal development."

28. Tuomela, *Human Action*, p. 110.

29. Ibid., p. 115.

30. Ibid., p. 20.

31. Ibid., p. 59.

32. Ibid., p. 115.

33. P. M. Churchland, "The Logical Character of Action-Explanations," *Philosophical Review* 79 (1970).

34. Beckermann, *Gründe und Ursachen*, pp. 107ff.

35. Ibid., pp. 110ff.

36. Churchland, "Logical Character," p. 225.

37. C. S. Chihara and J. A. Foder, "Operationalism and Ordinary Language: A Critique of Wittgenstein," *American Philosophical Quarterly* 2, pp. 281–295; and Brandt and Kim, "Wants as Explanations of Actions".

38. Beckermann, *Gründe und Ursachen* II, 6.4.

39. Ibid. II, 6.5.

40. P. Feyerabend, *Against Method* (London, 1975).

41. See R. Bernstein on the "displacement hypothesis," in *Praxis and Action* (Philadelphia, 1971), pp. 281ff. See also, J. Habermas's postscript to *Knowledge and Human Interests* (Boston, 1971).

42. For this reason, in the case in which the concept of experimentally relevant causal necessity exerts an ex post doubt on the supposition of the freedom of action that is understood intentionally, competition arises between determinism and the concept of the freedom of action in which, as von Wright states, the latter must always win.

43. In contraposition to W. V. O. Quine's "holism" thesis, one can admit, I think, that our entire system of knowledge (including the philosophical explication of the a priori presuppositions

of knowledge) is constantly confronted by experience. (This corresponds to the moment of truth in the "displacement hypothesis".) This corrects the Kantian view that a "transcendental difference" between experience and the conditions of the possibility of experience can be definitively set out in a complete system of transcendental philosophy. One cannot, however, acquiesce in the surrender of the transcendental difference, as such, in favor of an empirically conceived continuum in our knowledge. Rather, one can expect that this difference will be capable of sharper elaboration precisely to the extent that it is brought into question by the relativization of individual parts of the a priori of experience (for example, of the "methodical" a priori of Euclidean geometry and causal categories under the rubric of "protophysics"), or, more radically, by the distinction between the a priori of experience and that of reflection. So much, at this point, for the transcendental-pragmatic perspective. For an analogous argument against the possibility of replacing transcendental foundations with permanent critique as it is proposed by Hans Albert in the name of "critical rationalism," see my "Das Problem der philosophischen Letztbegründung im Lichte einer transzendentalen Sprachpragmatik: Versuch einer Metakritik des 'Kritsichen Rationalismus'," in *Sprache und Erkenntnis*, ed. B. Kannitscheider (Innsbruck, 1976).

44. Beckermann, *Gründe und Ursachen*, pp. 89ff.

45. Ibid., p. 91.

46. Ibid., p. 113.

47. The content of Max Weber's "rationalization" thesis is that such a proof is to be progressively established in modern Western civilization with regard to the principle of purposive rationality.

48. See K.-O. Apel, "From Kant to Peirce: The Semiotical Transformation of Transcendental Logic," in *Proceedings of the Third International Kant-Congress*, ed. L. W. Beck (Dordrecht, 1970).

49. Manninen and Tuomela, eds., *Essays on Explanation and Understanding* (Dordrecht, Holland, 1975), pp. 194, 197–198.

50. Ibid., p. 196.

51. In (2), I do not think that Tuomela recognizes that von Wright is not concerned with an objectively existing situation of the selection of means but, rather, with an agent's beliefs about the means at his disposal. It also seems to me that the word *necessary* should be replaced by *appropriate*, since, otherwise, the sentence states that there is no other means "necessary" for reaching $p$ instead of no other "possible" way of reaching $p$. This would contradict premise $(P_2)$.

52. Manninen and Tuomela, eds., *Essays*, p. 197.

53. Ibid., p. 403.

54. Ibid., p. 198.

55. Manninen and Tuomela, eds., *Essays*, p. 199.

56. Ibid.

57. Ibid., pp. 199ff.

58. Ibid., p. 201.

59. Ibid., p. 200.

60. Ibid., p. 201.

61. This seems to be the thrust of K. Popper and I. Niiniluoto's "propensity" conception of natural laws. (See I. Niiniluoto, "Inductive Explanation, Propensity, and Action," in Manninen and Tuomela, *Essays*, pp. 335–368.) It seems to me, however, that, according to Popper, the historical-innovative actions of such human beings as scientists must, in principle, always be able to change all "propensities" of the historical-social world. Precisely this is demanded as well by Kant and Peirce's postulate about realizing the principles of reason as ideal laws of the ideal human species-nature. Accordingly, neither can there be simultaneously universal and contingent probability laws in the sphere of human cultural reality. As Peirce assumed, the only thing that could be presumed to be pregiven here, as in the sphere of nature, would have to be the laws of "chance," in general, as the free play of spontaneity.

62. This is the chief argument against Niiniluoto's thesis; Manninen and Tuomela, *Essays*.

63. See my defense of the insights of critical theory, in "Reply to Lessnoff," in *Philosophical Disputes in the Social Sciences*, ed. S. Brown (Amherst, Mass., 1979).

# Part III, Chapter 1

1. See my programatic, and therefore provisional, statement in *Transformation der Philosophie* (Frankfurt, 1973), vol. II, part 2; partially translated in *Towards a Transformation of Philosophy* (London, 1980). Also see my "Programmatische Bemerkungen zur Idee einer transzendentalen Sprach-Pragmatik," in *Semantics and Communication*, ed. C. H. Heidrich (Amsterdam and London, 1974), pp. 79–108; "Zur Idee einer transzendentalen Sprach-pragmatik," in *Aspekte und Probleme der Sprachphilosophie*, ed. J. Simon (Freiburg, 1974), pp. 283–326; "Sprechakttheorie und transzendentale Sprachpragmatik zur Frage ethischer Normen," in *Sprachpragmatik und Philosophie*, ed. K.-O. Apel (Frankfurt, 1976); "Das Problem der philosophischen Letztbegründung im Lichte einer transzendentalen Sprachpragmatik: Versuch einer Metakritik des 'Kritischen Rationalismus'," in B. Kannitscheider, *Sprache und Erkenntnis* (Innsbruck, 1976), pp. 55–82; "Transcendental Semiotics and the Paradigms of First Philosophy," *Philosophic Exchange* 2/4 (1978); "Types of Rationality Today: The Continuum of Reason between Science and Ethics," in *Rationality Today*, ed. T. Gereats (Ottowa, 1979); "C. S. Peirce and the post-Tarskian Problem of an Adequate Explication of the Meaning of Truth," *The Monist* 63/3 (1980).

2. On the concept of knowledge-constitutive interests, or simply cognitive interests, see J. Habermas, *Knowledge and Human Interests* (Boston, 1971). See also, K.-O. Apel, *Analytic Philosophy of Language and the Geisteswissenschaften*, Foundations of Language Suppl. Series, vol. 5 (Dordrecht, Holland, 1967); "Scientistics, Hermeneutics and the Critique of Ideology," in *Transformation der Philosophie* (Frankfurt, 1973; English, *Towards a Transformation of Philosophy* (London, 1980) and "Types of Social Science in the Light of Human Interests of Knowledge," *Social Research* 44/3 (1977).

3. See the objections to Habermas's explication of the "technical interest in knowledge," N. Lobkowicz, "Interesse und Objektivität," *Philosophische Rundschau* 16 (1969), pp. 249–273; and in F. Dallmayr, *Materialen zu Habermas Erkenntnis und Interesse* (Frankfurt, 1974), pp. 169ff. and H. Schnädelbach "Über den Realismus," in *Zeitschrift für Wissenschaftstheorie*, III (1972), pp. 88ff. Also see Habermas's reply in the afterword to *Erkenntnis und Interesse* (Frankfurt, 1968, 1973).

4. On the problem of transcendental-pragmatic reflection, see the works cited in note 1 of the chapter, as well as the investigations by Habermas, Kuhlman, and Schnädelbach into the relation of reflection and discourse: J. Habermas, "Wahrheitstheorien," in *Wirklichkeit und Reflexion*, ed. H. Fahrenbach (Pfullingen, 1974), pp. 211–265; and "Was heist Universalpragmatik,"

in *Sprachpragmatik und Philosophie*, ed. K.-O. Apel (Innsbruck, 1976; English trans. in *Communication and the Evolution of Society* (Boston, 1979); W. Kuhlman, *Reflexion und kommunikative Erfahrung* (Frankfurt, 1975); H. Schnädelbach, *Reflexion und Diskurs* (Frankfurt, 1977).

5. This standard argument of scientism is always renewed by H. Albert, for example. It is incompatible with Popper's insight that innovative (thus, historically relevant) actions cannot be nomologically explained but understood only ex post.

6. For a critique of Gadamer along these lines, see D. Böhler, "Philosophische Hermeneutik und hermeneutische Methode," in *Fruchtblätter*, ed. Hartung et al. (Berlin, 1977).

7. This remains the case today, I think, despite Thomas Kuhn and Paul Feyerabend. One must look beyond the explication of theories in terms of abstract—thus incommensurable and, strictly taken, constantly false—semantic systems. One must, instead, conceive of the succession of theories in the pragmatic context of deepening and expanding the explication of nature as the basis for its technical domination.

8. M. Heidegger, *The Question Concerning Technology and Other Essays* (New York, 1977), pp. 19ff.

# Part III, Chapter 2

1. My criticism of hermeneutic idealism does not amount to a plea for the materialist hermeneutics proposed by H. J. Sandkühler and others at the meeting on "Explanation and Understanding" in Helsinki. (This was also the impetus behind the present investigation, as I mentioned in the Author's Preface. See H. J. Sandkühler, *Praxis and Geschichtsbewusstsein* [Frankfurt, 1973].) In Sandkühler's view, hermeneutics is to be projected as a methodology for "explaining" the "ideological superstructure" in terms of the conditions of the "base." I think this is mistaken, for two reasons:

(1) In exactly the same way as the positivist origin of scientism-objectivism, this conception skips over the dimension of communication with human beings as co-subjects of possible knowledge. Among other things, this means that texts regarded as elements of the "ideological superstructure" can no longer be taken seriously as the source of new truths, perhaps of truths that question the position of the subject of understanding. A countertest to the usefulness of Sandkühler's conception of hermeneutics lies in the question whether he could also accept it as the methodological foundation for the study of Marxist classics. The answer, I think, would have to be negative.

(2) Another reason for my rejection of "materialist hermeneutics" is that it eliminates the methodological difference between hermeneutics and the critique of ideology (in the sense of the genuine Marxist theory of a critique of "false consciousness"). In this way, it eliminates the heuristic-methodological point of historical materialism. If all validity claims by writers are seen as "ideology," hence made the object of "explanation" (and despite all "dialectical" mediation, in this context, this means the object of a deterministic causal explanation referring to the sufficient conditions of the base), then such an explanation can no longer take up the dialectical function of critically mediating a deepened human self-understanding by making mere "natural" determinants transparent. Indeed, where everything can be "explained" as materialistically determined, "critique," just as communication about validity claims, loses all meaning. The issue is precisely not the ontological question: materialism or idealism? This Leninist alternative is deeply "undialectical."

As an aside, it is noteworthy that Albert's conception of a scientific hermeneutic as the methodology for explaining "understanding" is basically, completely analogous to Sandkühler's objectivistic conception—and this is supposed to conform to Popper's philosophy of the "open society" and "critical conventionalism"? Briefly, the implicit philosophical foundation of the philosophy of the "open society," and, above all, of the notion of it as a "regulative principle" for social-historical progress, does not lie either in the ontological (or onto-semantic) objectivism that can grasp intersubjective understanding only as a theme for explanation or in the explication of truth in terms of the theory of correspondence. The latter must be either purely irrelevant from a logico-semantic, criteriological point of view or dogmatic from an onto-semantic-ontological one. It hypostatizes the assumption of a correspondence which, in view of the principle of "fallibilism" of both Peirce and Popper, can never be criteriologically redeemed. It seems to me that the required foundation for exposing the conditions of the possibility of what Popper calls "critical conventionalism" can lie only in a transcendental pragmatics (including a transcendental hermeneutics) of the presuppositions and regulative principles of reaching an understanding about meaning and forming a consensus about truth, processes that, in principal, are unrestricted.

For the corresponding conception of truth, see K.-O. Apel, "C. S. Peirce and the post-Tarskian Problem of an Adequate Explication of the Meaning of Truth," *The Monist* 63/3 (1980). In this work, by referring to Peirce, I have tried to eliminate some flaws in Habermas's path-breaking essay "Wahrheitstheorien," in *Wirklichkeit und Reflexion*, ed. H. Fahrenbach (Pfullingen, 1974), pp. 211–265.

2. The difficulties in connecting the methodologies of psychoanalysis and the sociological critique of ideology are articulated in K.-O. Apel et al., *Hermeneutik und Ideologiekritik* (Frankfurt, 1971). See also, A. Lorenzer, *Zur Begründung einer materialistischen Sozialisationstheorie* (Frankfurt, 1972), and *Die Wahrheit psychoanalytischer Erkenntnis* (Frankfurt, 1974); further, A. Lorenzer et al., *Psychoanalyse als Sozialwissenschaft* (Frankfurt, 1971). As far as a more precise theoretical development and resolution of these difficulties goes, it seems to me that little has been started.

3. On this figure of thought, see J. Habermas, *Knowledge and Human Interests* (Boston, 1971); and K.-O. Apel, *Analytic Philosophy of Language and the Geisteswissenschaften* Foundations of Language, supple. series, vol. 5 (Dordrecht, Holland, 1967), part IV. Also see my "Scientistics, Hermeneutics, and the Critique of Ideology," and "From Kant to Peirce: The Semiotical Transformation of Transcendental Logic," in K.-O. Apel, *Towards a Transformation of Philosophy* (London, 1980). See, too, the latter essay in L. W. Beck, ed., *Proceedings of the Third International Kant-Congress* (Dordrecht, Holland, 1972), pp. 90–104. Finally, see my "Types of Social Science in the Light of Human Interests of Knowledge," *Social Research* 44/3 (1977).

4. See K.-O. Apel, "Types of Rationality Today: The Continuum between Science and Ethics," in *Rationality Today*, ed. T. Gereats (Ottawa, 1979).

5. Insofar as the social sciences wish to attain not only empirically correct results but a true conception of the "nature" of human beings.

6. Thus, Habermas, "Vorbereitende Bemerkungen," Chap. 3. In contrast, see his self-revision in "Nachwort" to *Erkenntnis und Interesse* (Frankfurt, 1968, 1973), pp. 393ff., 411ff.; English translation, "A Postscript to Knowledge and Human Interests," *Philosophy of the Social Sciences* 3 (1974), pp. 157–189.

7. I have a rather pedantic concern with clarity and order in the philosophy of science with regard to the terminological determination of the methodological distinctions I have proposed (especially the characterization of the function of critical-reconstructive social science). Thus I have retained a mode of expression whose affirmative use seems to have lost its force in the present, although who knows for how long. The method followed here connects the emancipatory interest of knowledge to the idea of the counterfactual anticipation of an ideal—which, in spite of this necessary anticipation—constantly remains a "regulative ideal" "to which nothing empirical can (fully) correspond" (Kant). Until now, however, it was not allotted to this method to avoid either the truly utopian reproach of offering empty promises in the form of the "bad infinity" of progress or the anti-utopian reproach of distorting reality in a frightening way, in the sense of the terror of the ideal.

8. See especially E. Nagel, *The Structure of Science* (New York, 1961), Chap. 4.

9. See, for example, N. Luhmann, *Zweckbegriff und Systemrationalität* (Frankfurt, 1973); and Habermas and Luhmann, *Theorie der Gesellschaft oder Sozialtechnologie* (Frankfurt, 1971).

10. In *Explanation and Understanding* (Ithaca, 1971), pp. 16ff., von Wright seems to accept this, citing A. Rosenblueth, N. Wiener, and J. Bigelow, "Behavior, Purpose, and Teleology," *Philosophy of Science* 10 (1943); reprinted in *Purpose in Nature*, ed J. V. Canfield (Englewood Cliffs, N.J. 1966).

11. Its relation to the "subjective teleology" of human actions is clarified by the limit case of intentional action, that is, the case of basic action connected to the functioning of mediation by the "lived body." To understand the latter, we must presuppose more than the purposive-rational understanding of von Wright and Weber; we must not assume merely that a "practical inference" makes it possible to connect a volitional-cognitive complex with the decision to act. We must further assume a mediation of the "goal-realization" that is nomologically sufficient, as in the case of the objective teleology of a functional system. In this case, it is only the absence of the subjective intentionality of goal-setting that remains the criterion for distinguishing between subjective and objective teleology, and this apparently sharp distinction may possibly have to be questioned, given the depth-psychological category of unconscious goal-intentionality as displayed, for example, in psychosomatic symptoms. Because of the pathological disfunctionality of organ accomplishments that can be traced back to an unconscious intentionality, the objective teleology of healthy organ functions is not easy to make intelligible.

12. I have not considered the argument Bertalanffy raises against Ashby, according to which all system functions can be reduced to functions of system stabilization that are cybernetically interpreted.

13. See R. F. Kitchener's critique of Nagel's schema of reduction, in "On Translating Teleological Explanations," *International Logical Review* 13 (1976).

14. See P. Watzlawick, J. H. Beavin, and D. D. Jackson, *Pragmatics of Humans' Communication* (New York, 1967).

15. These alternatives set the parameters for the controversy between Habermas and Luhmann, in Habermas and Lubmann, *Theorie der Gesellschaft oder Socialtechnologie (1971)*. In *Legitimation Crisis* (Boston, 1975), Habermas elaborates a "sublation" of the opposition in terms of the "ethic of communication" as a superordinate standard.

16. See H.-G. Gadamer, *Wahrheit und Methode* (Tübingen, 1960), English, *Truth and Method* (New York, 1975).

17. Watzlawick, Beavin, and Jackson make this possibility and necessity clear for the case of social psychology, in *Pragmatics of Humans' Communication*.

18. See Habermas, *Legitimation Crisis*.

# Part III, Chapter 3

1. See, for example, Kant, *The Critique of Judgment*, para. 59, where he attains the insight into what he, like Thomas and Cusanus, considers the necessary "symbolic" use of language and connects it to a schematism of the concept of reason that is analogous to the schematism of the concept of understanding. Also see E. K. Specht, *Der Analogiebegriff bei Kant und Hegel*, Kantstudien, vol. 66 (Köln, 1953).

2. See my "From Kant to Peirce: The Semiotical Transformation of Transcendental Logic," in K.-O. Apel, *Towards a Transformation of Philosophy* (London, 1980), and *Der Denkweg von Charles Sanders Peirce* (Frankfurt, 1975; trans. by J. M. Krois as *Charles S. Peirce: From Pragmatism to Pragmaticism* (Amherst, Mass., 1981).

3. See my argument in "Reply to Peter Winch," in *Philosophical Disputes in the Social Sciences*, ed. S. Brown (Amherst, Mass., 1979).

4. See Z. Vendler, "A Note to the Paralogisms," in *Contemporary Aspects of Philosophy*, ed. G. Ryle (Stockfield, 1976).

5. See Wittgenstein: "If language is to be a means of communication there must be agreement not only in definitions but also (queer as this may sound) in judgments. This seems to abolish logic, but does not do so. It is one thing to describe methods of measurement and another to obtain and state results of measurement. But what we call 'measuring' is partly determined by a certain consistency in results of measurement." *Philosophical Investigations*, I, para. 242 (New York, 1953).

6. See Kant: "The objective criterion of truth is the agreement of representations with one another in a judgment according to universal laws of understanding and reason, i.e., in terms of intuitions and concepts. . . . The subjective criterion of truth is the agreement of one judgment with others, both in the same subject and in others." *Handschriftlicher Nachlass*, ed. Preussischen Akadmemie der Wissenschaften, No. 2128.

The latter definition is elucidated in Kant's *Logic* (*Introduction to Logic* [London, 1885], p. 47): "An external mark or an external touchstone of truth is the comparison of one's own judgment with that of others, since what is subjective cannot exist alike in all others, and hence semblance may be cleared up." Here, Kant mediates between the consensus theory of Aristotle and the Stoics and that of Peirce, for whom the issue is uncovering individuals' "idiosyncracies." Nevertheless, there can be no doubt that Kant, like Husserl, thought that the precommunicative structure of "transcendental consciousness" within every subject of knowledge was, in principle, sufficient to ground the intersubjective validity of knowledge. This was first disputed in Peirce's work, where the synthesis of the interpretation of signs now for the first time constitutes the intersubjective validity of our judgments "in the long run." Thus the first genuine consensus theory of the interpretation of meaning and truth is based on a semiotic transformation of the transcendental logic of knowledge. See K.-O. Apel, "From Kant to Peirce" *Towards a Transformation of Philosophy* (London, 1980), and "C. S. Peirce and the post-Tarskian Problem of an Adequate Explication of the Meaning of Truth," *The Monist* 63/3 (1980).

7. Ibid.

8. Plainly tragic is the classic combination of emancipatory socialism and a naive, scientistic, or technological concept of planning, a combination not yet affected by such insights. For an extreme example of this combination, see O. Neurath's *Empirische Soziologie* (Vienna, 1931), with an instructive introduction by R. Heselmann.

9. See K.-O. Apel, "Transcendental Semiotics and the Paradigms of First Philosophy," *Philosophical Exchange* 2/4 (1978).

# Appendix

1. See my "Types of Rationality Today: The Continuum of Reason between Science and Ethics," in *Rationality Today*, ed. T. Gereats (Ottawa, 1979).

2. K.-O. Apel, *Transformation der Philosophie*, vol. 1, Intro., pp. 35ff. See also, D. Bohler, "Philosophische Hermeneutik und hermeneutische Method," in *Fruchtblätter*, ed. Hartung et al. (Berlin, 1977).

3. See M. Weber, "Politics as a Vocation" and "Science as a Vocation," in *From Max Weber*, ed. Gerth and Mills (Oxford, 1947).

4. K.-O. Apel, *Transformation der Philosophie* (Frankfurt, 1973); trans. "The A Priori of the Communication Community and the Foundation of Ethics: The Problem of a Rational Foundation of Ethics in the Scientific Age," in *Towards a Transformation of Philosophy* (London, 1980).

5. K.-O. Apel, *Transformation*, vol. 2, pp. 358ff., and "Sprechakttheorie und transzendentale Sprachpragmatik zur Frage ethischer Normen," in *Sprachpragmatik und Philosophie*, ed. K.-O. Apel (Frankfurt, 1976).

6. K.-O. Apel, "Types of Rationality Today," in *Rationality Today*.

# Index

Index

# Index